SWEET AS SIN

SWEET AS SIN

THE UNWRAPPED STORY OF HOW CANDY
BECAME AMERICA'S FAVORITE PLEASURE

SUSAN BENJAMIN

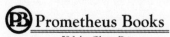
Prometheus Books

59 John Glenn Drive
Amherst, New York 14228

Published 2016 by Prometheus Books

Cover image © Martin Siepmann / Media Bakery
Cover design by Jacqueline Nasso Cooke

Inquiries should be addressed to

Prometheus Books
59 John Glenn Drive
Amherst, New York 14228
VOICE: 716–691–0133
FAX: 716–691–0137
WWW.PROMETHEUSBOOKS.COM

20 19 18 17 16   5 4 3 2 1

Library of Congress Cataloging-in-Publication Data

Names: Benjamin, Susan, 1957- author.
Title: Sweet as sin : the unwrapped story of how candy became America's favorite pleasure / by
    Susan Benjamin.
Description: Amherst, New York : Prometheus Books, [2016] | Includes bibliographical
    references and index.
Identifiers: LCCN 2015037700| ISBN 9781633881402 (pbk.) | ISBN 9781633881419
    (e-book)
Subjects: LCSH: Candy industry—United States—History. | Confectionery—United States—
    History. | Confectioners—United States—Biography.
Classification: LCC HD9330.C653 U5236 2016 | DDC 338.4/76641530973—dc23
    LC record available at http://lccn.loc.gov/2015037700

Printed in the United States of America

To my husband, Dan, and my father, Richard—loving guys who love to have fun

CONTENTS

CHAPTER 1
LOIS AND HOWIE, DAN AND ME

My husband, Dan, and I were in New York recently attending the Fancy Food Show. In case you've never been, it's an event of events if you happen to like food. There are thousands of vendors from all over the world with samples they not only give away but insist you enjoy. Never mind I was looking for candymakers, of which there was an abundant supply, but I also sampled from a multitudinous selection of Spanish olives and a much-too-good alcohol blend presented by a contingent from Mexico. After a two-hour stomach-settling respite, we met out friends Lois and Howie for dinner at a Korean restaurant near 35th Street. While we were enjoying buns, barbeque, and kimchee, I happened to mention that my mother hates candy. And that she's always hated candy. Even— no—*especially* when I was a kid.

Lois, who happens to be a psychotherapist, gave me one of those *aha!* looks. She knows my mother and I have problems and that I research and sell candy for a living. Ask me a question, and I'll steer it around to candy—it's my personal brand of narcissism. But despite what Lois may think, the reason I love candy has nothing to do with my candy-hating mother.

As for Lois, she enjoys your odd caramel or chocolate but was taking a time-out from sweets as part of a cleansing diet. I understood and took no offense, although personally I'd never do it. My husband, Dan, loves candy—especially bourbon balls—and he'd eat them at any given moment. In fact, he hides them from himself at home so he won't eat too many, though with uncanny skill, he still manages to find them.

Howie's different. In the interest of full disclosure, I interviewed Howie for this book because he has a connection through his grandmother to the makers of Bonomo's Turkish Taffy, the flat taffy that was invented in 1912. I've never met anyone else who realizes that Bonomo is someone's last name and not a corporate acronym, so this indirect connection is impressive enough for me. Even better, Howie was a Good Humor truck driver ages ago, and in Manhattan no less. Personally, Howie is all about nostalgia: childhood memories of the grandparents, aunts, uncles, and parents who handed out wintergreen Life Savers or lime-green sourballs.

I am telling you this because Lois, Howie, and Dan collectively make up the feelings that most of us have about candy. We love it, as Dan does—particularly the rich, luscious flavors—yet know as Lois does, that they're not exactly good for us in excess.

The more adventurous candy eaters may call candies "sinfully delicious," while the guilty among us use negative words such as *cavities*, *calories*, and *fat*. They say such things as "I shouldn't have," when they polish off a bag of nougats. For some, on the far end of the spectrum, candy and sin become deliciously literal: think *chocolate underwear*.

Who, though, at some level, doesn't experience that deep sense of connection, of belonging, that candy brings?

My mother, that's who. But here's the fascinating thing: my mother makes a distinction between candy and non-candy that gives her a loophole so she still gets to eat it. For example, she thinks that chocolates are candy but Life Savers are not. You know Life Savers right? The hard, sugar-based substance filled with flavorings and colorings that taste like candy? They, according to my mother, are useful—like when you have bad breath or a dry mouth. Candy, by definition, is not useful at all.

I don't agree with her conclusions, but she's right about one thing: Life Savers *were* for bad breath. Shortly after they were invented in 1912, Life Savers were marketed to saloon goers to cover their booze- and cigarette-smelling breath. I have no doubt that Prohibition helped buoy the popularity of Life Savers, landing them, decades later, in the most un-saloon-like place possible: the bottoms of thousands upon thousands of grandmothers' purses—where some, I'm willing to bet, still lie today.

CANDY LOVE: A CONFESSION

Once I returned home to West Virginia, quietly contemplating the Potomac and Shenandoah Rivers that flowed a few blocks from my home, I got to thinking: What does candy mean to me? Like most people, I found my love of candy as a kid. I grew up in Worcester, Massachusetts, which was a fading factory city with quite a few colleges (Clark University, Holy Cross, Worcester Polytechnic Institute) hidden in its folds.

My childhood wasn't exactly happy, but that's not something I want to get into. Suffice to say that I was one of those frightened, sickly kids with an ongoing illness that began with a case of scarlet fever. Sounds dramatic, I know. I wasn't exactly a favorite among my peers as a result; bad grades and days, sometimes weeks, away from school don't win you popularity, and I pretty much floated in a private bubble, trying to find ways to cope.

That's where penny candy came in. I loved it. It was tasty, it was colorful, and it was currency. With a bag of penny candy bought at Davy's Drugstore or Cotter's Spa, I could buy acceptance from the neighborhood suburban thugs. Or should I say thugettes? They made my young life miserable with their meanness, but in the end they were harmless, growing up to be social workers and receptionists at car dealerships.

Candy was also about fun. Already marketed to kids for over one hundred years when I came around in the late 1950s, candy tasted good, was texturally appealing, and was of my own choosing. At the candy store on my way to school, I got to select the jelly beans, Good & Plenty, and licorice whips and navigate the money to pay for them.

Later, at home, I would find places to hide my stash from my mother; candy was fun and delicious, but also contraband. Then, over the next few days, I would eat the sweets, parsing out the pieces, and all was good.

INTRODUCING MY FATHER

I wasn't the only family member who loved candy; my grandparents loved it, too. For them, there was a historic tie. Born into families that struggled financially, sugar was not readily available when they were growing up. My father's mother, my Nana, described times when they didn't have money for milk, let alone sugar. During World War I, the Great Depression, and World War II, sugar was rationed, and candy, even cheap penny candy, was a rarity they coveted.

Later, as my grandparents grew into prosperity, candy became a symbol of wealth. Also, given their age, candy still clung to its medicinal origins: my grandfather ate pepsin and wintergreen-flavored Canada Mints to sooth his ulcers, and my mother's mother, my grandma, gave me peppermint Starlight Mints for stomachaches. On the actual home front—the too-small house on Valley Hill Drive where I grew up—my father was the purveyor of sweets.

I have two vivid memories that demonstrate this best. One was his semi-regular trips to Friendly's Ice Cream. He'd take our orders: my mother liked root beer floats, my brothers liked ice cream, and I liked sundaes. I know this doesn't sound like candy, but it is. I had butter pecan ice cream, with marshmallow topping *and* hot fudge *and* whipped cream, which bridges the gap between ice cream and candy quite well.

The other is my father's car. My father, his brother, and my grandfather were partners in a manufacturing and wholesale hardware business my grandfather started after his hopes of being a chemist were dashed during the Depression. My father hit the road as the salesman while the other two remained at the factory, aka the "shop."

My father sold hardware, but you'd never know it from his car. While he was taking his after-work nap, I would raid the front seat, finding such treasures as candied fruit slices and marshmallow Peeps made by Just Born. I liked the Peeps best, probably because they were the most decadent. I helped myself to this treasure trove without asking.

My father never complained or, probably, noticed.

WHAT'S INTERESTING IS . . .

Given all these impressions of candy—Lois's, Howie's, Dan's, my parents', my grandparents', and mine—it's hard to imagine the history of candy is anything but frivolous. I see this in my stores, where we sell historic candy, arranged in chronological order from the first in history through the mid-1900s.

When my employees and I tell newcomers that we research the history of candy, some of them grin. A friendly, well-meaning grin, which says, "Well, isn't that *cute*." My employees are nice about it. They explain that candy is deeply embedded in our culture, influencing such things as slavery, the American Revolution, medicine, the birth of the FDA, war rations, marketing, the upsurge of the Industrial Revolution, and the shakedown of Prohibition.

As for me, I try to be nice, too, I really do. But deep inside I'm suppressing an urge to say "Knock that condescension off your face," for reasons Lois can probably explain best. But I don't. What I do say, slowly and clearly so they get the point, is that the story of candy is the story of everyone in general and all of us specifically, a convergence of many cultures and experiences that are also about the United States.

Then I talk about the American Revolution, Prohibition, and so on. By that time, in the course of ninety seconds, their smiles have relaxed into pleasant expressions of interest. And then, they get to know the backstory of candy, and they're glad that they did.

CHAPTER 2
SWEET AT THE START

T he history of candy in the United States begins with the Native Americans, although looking at the history books we read as kids, you'd never know it. These books portray the United States as having a quick false start with Columbus then beginning in earnest with the settlers. The Native Americans were present to greet the Europeans, much like a welcoming committee from a foreign planet: friendly and helpful, but prone to raiding their settlements and killing their families for reasons unknown.

However, the story of candy in America really does begin with the Native Americans. Many of their sweets were also enjoyed by early European Americans, though others remained in the Native American food tradition and are relatively unknown today. One such sweet is derived from corn, which is loved today at a clam bake but maligned as a sugar/syrup.

Depending on the tribe, Native Americans turned various parts of the corn plant into sugar by boiling or baking it. The Mohawk tribe, for example, would take green corn, let it ripen in water, and, after several months, enjoy it as candy, while the Pawnee mixed dried corn silk with ground corn for a sweetener. The Hopi of the Southwest ground corn with potash then boiled or baked it for a candy-like corn ball. On a more basic level, some tribes would strip the ears from the stalk before they robbed the stalk of its sweetness; then they would chew the stalk, much like a piece of candy. They also boiled the corn to create a syrup—that's right, corn syrup![1]

Succulents and cacti were another source of sweetness for Native Americans of the South and Southwest. Among them was sugar made from the agave plant, considered the hippest thing in sweeteners today. The agave also goes by the name "the century plant" because it lives a long life (although closer to only a quarter century) that ends with a single flower that shoots up fifteen feet in some species.

The century plant could just as easily be called the "phoenix plant" because new shoots cluster around its base to replace the dying stalk, and the plant is born again.[2] For candy, the Native Americans would cook the heart and leaves of the agave on hot stones for a number of days then eat them straight or pounded into flat, sweet cakes.[3]

Native Americans also ate the raw pods of the century plant and made a chocolate-like drink from the honey mesquite tree, a relatively small tree with one- or two-inch thorns and fragrant flowers. And from the fruit of the towering saguaro cactus, they made a sweet conserve and a mahogany-colored syrup, which is still used today by the Tohono O'odham tribe on the Mexico–US border.[4] The Apache, Pima, and Papago tribes ate the saguaro's wonderfully sweet pulp fresh or dried it for later.[5]

Among other plants were juniper, which the Utes, Apaches, and Navajos used as a spice, an ingredient in corn mush, in chewing gum, or as a candy; the prickly pear, which the Apaches made into a jelly; and stevia, which is yet another of the many "new" ancient sugars on the market today.

DID SOMEONE SAY *CORN SYRUP*?

The corn syrup that the Native Americans were using was basically ignored by the European settlers. It took Konstantin Gottlieb Sigismund Kirchhoff, a German scientist living in Russia, to discover that sugar could be produced from starch. His reason for the research wasn't what you'd think—it had to do with porcelain. In the eighteenth century, porcelain was made using gum arabic to hold the gold-leaf design in place. Gum arabic was later replaced with honey, which also acted like a glue.[6]

During the Napoleonic Wars in the late eighteenth and early nineteenth centuries, Russian citizens were faced with sugar shortages and turned to honey instead. This drove the price of honey up and its availability down, and porcelain makers were worried. Now what could they use? Kirchhoff's discovery of using starch to make a sticky glucose was the answer they were looking for, and the porcelain industry was saved. It was by *chance* not design, however, that Russians realized this sticky substance was actually an excellent replacement for the hard-to-find sugar around 1811.[7]

In the United States, experiments using starch to make sugar began in 1836 with corn, beets, and, for a short time, sorghum being the top sources. Corn syrup, less sweet than sugar, was primarily used to make candies, jellies, and other confections. By the late 1800s, the Glucose Sugar Refining Company was formed, and, in 1902, it merged with the New York Glucose Corporation to form an enormous and powerful entity called the Corn Products Refining Corporation.[8]

Their flagship product, introduced in 1903, was called Karo. It wasn't the first corn syrup to hit the market, but it had the broadest reach and the most aggressive marketing force.[9] So while some Native Americans were quietly using the corn they raised and harvested to make their own syrup, an industry of lab-made corn syrup was exploding.

THE PURE AND PURER MAPLE

Maple is the most famous and enduring sugar that Native Americans ate. It was more widely appreciated than corn candies, which people today mistakenly think is candy corn. Maple has numerous purposes all at once: with no added ingredients, it's a syrup, a sugar, and a candy. These candies appear in droves around the fall holidays, molded into Pilgrim-shaped pieces and feathered turkeys. Maple also appears in a variety of candy bars and in candy's unacknowledged cousin, sugary cereals.

By the time the European settlers arrived in North America, the Native Americans who lived in the cooler regions had been making maple sugar for hundreds of years. To make it, they would cut into a maple tree with a tomahawk or axe and allow the sap to flow into a container made of birch bark or other material. Then they collected the sap and boiled it in a hollowed log by adding blazing hot stones straight from the fire. New stones were added to keep the sap hot until it became thick and sticky. Next, the mixture was poured onto ice or snow where it cooled into solid form.[10]

While the Native Americans were busy making and enjoying sweets from the maple tree, some settlers were busy writing about them. The famous colonel James Smith wrote of them in an autobiography about his time as a prisoner, and adopted family member, of the Lenape tribe of Delaware. The text is aptly named *An Account of the Remarkable Occurrences in the Life and Times of Colonel James Smith (Now a Citizen of Bourbon County, Kentucky) During His Captivity with the Indians in the Years 1755, '56, '57, '58 and '59.*

The Lenape used another maple-sugar-making process, which involved

Fig. 2.1. Maple candies.

freezing the maple in the snow and letting the water in the sap separate from the sap itself, then scraping away the icy portion and refreezing the maple until it formed a maple-sugar block. This is what Smith reported:

> Shortly after we came to this place the squaws began to make sugar. We had no large kettles with us this year, and they made the frost, in some measure, supply the place of fire, in making sugar. Their large bark vessels, for holding the stock-water, they made broad and shallow; and as the weather is very cold here, it frequently freezes at night in sugar time; and the ice they break and cast out of the vessels. I asked them if they were not throwing away the sugar? They said no; it was water they were casting away, sugar did not freeze, and there was scarcely any in that ice. They said I might try the experiment, and boil some of it, and see what I would get. I never did try it; but I observed that after several times freezing, the water that remained in the vessel, changed its colour and became brown and very sweet.[11]

The settlers borrowed the Native American's maple-sugar-making process, with some adjustments. After they harvested the sap, they poured the mixture into three different kettles as it boiled down, filtering the maple with wool blankets.[12] Today, nearly 61 percent of maple sugar in the United States is imported, primarily from Canada, although plenty of American maple sugar makers are still around; many are located in Vermont.[13]

FROM MAPLE TO MEAT

As part of my research, I took the ninety-minute drive to Washington, DC, to visit the National Museum of the American Indian. I'd been there many times and always enjoyed the exhibits and artifacts and Native Americans in traditional clothing giving talks about their heritage. What appealed to me most, though, was the cafeteria: a sumptuous array of dishes from various nations laid out buffet-style so museum visitors can travel through the cuisine of many nations on a single plate.

It was in the gift shop that I had a breakthrough: the "Tanka Bar" made by the Lakota tribe at the Pine Ridge Reservation in South Dakota. "Tanka," as I later learned from Jason Stover , my contact at the reservation, is the brand name of a food the Lakota call "wasna" as well as a tribal name for the buffalo. Traditionally, the Lakota would dry buffalo meat and add dried chokecherry or buffalo berry, which is much like the chokecherry but smaller. The natural acid and sugar from the fruit preserved the meat so it would stay edible through long trips when the tribe moved around. Other tribes made a similar mixture that they called pemmican, which contained fat from deer, elk, or other animals, and fruit, frequently dried cranberry, which is in the Tanka Bar today.[14]

The connection between wasna and candy was an epiphany for me, albeit an embarrassing one since it's so obvious. The Native American's sugar also came from fruits and berries, which were used for their flavor, health benefits, texture, and preservative qualities. European Americans came to value fruits and berries later creating an industry from them, with fruit flavors, fruit-shaped candy, and glazed, creamed, and crystallized fruit pieces.

PERSONAL PERSPECTIVE: TIMOTHY KEADY,
WASNA AT THE RESERVATION

I met Timothy Keady at my shop when I was explaining the story of wasna to visitors. He told me he had made it many times, as had his grandmother, on the reservation where he grew up. When he left the shop, he promised to keep in touch. A few weeks later, I received this letter:

> My name is Timothy Keady. I am half Comanche Indian on my father's side. My grandparents raised me. I have practiced a Lakota Sioux tradition since there are few Comanches in the Northwest, but many Lakota. I am a drummer and singer in the Sweat Lodge and have vision quested four times . . . As Lakota, we use something for ceremonial use (and may be eaten otherwise) called "wasna." Heaven knows how old the recipe is.

> <u>Wasna:</u>

> 1. Two pounds buffalo steak cut into thin strips and dried by the fire
> 2. One pound dried chokecherries
> 3. One pound suet

> Chop and crush dried buffalo and dried choke cherry into a fine dice (not quite powder, more granular).

> Melt suet until totally liquid.

> Using a tea cup, fill it half full of buffalo-cherry mixture

> Drizzle a small amount of suet at a time until just sufficient to make a ball or patty that holds together without crumbling.

> (I got this recipe from a very old Lakota woman who mixed this wasna with her bare fingers. I would advise you to use a spoon or Popsicle stick!)

> 1. If you can't get buffalo steak you can use jerky. Watch the seasonings of preservatives as they will affect flavors.
> 2. My grandmother would dry berries, fruits, etc. on the tin roof of the spring house. Usually took about ten (very warm and dry) days.
> 3. Buffalo is very lean by nature. You probably won't be able to collect enough buffalo suet in a hurry. Your butcher can usually provide you with beef suet inexpensively.

Once you have made your wasna, store it in a paper bag in a cool place. Us modern Native Americans prefer the "fridge" but I've kept it up to 45 days in a dark, cool place.

Also note that once "civilized" on reservations, Native Americans were given sugar rations. Of all the rations, coffee and sugar were the most reliable. Most of the natural berries and fruits were eaten as found or dried for later use. It wasn't until white traders and posts came into being that actual wheat grains were available.

CHAPTER 3

SUGAR FROM FRUIT AND FRUIT FROM FRUIT

J ust as I was writing this, my brother Mark, a farmer in western Massachusetts, called to say hello. We were talking about candy when, naturally, the topic of our father came up. My father had a big temper and a big voice but also a big appetite for good times, and, as I mentioned earlier, sweets were part of it.

During my father's trips selling hardware from one New England town to another, he'd hang around his customers' stores with other men who wandered in, talking about God only knows what. These hardware stores were classic American hangouts: they weren't the Home Depots or Lowes of today, but the real thing with worn wooden floors, and nails, screws, and bolts stacked in cardboard boxes. Greasy or otherwise manhandled tubs of chewing gum, peppermints, and other penny-size candies sat by the register. On trips with my father—when he'd drop me off at summer camp or college as part of his route—I don't remember seeing a woman enter those doors, ever. These stores were definitely a man's home base.

For Mark, the real treasure trove in my father's car wasn't the candy but the fruit stuffed in brown paper bags (sometimes half-filled with my father's pits). My father got the fruit at farm stands along the road, freshly picked, carelessly weighed, and sold by the farmers or a young kid—usually a son, daughter, or neighbor—who manned the stands. But, as my brother pointed out, fruit is pretty much the same as candy; fructose *is* sugar, after all.

CAINE AND ABEL: A CANDY COMPARISON

In the biblical story of brothers Caine and Abel, Abel was the overseer—the protector tending his sheep—while Caine was the farmer—planting seeds, harvesting crops, and more or less changing things. Abel observed. Caine moved things around and made changes. Just about everyone knows how the story ended, and the story of the Native Americans and the Europeans is a little like that: the Native Americans were, much like Abel, stewards of the land, while the Caine-like European Americans were all about change.

Generally, the story has four stages. The first concerns the Native Americans who used fruit that grew wild and unadorned. In the second stage, European Americans arrived and "discovered" these products, much the same way Christopher Columbus discovered the "new land." In stage three, the European Americans found ways to control or in more familiar language, "cultivate" the fruit. Finally, in the fourth stage, those very same European Americans marketed and turned a profit from the newly controlled products.

THE CAPED CRANBERRY

One of the most significant native berries is also one of the most understated: the cranberry. Originally, the cranberry grew in bogs and marshes all over the country, from Cape Cod, Massachusetts, the top cranberry producer today,[1] to Oregon, Wisconsin, and British Columbia. The Indians of the east called it "sassamanesh;" the New Jersey Leni-Lenape, "ibimi;" and the Wisconsin Algonquin, "atoqua."[2] The European settlers conjured the current name "cranberry" based on the fruit's pink blossoms, which they thought resembled the head and bill of a crane.[3]

For the Native Americans, the cranberry—with its sweet-sour flavor—was wild and readily available in the fall and served many purposes. With their high sugar content, cranberries stored well in the winter in dried cakes and acted as a preservative in such foods as pemmican. Some tribes used cranberries to treat a range of ailments—from arrow wounds[4] to fevers.

As we're reminded each fall, the Native Americans introduced the settlers to the cranberry as a food, sweet, and medicine. Other European Americans soon caught on: Whalers and sailors discovered that cranberries fight scurvy, so they loaded up with stores of the berries for their travels. Years later, Ulysses S. Grant sent cranberries to Union soldiers at the Siege of Petersburg.[5] During World War II, the US government sent troops a variety of fruits and candies, including one million pounds of dried cranberries each year.[6]

But for the average plant-loving European American, the cranberry wasn't quite good enough. It was too wild, too unpredictable. In his famous botanical text of 1919, *Sturtevant's Notes on Edible Plants,* Edward Lewis Sturtevant described how European Americans took control of this untamed element:

> [The cranberry] was eaten by the Indians of New England. The fruit is boiled and eaten at the present day by the Indians of the Columbia River. . . . The fruit is an article of commerce among the tribes of the Northwest. About 1820, a few vines were cared for at Dennis, Massachusetts, but not until about 1840 can the trials of cultivation be said to have commenced, and not until 1845 was the fact established that the cranberry could be utilized as a marketable commodity. . . .[7]

One of these mid-1800s architects of the modern cranberry was a New Jersey Quaker named James Fenwick. Fenwick experimented with a small cranberry bog at a place known as Skunk's Misery (likely named because the bog tended to be on damp, unusable land). But this wasn't an ordinary bog. Fenwick's early cranberry experiments at Skunk's Misery were so successful that in 1857 he purchased 108 acres along a track of land called Cranberry Run. Here's how he described it:

> There have been seen at one time as many as sixty covered wagons with horses hitched to trees around the edges of these meadows. These wagons brought farmers' families who were busily engaged picking cranberries. Surely there can be no place better adapted to their cultivation than this where they have grown and produced fruit generation after generation.[8]

No better place, indeed. Fenwick soon constructed a cedar rail fence around the field and kicked out those happy farmers and their families. This land, and the hundreds of acres he later added to it, became the Whitesbog cranberry farm.

About ten years later, Joseph J. White, a full-time engineer and cranberry farmer, set eyes upon Fenwick's daughter, Mary. He revealingly described her as "a comely virgin . . . daughter of James A. Fenwick, a pioneer cranberry grower." So what are the odds that White would wed Mary and eventually fold in Fenwick's land, creating an unheard of three-thousand-acre cranberry farm? Extremely high. But Mary was more than a comely virgin. She was also an artist who illustrated White's book on cranberry cultivation. It became a cranberry classic.

About twenty years later, one of White's seven children, Elizabeth, became involved in cranberry production, ultimately shaping the American berry scene. While White worked in the professional engineering world, Elizabeth operated the farm, cultivating the wild cranberry into an obedient, harvestable fruit. What kind of woman was Elizabeth White? It's hard to say. I contacted the archivist at the Whitesbog Museum, a practical but flawed gesture given that archivists, especially the volunteer kind, don't devote their time keeping alive the memory of people they *don't* like.

To no one's surprise, the archivist sang Miss White's praises, even pointing out that in 1911, the National Child Labor Committee accused cranberry growers of mistreating migrant workers and the children who worked alongside them. In November 1913, right around the Thanksgiving holiday, *Good Housekeeping* published an article titled "Who Picked Your Cranberries?"

Whitesbog was the main focus of the article since it produced roughly one-third of the cranberries in the market. Elizabeth made a case that the migrants, primarily Italians from South Philadelphia, were able to exchange poverty and filth for fresh air, reasonable pay, and a clean, wholesome environment by working in the bogs. It was true that their kids were working with them, and not in school, but it was only the older kids, and they worked at a pace that their parents determined.[9] The verdict on Miss White is still out.

That's when Joseph J. White stepped in. He became active in the American Cranberry Association, which merged with other groups to become the influential American Cranberry Exchange. The group, established to address problems facing cranberry growers, set standards for grading and inspecting cranberries, but their main and most influential focus was marketing.[10] They adopted the trademarked name of "Eatmor Cranberries,"[11] and their message was clear: cranberries are *not* just for Thanksgiving.

One 1922 newspaper ad, typical of their campaign, reminds readers that cranberries are perfect for breakfast, lunch, *and* dinner.[12] For skeptics or the cranberry-challenged, their advertisements in newspapers and booklets circulated to housewives contained recipes such as cranberry ice and cranberry meringue pie; recipes so luscious that even I, who won't so much as broil without a fuss, would consider making them.[13] As for the claims: "Cranberry has no waste—all of the fruit is used," and "They require no labor to prepare—and little cooking." Perfect: economical and effortless! What could be better?

THE CRANBERRY TODAY

The Eatmor Cranberries campaign pushed the fruit into more American kitchens and onto more dinner plates, but it took decades for the cranberry to wriggle its way off the Thanksgiving table and into the foods of Americans year round. In terms of candy, even today, the cranberry can't seem to shake the pilgrim association entirely. You can see this in candies such as Jelly Belly's cranberry sauce jelly bean[14] and sugar-free "Ice Chips," which contain "hand-crafted juicy cranberry" sweetened with xylitol and claim, "You'll want to break out the rest of the holiday feast as this wonderful candy melts in your mouth. Tart, tangy, exciting your taste buds and carrying your thoughts back to past celebrations."[15]

The cranberry has found a non-Thanksgiving niche among people who eat healthy candy with companies such as Dove—whose chocolate promises "real cranberries" dipped in silky smooth dark chocolate[16]—and Kind—whose cranberry candy bars contain almonds and antioxidants. In case you're unsure of the Kind bar's health value, they add this convincing bit in their advertising: "Each bar contains 50% of the recommended daily intake of Vitamins A, C, and E, which fight free radicals, and help maintain the immune system and healthy skin." They also have a tagline that says: "Snack like there is a tomorrow."[17] A little dark, maybe, but I get their point. Viva la cranberry!

MY COUSIN THE BLUEBERRY

A cousin of the cranberry, the thirteen-thousand-year-old blueberry grows around the world spreading its roots from Alaska to the jungles of South America.[18] It's a plant hefty, sturdy, and steadfast enough to endure long winters. The Alaskan Indians preserved blueberries in seal oil,[19] and the Native Americans of the Northeast dried them for the winter. No wonder one legend, which calls the blueberry a "star berry" for the star shape at the bottom, claims that the Great Spirit sent the fruit to help humans during a time of famine.[20]

To get more information on the blueberry, I contacted Joel Rohbe, who was referred to me by some folks at the Red Lake Nation, home of the Ojibway tribe in Minnesota. He told me that the Ojibway have eaten nothing but wild, uncultivated blueberries. "You should see," he told me, "there are acres and acres of them. All the land as far as you can see, everywhere, turns blue." To ensure the berries' growth, the tribe burns a portion of the fields every year, which enables the berries to die back and return with new, invigorated life.[21]

As we spoke, I remembered harvesting blueberries with my mother and brothers at Mount Wachusett in Massachusetts when I was young. We picked the berries one-by-one and dropped them in a bucket with a plunk. (Or maybe I just *think* I heard a plunking sound; it adds a nice background to the memory.) What I know for sure is that one of my mother's friends confronted a bear while gathering the fruit. The story isn't exactly dramatic: the bear survived, she survived, and I assume the berries in the area were eaten by both of them.

PERSONAL PERSPECTIVE:
MARK BENJAMIN, BURNING BLUEBERRIES

To follow up on my recollections, I called my brother Mark. Not only was he a witness to our blueberry outings (which he didn't remember that well), but he had spent at least part of his farming life harvesting and burning wild blueberries. Here's what he said:[22]

The blueberries were at the top of a small Berkshire mountain. We burned one-third of the field every year to take off the extra dead woody matter and allow for fresh green growth that would have the most blueberries. We start in late winter, when the snow melts away from the main parts of the field but remains on the edges near a stone wall which stops the fire. Sometimes, at the ridge line, we can see a snowstorm coming from out west.

When we're sure it's safe and the land is dry enough, we burn a ten-foot perimeter with propane tanks that we carry with us, so the fire won't take off. This is called a black-line, or black-burning.

When we have a decent wind, we create a wall of fire. It's quite an experience because you get the feeling the fire is a living thing. It's like you're doing a dance with fire and wind, the way they interact, and you kind of read where the fire needs to go and get a sense of how you're leading the fire along.

You're working alongside other people and trying to keep the smoke from getting in your own way and other people's way. It can be especially hard when the wind is shifting. One of my fondest memories is when I was making different spots of fire a few yards apart and all at once the little patches started coming together in one big ring: I stepped outside the fire, it was a promontory, it created a vortex, all of it coming together and the smoke rising up in a spiral.

The blueberries in the area where we burned wouldn't come back until the following spring. We burn them so they get fresh green growth and berries that come in a year.

● ● ● ● ● ● ● ● ● ● ● ● ● ● ●

Since they first discovered the blueberries, the European Americans considered them a renegade fruit, growing of their own will and impossible to transplant or cultivate. Then, in 1910, Frederick Coville of the US Department of Agriculture published a report called "Experiments in Blueberry Culture" in which he unearthed the bizarre error in this thinking: the professionals were planting the bushes in the richest, most pampered soil possible. But blueberries don't like rich, pampered soil. They like the gritty stuff. Or, as Coville said:

> The idea rests on the unsuccessful experience of those who have taken up wild bushes and set them in well-manured garden soil. These are exactly the conditions . . . under which blueberries become feeble and unproductive.[23]

Instead the plants prefer swamps, sandy lands, or porous, often gravelly loams. In other words, the blueberry enjoys areas that other plants (with the exception of its cousin the cranberry) can't handle.[24]

The problem was solved and the blueberries grew, but no one particularly cared. This was a problem for European American growers, to whom good fruit meant good profit. Unfortunately, the blueberry was so small it took forever to harvest. Worse, common harvesting tools injured the blueberries, causing them to ferment en route, making them unattractive and unsalable.

So, Coville came up with a big idea: cultivate bigger blueberries. "Large size and abundance mean a great reduction in the cost of picking. Large size means also a higher market price, and when taken in connection with good color and good market condition it means a much higher price," he wrote.[25] And so, the search for the big, bold cultivated blueberry began.

At that time, a well-to-do cranberry farmer read Coville's report and immediately reached out to him; the blueberry had many similarities to the cranberry—including the same soil and climate preferences—and she was intrigued. The farmer was Elizabeth White, and she was willing to supply all the means: funding, land for experiments, knowledge, and expertise. How could Coville resist? He couldn't, and so together they began an effort to market and sell the blueberry by changing it. Five years later, in 1916, they had cultivated and produced their first crop.

By the 1920s, while Elizabeth White had one foot in the blueberry world and one in the cranberry, women at home were struggling in the kitchen. New appliances were cropping up, and the pressure was mounting for expert cuisine that would essentially define women as good wives and mothers. Around this time,

Washburn Crosby, a Minneapolis flour company, ran a contest inviting women to complete a jigsaw puzzle and send it in. If the pieces fit, they'd get a pin cushion shaped like a flour sack.

The puzzles flooded in and with them came letters asking the flour company for advice on household cooking matters. The company had their home-economics staff respond with sound, practical advice, all signing their names "Betty Crocker." Why "Betty Crocker"? "Betty" was homey and trustworthy and "Crocker" was the name of a loyal company executive. As for Washburn Crosby, they eventually became known as General Mills.

Soon, Betty Crocker (or, more accurately, the Betty Crockers), was writing a newspaper column, starring on her own radio show, and ultimately shining on the television screen. She had plenty to say about all matters relating to food and was the most reliable voice to say it.[26] In a column in 1931, she retold the blueberry story, whose victory over wildness was the quintessential American tale, with a culinary twist and plenty of artistic license. Here's what she wrote:

> Blueberries are wild things—the last of our American berries to yield to cultiva-
> tion. In fact, back in New Hampshire, in 1906, when Dr. Frederick V. Colville
> suggested transplanting the big, silvery berries from the pasture of his farm, the
> neighbors shook their heads . . . why the very idea of having whole fields of culti-
> vated blueberries from those wild things! Blueberries just couldn't be cultivated.
> But Dr. Coville wasn't discouraged, not even when the first blueberry bushes he
> transplanted to good garden soil withered and died, just as his neighbors said
> they would. Not even when they died a second year. It was then that he made
> a discovery that blueberries demand an acidic soil, preferably a mixture of peat
> and sand. They simply refuse to grow in anything else.
>
> After that, the cultivation of the blueberry went on without setbacks. The
> result was huge juicy berries with the circumference of a dime or nickel—or
> even a quarter. These are the ones that go to market in swanky little boxes with
> cellophane tops.
>
> During the last 30 years, Dr. Coville and those working with him have
> grown over 60,000 pedigreed seedlings . . . grown all the way from Maine to the
> Carolinas. Out of these only twelve have been chosen as worthy of being named
> "varieties." A few of the names given to these varieties are Concord, Pioneer,
> Jersey, Stanley, and Rancocas.[27]

Many of the names, as it happens, had more communal, down-to-earth origins. For example, one variety was named for the "Pineys," who lived among the trees and swamps.[28] Elizabeth White figured out how to tap their knowledge, as she said in a 1953 interview:

> As I was hunting wild blueberry bushes I learned that the old blueberry pickers that were going to the different swamps recognized a difference in the class of bushes in each swamp. For instance, in Iricks Swamp I was told that the majority of the berries were pear-shaped and I was told that in Feather Bed Swamp the majority of the berries were very blue and flattened.[29]

White loaded up the "Pineys" with labels, collection bottles, and an aluminum gauge, and sent them into their native terrain to find the best blueberry plants to propagate. In return, they were given $2.00 per bush, plus the time necessary to relocate the plant. White named the bush for their finders. She said:

> In getting the early bushes I tried to name every bush after the finder. And so I had the Adams bush found by Jim Adams, the Harding bush that was found by Ralph Harding, and the Dunphy bush that was found by Theodore Dunphy. When Sam Lemon found a bush I could not name it the Lemon bush so I called it the Sam. Finally, Rube Leek of Chatsworth found a bush. I did not know it was anything special at that time and I used the full name in my notes. . . . Coville called it the Rube which I thought was a poor name for an aristocratic bush. He finally suggested that we call it the Rubel. And the Rubel bush has really been the keystone of blueberry breeding.[30]

In the end, the old world Pineys helped create a new world industry, and White defended them against criticism that they were slow-witted, uneducated, and inbred.[31] The plants in Whitesbog alone were incredibly profitable: in 1927, a sixty-acre crop was worth about $20,000. At its peak, Whitesbog had ninety acres of blueberries.[32]

Elizabeth White, like her father, recognized that cultivating the uncultivated wasn't enough. You had to market your goods and make money from them. Among other efforts, she was the brains behind the packaging Betty Crocker referred to as " swanky little boxes with cellophane tops." White recognized that the plump blueberries they worked so hard to create were lost behind the brown paper bags they were wrapped in. So, she covered them with imported clear tops. In 1917, she had another marketing brainstorm: sell the blueberry bush to gardeners and farmers.[33] The effort was a success.

Ultimately, however, White's contributions went unrewarded. She told her father that when he died, she wanted to be president of J. J. White, Inc. Instead, he left the company to his son-in-law. Elizabeth stayed involved in the company, but the meetings were acrimonious.[34]

BLUEBERRIES AND CANDY: AN AWKWARD UNION

In the candy world, the blueberry shines—albeit in a more psychedelic-shade-of-blue sort of way. While brands like Dove and Brookside offer healthy candy bars, such as one with blueberries in good-for-you dark chocolate and one with even-better-for-you acai berries, the range of tacky blue candy is astonishing. It must be the synthetic coloring that gives it this edge because, I can assure you, the relationship between the tacky stuff and the real deal, no matter how cultivated, is nonexistent.

Here's a rundown of a few of the more "colorful" blueberry candies: purple milk-chocolate-covered blueberries (why purple, I don't know); Barrels of Yum! Blueberry Crumble, which are vaguely reminiscent of root beer barrels but with a startling hue; blue (if you can call it that) blueberry gumballs; blue Pixy Stix; Jelly Belly blueberry gumdrops, which actually look like raspberry candies colored with food dye; and the pièce de résistance, blueberry-flavored Jelly Belly jelly beans that are served up in a ceramic blueberry-pie-shaped candy dish.

Elizabeth? Elizabeth White? Where are you?

THE VERDICT ON ELIZABETH WHITE

I must plead bias. I am always impressed by women who buck the system, over-come obstacles, and make their way in a man's world. That's what Elizabeth White did. Besides, White's subsequent work, including her work on behalf of migrant workers, tells me she was brave, successful, and, more to the point, a good person. In other words, she's OK. The archivist can rest.

THE SPY AND A NATIVE FRUIT,
WITH ROOTS AROUND THE WORLD . . .

Today, strawberry is one of the most popular candy flavors in the nation. It's in chewing gum, hard candies, jelly beans, taffy, Caramel Creams, and licorice, which is now branded as "Strawberry Twists." The list is practically endless and new additions are always on the way.

The story of the strawberry, unlike that of the cranberry and blueberry, involves three continents, numerous ships, and a healthy dose of intrigue. In North America, strawberries were tiny nuggets that remained a humble yet wild fruit while other plants were tamed and potted. Wild strawberry plants carpeted the land, offering their fruits with abandon, especially after a forest or field was burned to clear it. Strawberry plants held special meaning for Native Americans because they were the first to produce fruit in spring. No part of the plant was forgotten, overlooked, or thrown away. Depending on the tribe, the leaves were boiled into tea, the roots were used to relieve stomach problems, and the fruit was consumed for health and pleasure.[35]

Thomas Jefferson, whose botanical prowess is legendary, grew strawberries in his garden. In 1767, he wrote in his *Garden Book* that "100 fill half a pint," which indicates how remarkably small these berries were.[36]

Three events occurred to change the legacy of the strawberry. First, an American strawberry—the Virginia strawberry (*F. virginiana*)—appeared in France in the 1600s and made its way around Europe from garden to garden without much fanfare.[37] How it arrived there no one exactly seems to know, but it showed up in a manual of botany compiled for Louis XIII in 1624.[38]

A second event occurred in 1771. King Louis XIV of France sent a spy, Lieutenant Colonel Frézier, to Chile to gather information about the Spanish who had clearly gained control over the nation. The royal family was enamored with Frézier because of a book he wrote while he was an infantryman in the royal service. In it, he explored the many possibilities of munitions, including a favorite for celebratory events: fireworks, or in other words, armaments for fun. His book on the subject became a standard of the time.[39]

By the time he left for Chile, Frézier was an experienced and enthusiastic officer and an excellent spy. He hobnobbed with his targets, posing as a merchant sea captain and visited garrisons, forts, and armaments as an eager tourist. He befriended Spanish officers, observed the native people, and studied the native terrain, drafting detailed maps to bring home. All of this he recorded in copious notes, which later became another popular book that was read throughout Europe.

And there, among riff-raff and royalty, Frézier discovered the Chilean strawberry. The plant had one distinguishing quality compared to its European and North American cousins. As Frézier put it in a 1917 English translation: "The fruit is as big as a walnut or a hen's egg."[40] In other words, unlike the petite varieties at home, the Chilean strawberry had heft. In addition, the flowers were enormous, the runners were long, and the berries didn't bow down like other varieties, but thrust their seeded chins up to the sun. As for the downside—it was less flavorful than the other varieties.

Regardless, Frézier nursed the strawberry on the 160-day voyage back to France, during which he, and the plant, survived storms, churning waves, and the threat of pirates. It's worth noting that the French ship on which he sailed enjoyed pirating as much as anyone else but, due to time constraints, resisted the temptation to target a small, Portuguese fishing boat.

Once the Chilean strawberry plant was settled in France, safe among botanists and gardeners, a third event happened that would make today's strawberry complete: it co-mingled with the *F. virginiana*. How exactly it happened, no one seems to know, but the prevailing thought is that the union was accidental. The culprit could have been a French botanist, perhaps Frézier himself,[41] or it could have been the botanist and director of the Netherlands East India Company, George Clifford.[42] Whoever it was put the Chilean variety next to the Virginia berry and soon an amazing hybrid was born—a big, robust, and tasty fruit.

One more note about Frézier: his name is derived from the French word "fraise" meaning "strawberry." His ancestor Julius de Berry gave the king of France a gift of strawberries in 916. As a thank you, the king knighted Berry and changed his name from Berry to Fraise, which later became Frézier. As for the coat of arms—the king gave him three stalks of strawberries. Whether Frézier was aware of this or not, is anyone's guess. He never mentioned it in his writings or referred to it in any way.[43]

HOME, AGAIN

In the early nineteenth century, strawberry cultivation was booming in Europe, but in the United States it merely trotted along. Around Boston, strawberries were primarily grown in gardens by amateurs who hoped for the best. In New York, the plants were more or less dropped in sandy soil in fields and on mountainsides and left to fend for themselves. In North Carolina, amateurs wrote articles and experimented with the plant, but not much came of it.[44] Other efforts to create hybrids brought so-so results.[45]

In 1834, Boston horticulturist Charles Hovey changed all that. Hovey was born in 1810 in Cambridge, which was at that time a rural town.[46] Nearby Boston, however, was a center of horticultural activity. The influential Massachusetts Horticultural Society was newly formed, marking the separation between horticulture and agriculture. It is still around today. Hovey, whose father owned a grocery store and property in Cambridge when Hovey was a boy, went on to start a nursery and then a seed operation; he also founded and edited the first horticultural magazine, which operated for forty-some years.[47]

Hovey cross-pollinated a number of strawberry varieties to come up with the remarkable "Hovey" strawberry. It's DNA, however, is unknown since Hovey lost the markers indicating the cross of the berry.[48] Regardless of its lineage, the orphan plant was a star: at the Massachusetts Horticultural Society exhibition in 1835, strawberry lovers were dumbstruck by the size and quality of the fruit. It was deemed "perfect" and viewed as the first worthy cultivated strawberry, the one the nation was waiting for. In 1840, a dozen of the plants sold for the vast sum of $5.00.[49]

The Hovey berry lived up to the expectations of gardeners, with whom it remained a hit through the late 1800s,[50] and to this day, Charles Hovey remains the father of the strawberry in the United States.

CHAPTER 4
ROOTS, BARK, AND BEANS

My father's job required him to travel from town to town selling his hardware to small and occasionally large shops. Essentially, he was a sales rep, and the business he represented jointly belonged to my father, grandfather, and uncle. But the nation's first traveling sales rep was John Bacon Curtis, a man just about no one's ever heard of. His product was chewing gum. More specifically, it was the first commercial chewing gum. It was made from spruce tree resin and was wrapped and labeled with a European American finish.

The Native Americans of Maine had been chewing hard wads of tree resin for ages,[1] as did other native peoples worldwide. Scientists in Sweden discovered one of the oldest samples—a 9,000-year-old chunk of birch tree gum—about twenty years ago. There's some sort of poetic justice in knowing that the tooth marks in the gum belonged to a Neanderthal teen.[2] A few years later, a British archeology student in Finland found a chunk of 6,500-year-old birch tar, also with tooth marks.[3]

Those were prehistoric specimens. The first example in *written* history is the mastic resin of Greece, which appeared in a first-century text by botanist and physician Dioscorides.[4] Unlike birch and spruce resins, which hardly anyone chews or otherwise ingests anymore, mastic resin is still popular. It shows up as an ingredient in Turkish delight, toffees, both hard and jelly candies,[5] and, of course, as its naked chewable self. The resin pearls have a gorgeous, rich, yellow hue; the stuff of jewelry. Most mastic trees grow on the Greek island of Chios; the tree is squat with knotted limbs, much like an overgrown bonsai.

Why people chewed gum is another matter. They believed it had health value, and they were right; according to scientists, some resins have antibacterial and antifungal properties that can eliminate plaque, heal gums, and even cure peptic ulcers. The Neanderthal tar contains antiseptic compounds called "phenols" as well as xylitol, the sweetener in Ice Chips, the cranberry-enriched good-for-you candy. Xylitol, it turns out, fights tooth decay.[6]

Fig. 4.1. John Bacon Curtis. *Image from Wikipedia, user Doug Coldwell.*

As for the Native Americans, they took resin on long trips when fishing, hunting, or exploring. In addition to its healing powers, it moistened their mouths, cleaned their teeth, exercised their jaws, and even healed skin irritations and sores. In an interesting twist to the problem of gum stuck to the bottom of shoes, the Native Americans used spruce resin as an adhesive, particularly useful when repairing canoes.

John Bacon Curtis probably wasn't the first European American to discover the chewing value of spruce resin, but he was the first to care about it. It was either Curtis's time as a "swamper," clearing underbrush and forests to make way for roads, his familiarity with the Native American's use of spruce resin, or both that gave the twenty-one-year-old an idea: Why not package spruce resin and sell it to everyone who will buy it? With help from his reluctant father, he tested numerous production methods. They settled on boiling the spruce on the kitchen

Fig. 4.2. Chunks of spruce resin.

stove, cleaning it, cutting it into strips, wrapping it, and, finally, sealing it with their own label. They named their creation "State of Maine Pure Spruce Gum."[7]

Legend has it that for two days, Curtis went from store to store trying to sell his new product but nobody was interested. On the third day, he found a shop willing to try it. The gum didn't sell well at first, but eventually gained a limited following—it didn't bring in enough money to support the family in style but, evidently, there was enough of a profit to give them hope. In 1850, Curtis took the gum, along with some patent medicines and other goods, on the road, joining up with one of the many wholesale peddlers who were out at the time.

Curtis had three things going for him: he was aggressive, energetic, and self-assured. A biography published in 1909 quotes him as saying: "When the other fellows thought I was in bed, I was on the road. By driving nights I got in ahead many times, and had the trade all to myself."[8] Within a year, Curtis had earned $6,000 selling his new, tree-tasting product throughout New England.

Inspired, Curtis expanded his time on the road while his father oversaw the gum production at home. Their resin came from a new group of workers known as "pickers," which an 1889 *New York Times* article described in this way:

Very few people know how extensive [spruce gum picking] is, or how many people depend on it to help out a scanty living. . . . Most of the Adirondack gum pickers are gum pickers from necessity, not from choice. They are a nondescript class. . . . They are found among farmers, mechanics, lumbermen, guides, and even some of the young and robust maidens who dwell on the borders of the woods.[9]

Sound familiar? The pickers filled the same role as Elizabeth White's "Pineys" but with a different process. Pickers would score a tree with a knife, causing sap to slowly bubble up to fill and heal the wound. Months later, the pickers would return with axes, long poles with scrapers, or buckets with sharp edges, which they would use to pry the hardened sap from the bark. The pickers, as well as other lumbermen and forest workers, might spend days, even months, in the woods. During that time, they made little boxes with sliding tops, often etched with a design, called "gum books." They filled the interiors with chunks of spruce gum that they later gave their sweethearts back home.[10]

Curtis, meanwhile, broadened his territory, breaking historic ground as the first Easterner to set up commercial relationships in the Wild West and, as I mentioned, as one of the first—if not, *the* first—sales reps in the nation. When you imagine an early salesman, you might think of train rides, à la the musical *The Music Man*, with crafty hucksters huddled together in coach class; or saloons with beds on the upper floors for the weary (and intoxicated) traveler; or a lone salesman flying through the night with his horse and carriage.

But for the first chewing gum salesman, the narrative is entirely different. Curtis's travels predated much of the railroad system in the United States, or, as he stated: "In

Fig. 4.3. A gum book filled with spruce resin.

those early days Chicago had but one railroad and nothing but wooden sidewalks, through the cracks of which when the ground was wet the water was projected upward in streams that copiously sprinkled the passer-by."[11]

This usually meant he traveled by stagecoach or by water—on rivers, canals, and lakes. Here's what Curtis said about the matter:

> I have passed hundreds of nights camping out on long trips, with only a blanket for a covering and the ground for a bed. We, who drummed the trade in the West then in behalf of Eastern houses, did not mind that, but we did object to the rattlesnakes sometimes. It didn't pay to have them get too familiar. We were happy when we could travel by canal-boat or by steamboat, but the dreadful Western stages were what tried our patience. Time and again, but for the fact that my samples and baggage had to be carried, I should have preferred to walk, and would have beaten the stages under ordinary circumstances. Many times I did walk, but it was beside the stage, with a rail on my shoulder, ready to help pry the stage itself out of the mud.[12]

Despite the harsh travel conditions and, for that matter, the year it took for his customers to pay him, Curtis was a stunning success. To keep up with demand, he invented a gum-making machine that enabled his father to produce the gum faster and easier than by hand. In 1852, the Curtis & Son Company opened the nation's first chewing gum factory. With about 150 employees, they were able to produce 1,800 boxes of gum each day. The chewing gum industry was born!

Why Curtis stopped making chewing gum isn't clear. Before he did, he experimented with flavors—such as licorice—and ingredients—including paraffin wax, the parent to the wax lips kids still enjoy today. Competitors cropped up throughout Maine and beyond, but Curtis remained king. One reason that Curtis quit making gum may have been the death of his father in 1869, which changed the nature of their business. Another reason could have been that spruce resin, in spite of the boiling and added flavoring, still had a strong flavor and bitter aftertaste; with the appearance of new and fanciful chewing gum flavors as the commercial candy industry grew, spruce just couldn't compete.

It's also possible that Curtis—who went into dredging, ship-building, mining, and, finally, farming—was a true entrepreneurial spirit who loved the adventure of breaking ground but had no interest in staying there. And he was a good entrepreneur—his many endeavors made him a very rich man, and he died that way at the age of seventy in 1897.[13]

Regardless, his chewing gum legacy lived on. The machinery he invented (but never patented) is the basis of gum-making machines today. The chewing gum industry that he started blossomed, and his spruce resin continued to play a part. In 1892, a baking powder salesman decided to offer spruce gum as a free gift to encourage people to buy his product. It turned out that customers were more interested in the spruce gum than the baking powder, and the salesman switched careers. He went on to become the most powerful player in the gum industry and one of the most powerful men of his time. This salesman's name was William Wrigley.[14]

EATING THE TREE

Just about everyone I know enjoys a good apple or orange, but the only other advantage from the tree is shade on a hot day. Not so with the Native Americans, who believed in using the whole of a tree: the bark, the roots, and the leaves. A perfect example is the sassafras tree. You may have seen one—perhaps even pulled one out of your garden, depending on where you live. The sassafras has large mitten-like leaves and can have a towering presence. In candy, it appears in such choice bits as root beer barrels and sassafras sugar sticks.

For several Native American tribes, including the Cherokees, Chippewas, Choctaws, Creeks, Delawares, and Oklahomas, the sassafras had many uses. The roots in particular could purify blood, correct "overfatness," treat rheumatism, or be used as an eyewash, mouthwash, or cough medicine.[15] They frequently added spices, herbs, roots and other ingredients, sometimes up to fifty of them, and created a "root tea." When the settlers arrived, they discovered the tea, and, in the inimitable European American style, changed it into a tasty and healthful drink.[16] The eighteenth and early nineteenth-century versions of the tea also contained roots from the spruce tree, among others, with a dash of alcohol.[17]

Root tea was eventually transformed into root *beer*, with one European American standing out as the likely inventor: Charles Hires. His product was "Hires Root Beer." Like Elizabeth White's grandfather, as well as the renowned chocolate-making Cadbury and Fry families of England, Hires was a Quaker.

At twelve, Hires apprenticed at a pharmacy in his home in southern New Jersey, then moved to the bright lights of Philadelphia.[18] By the time he was eighteen, he had become a pharmacist, operating his own store. When Hires first tasted root tea is a mystery. Most accounts say he was on his honeymoon and discovered the root tea at a hotel where the owner served it. Her version contained a mix of twenty-six roots, berries, and herbs. Back in Philadelphia, Hires figured out a way to make root tea powder, which customers had to boil in water, strain, mix with sugar and yeast, and let ferment before they could drink it. The original package claimed the powder was "made from finest grade Honduras sarsaparilla, ginger, sassafras, hops, and other healthful and scientifically blended roots, barks and berries."[19]

Hires's new product had problems. One was the name. "Root tea" was fine but it lacked pizazz. Given that the temperance movement was gaining momentum, and alcohol was winning the hearts of oppositional consumers, why not call it *beer*? So, the fermented healthy tea became a fermented healthy beer. But Hires was a Quaker, and many Quakers, including Hires, would become die-hard prohibitionists. In short, Hires, the man who renamed his drink "root *beer*," was a teetotaler.

Not a problem. In fact, the name "root beer" became an asset since Hires branded it: "The Temperance Movement's Drink." According to one ad from 1888 in the *New York Times*, "Hires improved root beer . . . makes five gallons of the most delicious and wholesome temperance drink in the world."[20]

By "wholesome" this ad, and many others like it, was understating the point. A sidebar alongside the ad reinforced the point, proclaiming: "It is an acknowledged fact that the Beer made from this package is superior to all other so-called Root Beer made from oils, extracts and old or inert roots and herbs, because the roots and barks used in this compound are always fresh and carefully selected, hence it strengthens and purifies the blood." In case you're skeptical, it also said: "Its merits are endorsed by thousands, now using it, who are willing to testify to its superiority over all others."[21]

In addition to ads, Hires launched his beer powder at the Philadelphia Centennial Exposition of 1876. Within four years, he stopped making the powder and began to sell premade extract in glass bottles instead. Customers still had to boil the mixture, but that was easy, relatively speaking. Thirteen years later, Hires was selling three million bottles of extract each year, and by 1893, he was selling bottles of ready-to-drink root beer.

Whether it was a temperance drink, a healthy beverage that was good for the blood, or a cure for a variety of health issues (too many to list here), Hires was an expert at what mattered most: telling people about it. His ads were everywhere, portraying healthy, happy beverage drinkers. And, while Hires did place the first full-color ad in the back pages of *Ladies' Home Journal*[22] and featured plenty of wholesome kids and very Victorian mothers in all of his campaigns, there was no question about the audience he was actually trying to attract.

Root beer was no ladylike strawberry boiled sugar. Root beer was all about *men*. One ad announced: "To Farmers and Laboring men! It is indispensable in the Summer month in warding off the effects of heat"[23] In 1915, the *American Druggist and Pharmaceutical Record*, which, in true fashion of the times, devoted itself to both candy and medicine, told pharmacist readers:

> In a distinctly business section of the town, where men are in the majority, it is most advisable to cater chiefly to men by offering those drinks in non-alcoholic class which makes the strongest appeal to men. In this category may be mentioned such "solid" thirst quenchers as lemonade, limeade, orangeade, and other sour and bitter drinks . . . ginger ale combinations, root beer, buttermilk, malt.[24]

In case you're wondering, women were clumped together with children who enjoy "chocolates, ice cream sodas, sundaes, sorbets, sherbets, parfaits, ices and other delicacies."[25]

There's no question that Hires was a man full of contradictions. He sold "beer" yet was ultimately a prohibitionist. He was a Quaker, a believer in truth, yet falsely advertised his drink. And, oddly enough, as a member of the pacifist Society of Friends, he signed a pro-war statement during the First World War in 1918.[26]

You may be wondering when "root beer" became "root beer candy," one of the most beloved of penny candies and, from my observation, a favorite wherever it's sold today. My hunch is that root beer candy started at home, where women, the primary at-home candymakers, added root beer flavoring to boiled, or hard, sugars. It's also possible that the candies were first made in apothecaries, where pharmacists added flavorings and sugar to hide the bitter taste of medicine. Or, just as likely, pharmacists may have added the root beer extract *as* medicine, then, realizing it tasted good, ate it as candy.

Ads for root beer candy started surfacing in the late 1920s and had a definite presence after that. One, advertised in the 1930s, was called "Hires's Diced Root Beer Candy."[27] Some had brand names, others were nameless, and most were sold by the pound. By that time, there was a sea of root beer companies making candies, typically root beer barrels. Some of these companies are still around today; two of the most popular being A&W and Dad's.

A&W: BORN OF VICTORY

One of Roy Allen's first ventures selling root beer was a stand he set up at a parade for Great War veterans in his hometown of Lodi, California. Inspired by its success, Allen took on a partner, Frank Wright, and named their company A&W for their last names. A&W added a new offering: a "drive-in" where "tray-boys" delivered the customers' orders directly to their cars.[28] The drive-in was the 1921 brainchild of a Texas restaurant chain called the Pig Stand. Ten years later, one Pig Stand restaurant in Los Angeles opened a "drive-through," where customers placed their orders, paid for their meal, picked up their bagged and waiting food, and then drove away.[29] Sound familiar?

In 1924, Allen and Wright's partnership dissolved. Still Allen continued to call his restaurant A&W and developed a new business model which he called the "franchise." The idea took off, and in less than ten years there were 170 A&Ws nationwide. By the end of World War II, around the time that Allen retired and sold his business, that number had swelled to 450.[30] One of the early A&W franchisees was Willard Marriot, the Utah-born entrepreneur and father of the Marriot hotel chain.[31]

A&W switched hands many times after that. Eventually A&W root beer found its way onto grocery-store shelves in newly minted bottles and cans.[32] As for the root beer barrels, the company stopped making them in 2011 after licensing issues got in the way. Today, shops sell Brach's root beer barrels *made* with A&W root beer.

DAD'S ACTUALLY HOMEMADE (AT LEAST AT FIRST) ROOT BEER

The story of Chicago-based Dad's Root Beer is classically American. In the 1930s, two men, Barney Berns and Ely Klapman, made their own root beer in Klapman's basement. Evidently they enjoyed the taste and figured others would enjoy it too, because they opened up a business. As for the name: at that time, the newest thing for dads everywhere, including Klapman's, was making root beer at home.

Over the next twenty years, Dad's Root Beer spread across the Midwest thanks to advertising and marketing campaigns. Soon it became one of the most popular root beers in the United States.[33] No longer promising healthy, thirst-quenching drinks that doubled as a cure, Dad's was all about fun. The company leveraged the popular "giveaway" routine, like with their 1953 campaign promising a set of three Quikut steak knives, "a $1.50 value, yours for only 50c plus two of Dad's Root Beer bottle caps."[34] Dad's also gave away samples at events such as Gold's of Nebraska's Food Show in 1954,[35] and they sold smaller sized "Mama" and "Junior" bottles. Purchase Papa's half gallon size and get Mama's quart for a penny.[36]

In the late 1940s, the Atlanta Paper Company invented the now-famous six-pack container for sodas; Dad's was the first to use it. Later, Ely's son, Jules Klapman, took the business worldwide.

For all the root beers that surfaced over the years, it's worth noting that Hires had tried to get a patent on root beer in 1879 but lost because generic words are not patentable. He's the man who started the industry, though for all of root beer's success, we ultimately have the Native Americans to thank.

WHAT ABOUT THE BEANS?

Boston Baked Beans would seem like another candy connected to Native Americans. However, a reality check is in order. Beans *were* important to the Narragansett, Penobscot, and Iroquois tribes, who baked navy beans (later named for their role in the Navy) in a pot or wrapped them in deerskins with venison, bear fat, maple syrup, and possibly berries, much like pemmican. And Native Americans *did* teach European newcomers how to bake beans, with the settlers gradually changing the recipe to include molasses instead of maple syrup and salt pork instead of bear fat.[37]

But Boston Baked Beans actually have nothing to do with Native American beans or, for that matter, Boston. The candies are basically sugar-coated peanuts mixed with various flavorings and colorings; none of these ingredients were available in North America at this time. The "beans" are not even made by a Boston company but by the Illinois-based Ferrara Company, which produces 38,600 pounds of the candy each day.[38]

A LAND RICH WITH PLENTY

With all the ingredients that go into candy, it's astonishing how few originated in North America. Many of the native plants are relatively unfamiliar, such as

Fig. 4.4. Boston Baked Beans.

ginseng, which most people think is only found in China (although it also grew there); the persimmon, which grew in the south; and wintergreen, which is a popular flavor and whose berries, called "teaberries," are used in sweets such as Clark's Teaberry Gum. Most of the other ingredients—the orange, lemon, lime, peppermint, and spearmint flavors—came to North America with European settlers who discovered them elsewhere.

CHAPTER 5

ALL THE FOOD IN THE WORLD

The candy and fruit my father ate in his car were primarily newcomers to the nation, brought over in the sixteenth and seventeenth centuries. With the arrival of Europeans, the culinary landscape of the Native Americans started to shift, sprouting such things as citrus and almond trees, and pink-and-white-flowered marshmallow plants; and buzzing with honey bees, a European import from Africa.

Today, the candy aisle of your average grocery store showcases these changes . . . with a vibrant industrial flair. We have bright orange and lemon slices, marshmallows twisted into Santa Clause and bunny shapes, and almonds lost within layers of chocolate. But artificial or organic, love them or hate them, they are ours.

TART-AND-TANGY TANGO FROM CHINA TO SPAIN

While Europeans took the fruits that existed in North America and changed them into something more profitable, they also jumped from one continent to another, planting seeds as they went. One example is the peach, a succulent, seasonal favorite that endures cold weather but is also a luscious warm-weather treat. Peaches originated in China, where people enjoyed them some four thousand years ago. From China, peaches were carried by caravan to India, Persia, and Rome. The fruit didn't reach the United States until 1565, when Spanish explorers brought it to Florida.[1]

The Cherokee and Creek Indians were among the first to plant lush orchards with peach trees (and also with fig, apple, and orange trees). But when the European Americans discovered gold on Cherokee land, they promptly destroyed the orchards and exiled the inhabitants leaving only archeological evidence for eighteenth-century investigators to find.[2] Still, by the American Revolution, peaches were so prevalent that new European arrivals, like many Americans today, likely assumed they were native.[3]

The peach showed up in various confections starting in the eighteenth century. Eliza Leslie's *Directions for Cookery in Its Various Branches*, first published in 1817, used the fruit in all its parts: the pit (broken and boiled), the leaves, and the flesh.[4] The pit is said to have a cherry flavor—tasty but deadly in large doses, given that it's poisonous.

Today, the peach is primarily used as a flavoring in candy, not unlike another favorite, the orange. Throughout the eighteenth and nineteenth centuries, oranges, and also lemons, were confections in their own right—particularly when it came to their peels. Martha Washington's cookbook contains a recipe in which fruit peels were boiled repeatedly until the bitterness was more or less knocked out of them and a sugary coating had formed.[5]

Like the peach, we have the Spanish to thank for the arrival of the orange. The orange had been cultivated in China for more than four thousand years and edged its way across the world with explorers who planted their seeds as they went.[6] In this case, it was Christopher Columbus who brought the seeds with him on his second voyage to the Caribbean islands.

The seeds that Columbus carried were for a bitter type of orange; this was not necessarily a bad thing, as many early confectionery recipes specifically called for bitter oranges. Other explorers planted oranges in Florida as well, including sweet oranges, which were also native to China and are the oranges we eat today. Florida was sparsely populated, and, in spite of Martha Washington's culinary interest, the orange was more or less ignored. In fact, Jesse Fish, an early Floridian, was the only large-scale orange grower during the eighteenth century. By the early nineteenth century, though, the orange took off with abandon.[7] One early chewing gum was Thomas Adam's orange flavor—make that *sour* orange—which followed on the heels of Tutti Frutti.[8]

HERE BUT NOT HERE . . . DE LOVELY, DE ROSE

When the tired, beleaguered settlers stepped onto the "new land" they didn't see any roses for their gardens. But, they must not have looked very closely: the United States is home to twenty-six varieties of roses that grow from coast to coast. Instead of harvesting these native plants, the new settlers and the Europeans who followed, imported their own roses from England, France, Holland, and elsewhere.

By the eighteenth century, gardeners and professional nurserymen were developing hybrids, something the Chinese had been doing since time immemorial. One of the Chinese roses had an enviable trait: it flowered from spring through fall, whereas the attractive European variety only flowered once. The growers got to work bringing the two together, and a beautiful long-flowering rose was born. Many other hybrids followed, hundreds in fact, and the rose bush, a "new" plant that was already in the United States, spread out across the nation.[9]

But why the rose? This ornamental flower has long been admired for its medicinal and culinary value, starting with the Ancient Egyptians, Greeks, and Romans, and, on a larger scale, with the Persians of the ninth century.[10] The rose found its way to Europe with the crusaders in such culinary (and medicinal) pleasures as Turkish delight and marzipan, which was first made thousands of years ago.[11] In the eighteenth century, the rose appeared in tea biscuits, cakes, and other sweets. Confectioners also created a delicious confit with floating rose petals in a sugar base, reminiscent of Turkish delight but with a jellylike consistency. All these candies can still be found today, though primarily on the shelves of specialty stores.

Rose petals hold their own special place in the historic confectionery world. The idea of using flowers in candy, or even *as* candy, began in the Middle East, where they were pulverized and coated with sugar.[12] This trend continued throughout the eighteenth and nineteenth centuries in the United States, where recipes appeared in Martha Washington's *Booke of Cookery*[13] as well as in the work of African American cookbook author Rufus Estes about one hundred years later.[14]

So, how did the rose lose its confectionery stature? As a flavor, the rose lost out to vanilla. As a candied sweet, it's hard to say. My hunch is that the rose petal was too delicate and sensitive to mass produce once the Industrial Revolution took hold. Today, most candied rose petals in the United States come from France, although some are prepared at home or, now and then, by boutique confectioners.

As for the petals the locals are using: the vast majority are from imported roses and this might be good news for the native plants. Barring urban sprawl or suburban development, native roses may be growing unpicked and unencumbered wherever soil and climate allow.

A QUICK WORD ABOUT THE VIOLET

The violet is a native flower. But the concept of candying violet petals is purely European, and the methods for doing so are pretty much the same as for rose petals. What separates these two flowers are three things: their flavor, their place of origin, and Napoleon Bonaparte. Napoleon and his wife, Josephine, were enamored with violets, which became a French favorite during their lifetime. Once Napoleon fell from favor, the French love of violets fell, too.

ALL ABOUT THE ROSE WATER KILLER

It's true that vanilla killed the rose flavoring, but only indirectly. In short, once vanilla became available, people preferred it, and rose flavoring more or less died of neglect.

Vanilla comes from an orchid, the *Vanilla planifolia*, and has never grown on a large scale in the United States. In fact, for centuries, it never left its Mesoamerican home. Then came Spanish explorer Hernán Cortés who discovered the pod in a chocolate drink Emperor Montezuma gave him. Like cacao, another favorite of Montezuma, vanilla is considered an aphrodisiac and a helper should impotence get in the way.[15] In 1772, German physician Bezaar Zimmermann wrote: "No fewer than 342 impotent men, by drinking vanilla decoctions, have changed into astonishing lovers of at least as many women."[16]

The Spaniards kept the vanilla orchid to themselves, where it remained until 1791 when it was smuggled onto the island of Réunion, part of the Bourbon Islands. Unfortunately, when it came to performance, the orchid had its own problems: it could only be pollinated by the stingless *Melipona* bee, which could not survive outside its Mesoamerican homeland. Whatever pollination occurred was unpredictable; more a matter of luck than desire.[17]

Botanists got to work. In the 1830s, Charles Morren, a professor of botany from Belgium, figured out how to hand pollinate the plant, but his method was slow and ultimately expensive. Then came Edmond Albius, a French slave and an orphan whose mother died when he was born and whose father was never present. The slaveholder, Féréol Bellier-Beaumont, had a special fondness for the boy. The two would walk through the plantation gardens, Bellier-Beaumont teaching Edmond the intricacies of plant reproduction as they went. As it happened, Bellier-Beaumont was in possession of the vanilla orchid, which he had received from the French government years before.[18]

One day in 1841, Bellier-Beaumont taught Edmond how to pollinate the watermelon plant. Soon after, Edmond applied the principles to the vanilla orchid, taking a stick and moving the pollen from the orchid's male anther to its female stigma with a quick flick of his thumb. The vanilla was pollinated. At that moment, the vanilla industry was born. Edmond was twelve years old at the time; his method is still used today.

In 1848, the French outlawed slavery. Once freed, Edmond married and took a job as a kitchen servant. One day, a robbery occurred while he was working. Jewelry

Fig. 5.1. Edmond Albius.
*Image from Wikipedia,
user B.navez.*

went missing, and Edmond was blamed and sentenced to five years of hard labor. Bellier-Beaumont came to his defense, saying: "If anyone has a right to clemency and to recognition for his achievements, then it is Edmond. . . . It is entirely due to him that this country owes [*sic*] a new branch of industry—for it is he who first discovered how to manually fertilize the vanilla plant."[19]

The judge agreed. While Edmond was released, he was never compensated for his discovery, although Bellier-Beaumont lobbied on his behalf. Edmond died in poverty at the age of fifty-one; the vanilla industry soared.

THE FLIGHT OF THE HONEY BEE

Most people today believe that honey bees are a native insect, but they're actually from Africa and were brought to Jamestown colony by the British around 1622. Their detritus, honey, was used from the Mideast to Asia, as a part of funeral rites (some believed it warded off demons), in marriage rituals, as a love charm, and as an aphrodisiac. The Egyptians also mixed honey with lemon as a contraceptive,[20] although I can't vouch for its effectiveness.

Many early candies were also honey-based, such as pasteli, the first brittle, which consisted of honey with sesame seeds and, occasionally, lemon. This delightful treat, still sold in candy stores and supermarkets today, was likely the food Homer referred to in the *Iliad* as "honey and sesame pie."[21] Another honey-based original was nougat, a soft, sweet honey mixture with nuts—typically almonds or walnuts— suspended inside, dating back to the Roman food writer Apicius in the first century CE. Nougat candies still available today include torrone in Italy, which originated in the fifteenth century; nougat in France, circa the sixteenth century; and turrón of Spain, which is roughly five hundred years old.[22]

Fig. 5.2. Sesame brittle.

Native Americans called the newcomer honey bees "the white man's fly." The bees migrated ahead of the settlers; when tribes further out saw the swarms and heard the thunderous humming of the bees, they knew the Europeans would soon follow. Over the years, the bees swarmed further west, but stopped at the Rockies. To help them along, botanists, including C. A. Shelton, carried them to California, traveling from the East Coast, across Panama, then over to the Pacific Ocean in 1852. The trip wasn't easy for the bees or, I imagine, the travelers, and many died, but enough survived to eventually thrive.[23]

Early on, the colonists used honey as a stain remover for clothes,[24] and, more to the point, as a sweetener that was cheaper than sugar or molasses since they kept bees at home.[25] They also used honey as a flavoring and an ingredient in a variety of sweets including brandied peaches, fruit butters, marmalades, and gingerbread, among others.

The honey bee would also become significant to the abolitionists' "free

Fig. 5.3. A beehive.

produce movement." As the name implies, this movement, primarily started by female Quakers in the early 1800s, promoted food and fabrics not made by enslaved workers. In 1830, the Quakers launched a Free Produce Association in Philadelphia, and, soon after, women of the African American community formed the Colored Female Free Produce Society of Philadelphia.[26]

Among other initiatives, the African American women encouraged "colored capitalists" to buy from "free produce" stores. An African American publication, *Freedom's Journal*, carried an article indicating that every twenty-five people who used cane sugar found work for one slave.[27] The women activists dispersed recipes that replaced cane sugar with free produce—frequently honey.

Honey could never be mass-produced, so it never took off to the same degree as sugar beets and sugarcane. Its history as a newcomer to the nation is long forgotten, and much of today's commercial honey is imported from China. Home beekeepers have created an interesting cottage industry, helping the immigrant bee, and its honey, survive.

OH THAT FLITTERING, FLUTTERING PEANUT

The peanut is another non-native plant, which most people believe originated in Africa. Actually, the flight of the peanut plant began in South America, where it was eaten by the Mayas of the Yucatan, the Incas of Peru, and tribes throughout Brazil. The peanut, which is actually not a nut, but a pea, was discovered by the conquistadors who carried it back to Europe. The Spanish, who considered it beneath their culinary tastes, carried the peanut to Asia, where it was appreciated in a variety of foods,[28] while the Portuguese carried it to West Africa. From there, slave traders loaded it on ships, along with their human cargo.[29] Thus, the peanut returned to the Americas, where it once began.

For roughly one hundred years, the enslaved people were the only North Americans to eat the peanut, which they ate raw, boiled, or roasted. In the late 1700s, vendors roasted them in northern cities,[30] although the peanut was relatively unknown. In the early 1800s, commercial peanuts were being grown in Virginia and used as, among other things, a substitute for cocoa.[31] By the mid-1800s, peanut production began in earnest thanks to the wonders of steam-powered machinery.[32] During the Civil War, Union soldiers discovered the peanut and brought them north. The era of the peanut was launched.

And boy did peanuts take off. They became a source of both nourishment and fun, often at the same time. P. T. Barnum's circus wagon sold "hot roasted peanuts," and spectators at baseball games—the recreational passion of returning Union soldiers—bought them from hawkers. Soon vendors were selling them at festive events and suburban street corners, joining forces with another fun favorite: popcorn.

In the early 1900s, thanks to new machinery that improved everything from planting to picking to cleaning the kernels, the peanut seemed to be everywhere,[33] including in the quintessential American candy: the tasty and delicious candy bar. These confectionery wonders arrived on the scene in 1912 and were marketed as an inexpensive meal in a bar, and a healthy energy food. Not surprisingly, its off-spring include such un-candy-like creations as protein bars, nutrition bars, and, remarkably enough, *diet* bars.

As for peanut butter, many lay claim to inventing this American standard. One was the influential health-food advocate Dr. John Harvey Kellogg. Peanut butter satisfied his requirements as a strict vegetarian and his belief that food must be chewed extensively before being swallowed. The ground-up peanut pretty much did the work for you. As an interesting side note: Kellogg was a speaker at the Tuskegee Institute in Alabama, where peanut advocate and scientist George Washington Carver attended.[34] Chocolates with peanut butter filling were soon among the most popular candies sold. This was ironic since Kellogg had strong feelings against chocolate. = And why? Because it stirred sexual desire (and he was against sex, too).

Today, peanuts are the nation's twelfth most valuable cash crop, and peanut candy is among the most popular products.[35]

THE BEGINNING OF EVERYTHING: THE ELEGANT ALMOND

It's impossible to discuss confectionery immigrants without bringing up the almond. This popular nut, with its pleasant taste and pop-in-your-mouth size, is so at home, you'd think the tree was native. But, it's not. Like the peanut, the almond isn't exactly a nut, either. It's a drupe, which is a type of fruit.[36] Its cousins are other mostly immigrant fruits such as the peach, the cherry, the apricot, and the plum. Nonetheless, people have been enjoying almonds for thousands of years; samples eaten in 10,000 BCE were found in the Franchthi Cave of Greece.[37]

So valued is the almond tree that it's been a symbol of sweetness and fragility since prehistory. In the Bible, Aaron's rod blossomed and produced almonds, while the Roman's threw almonds at weddings as a fertility charm.[38] This reflect the almond's flowering cycle: the tree is the first to flower, which announces sweet beginnings, but it is vulnerable to frost. The almond tree first arrived in the United States with Spanish Franciscan padres on the California coast in the mid-1700s, but it was another hundred years or so before the almond began to flourish.

In terms of candy, the almond was embedded in the age-old nougat, described by one tenth-century text as being "as soft and sweet as lips."[39] It was also central to the almond-based marzipan, used in "subtleties," where men, animals, trees, castles, and other shapes were part of medieval feasts. Today, marzipan appears in the shapes of fruits, flowers, and other forms, with exuberant colors.

Two other almond-based candies are classics. One is the candy-coated almond, known in the United States as the Jordan Almond, aka the Italian "confetti" and the French "dragee." These candies were thrown in Roman weddings and are still served at American weddings today. The other candy is the Hershey's Bar with almonds. It's not exactly ancient, but it is old, dating back to the turn-of-the-century when Hershey created one of the first candy bars that was not made of solid chocolate.

MARSHMALLOW

Yes, the marshmallow really is from the marshmallow plant. That's what I say every time someone asks me about the marshmallow, which is often. Maybe it's the sticky texture that equates the marshmallow with something other than a plant? Even stranger, perhaps, is the marshmallow's incredible background. The marshmallow plant, or *Althaea officinalis*, is a relative of the hollyhock, with pastel-colored, papery flowers.[40] The plant, especially its roots, has a sticky substance that once gave marshmallow its taste and texture. Today, the root is widely available as a tea: the mucilage is like a syrup in hot water but thickens into a strangely sweet gel when cool.

The marshmallow plant originated in Europe and West Asia, where the ancients used it to treat coughs and sore throats. The marshmallow was also a sweet that ancient Egyptians boiled with sugar or mixed with honey around 2000 BCE.[41] The result must have been very thick, very sweet, and very hard to make given the stickiness of the plant.

Fig. 5.4. Marshmallow root.

When marshmallow appeared in the United States is unclear, but marsh-mallow candy originated in France around 1850 when confectioners blended the mallow root with egg whites, sugar, and water. By the mid-1800s, cookbooks such as the *Complete Confectioner*, written by Eleanor Parkinson in 1864, contained recipes such as this:

Pate de Guimauve

Take of decoction of: marshmallow roots 4 ounces; water 1 gallon.

Boil down to 4 pints and strain; then add gum arabic 1/2 a pound; refined sugar 2 pounds.

Evaporate to an extract; then take from the fire, stir it quickly with the whites of 12 eggs previously beaten to a froth; then add, while stirring, 1/2 ounce of orange-flower water.[42]

Within thirty years, marshmallow candy was being advertised as a penny candy. The recipes remained unchanged except for one omission: the marshmallow root. In its place was an ingredient that took the food world by storm: instant gelatin.

To understand instant gelatin, you have to understand the process of making the non-instant gelatin, which was typically made by women at home who would spend long days boiling cow hooves in their hot kitchens, a process that was demanding and tedious. Instant gelatin put an end to all that, although the early efforts were hardly triumphant. In 1845, industrialist, philanthropist, and inventor of the steam locomotive Peter Cooper made what he called "portable gelatin."[43] He didn't do much with the product beyond patenting it, probably because he was actually trying to make glue.[44] Others soon followed, including the Scottish import, Cox Gelatin; Boston's Plymouth Rock Gelatin Company; and Charles Knox's instant gelatin, the most successful of the batch.

Charles Knox's success was due to many things—the quality of his gelatin being only one of them. He was an aggressive and creative marketer, who initially hired salesmen to go door-to-door and teach his target audience—housewives— how to use the stuff. Then there was his wife, Rose. Knox initially started making instant gelatin after observing his wife's struggles with the real thing.

Yet, it wasn't until Charles died that Rose really blossomed. She took over every aspect of the company, doing away with Knox's other ventures and toning down his marketing campaigns. Among her efforts, she set up test kitchens and published hundreds of free Knox gelatin booklets loaded with recipes, a popular giveaway at the time. Mrs. Knox made Knox Gelatin one of the leading instant-gelatin manufacturers, which it remains today.[45]

Gelatin enabled candymakers to do something they probably yearned for: kick the marshmallow plant out of the marshmallow. It was too sticky, too unmanageable, and too expensive to use. They replaced it with gelatin and, in words Peter Cooper probably would have been proud of, it was full steam ahead. The marshmallow was fun, tasty, and eclectic, effortlessly crossing the lines between candy and other foods. Newspapers had ads for such unlikely possibilities as pineapple parfait with marshmallows, almond-marshmallow fudge, and marshmallow delight with more ingredients than you'd want to know.[46]

The marshmallow also appeared in the candy bar, the S'more, and as part of a turn-of-the-century phenomenon, the marshmallow roast. One article in 1892 described marshmallow roasts as the "Latest Diversion to Amuse the Summer Girl" and provided detailed advice on how to brown a marshmallow without burning it. "When done they are morsels for the gods," the author wrote. "Resembling in flavor the most excellent meringue, with a delicious nutty and crusty outside. They are a sort of sublimated combination of candy and cake, all in one bite."[47]

If you are not convinced, the author adds: "Marshmallow roasts are an excellent medium for flirtation, mutual regard between a young lady and a young gentleman being appropriately exhibited by nibbling the marshmallow off of each other's sticks."[48] Personally, I never considered the marshmallow in this way, but it does give you something to think about.

FLUFF AND CHICKS:
TWO CLASSICS IN MARSHMALLOW HISTORY

No discussion of the marshmallow is ever complete without looking at two marshmallow favorites, both as far removed from the sappy root as you can get. The first is Marshmallow Fluff. I remember it well from my own experience at my nana's house. My nana was my father's candy-loving mother who, according to my mother, would sneak me into the backyard and covertly pass me sweets.

That, I can assure you, was nothing compared to the goings-on in her kitchen. From a corner cupboard she would withdraw a white bottle of Marshmallow Fluff, dig in with a mega-sized tablespoon, and hand me an otherworldly heap of creamy, forbidden marshmallow. She knew exactly what she was doing. I was in heaven.

While my nana died almost twenty years ago, the company that makes Fluff is still around and still in Massachusetts. It all started in 1917, when confectioner Archibald Query first made the concoction in his Somerville kitchen. He sold it door-to-door but lost momentum due to shortages from World War I. A few years later, Query joined forces with two entrepreneurs, H. Allen Durkee and Fred L. Mower, and started again, calling the confection "Toot Sweet Marshmallow Fluff." Query soon sold his partners the confection for $500, a decision he would later regret. They renamed the company Durkee-Mower Inc., which is still its name today. The company is also the proud parent of the Fluffernutter, the famous marshmallow-fluff-and-peanut-butter sandwich.[49]

JUST BORN, AGAIN

The Marshmallow Peeps, the ones that I found in my father's car all those years ago, are a fascination and an enigma. They don't seem to spoil; they just grow hard over time. They also don't have much taste but make up for it with texture. And they are called chicks, but they don't have wings.

The chicks are a product—make that *the* product—of the Just Born company. Sam Born was a Russian immigrant who went into candy making in 1910 in Brooklyn, New York. A few years later, he opened a retail store, helping to bring French chocolates to New York. He announced the freshness of his sweets with a sign saying "Just Born."

Adding to the not-real religious undertones, Born moved his company to Bethlehem, Pennsylvania, to save money during the Depression.[50] In 1953, the company bought Rodda Candy Co. of Lancaster, Pennsylvania, mainly for its jelly bean business. Rodda did have a line of marshmallow chicks that a dozen or so women squeezed into life from pastry bags—a slow, difficult process that was not very rewarding. By the mid-1950s Sam's son, Bob, an engineer and physicist, made a machine that produced the Peeps quickly. There was only one problem: the little Peep-wings got in the way. Off went the wings, and more and more wingless Peeps have been mass-produced every year, with totals reaching one billion during Easter season alone.[51]

LIGHT UP A LICORICE, ANYONE?

When John Josselyn brought the licorice plant to Boston from England in the sixteenth century, he described it as a "precious herb."[52] He gave the root to the Native Americans, explaining that they could ferment it into a drink that would cure colds or chew it to clean their teeth. The Blackfoot Indians later used the root to cure earaches. Licorice is an amiable plant that prefers sun but can handle shade and dies back in the fall so it's not affected by frost. It was likely a native of the Mediterranean, but grew in many parts of the world.

It also grows in the United States, but apparently not enough according to some outspoken nineteenth-century growers. Like the Native Americans, the European Americans considered licorice medicinal and used it for everything from a diuretic to a cure for respiratory ailments. But that wasn't the reason American growers wanted the licorice plant. The real reason was that licorice was an important flavoring for tobacco. In fact, by 1876, three-fourths of all licorice entering the country was used for tobacco.[53]

One article published in 1888 explained: "It may be surprising to know that the United States uses annually 20,000,000 pounds of licorice in her tobacco factories. . . . Besides what is used in tobacco factories, the article is largely used for other purposes. This country annually pays out about $7,000,000—a big sum that would be at home if farmers would only grow the plant."[54] The article went on to state how easy the plant is to grow and harvest but to no avail; licorice growing remained a cottage industry.

While the tobacco industry was lobbying to grow more licorice, children were eating it as a penny candy. Two licorice favorites of today got their start at that time. One was the Licorice Allsorts, a British confection made in 1899 by Bassett's Candy. The candy was created when a company salesman was calling on a difficult customer. He neatly set out numerous trays of licorice candy, but they toppled over, pieces comingling into an assortment of "all sorts" of licorice. The customer actually liked them.[55]

The other licorice candy was, believe it or not, Good & Plenty, which is owned by Hershey today but remains the nation's oldest brand of candy. The key to its survival is likely two American icons. One was Choo-Choo Charlie, the cartoon engineer whose train pulled dining cars as he

Fig. 5.5. Licorice root.

proclaimed Good & Plenty "really rings my bell" in television ads. The other is the real-life engineer Casey Jones.

Jonathan Luther "Casey" Jones (1863–1900) was born in a racially charged nation at the time of the Civil War and reveals the best of America. Jones and Sim Webb, his African American friend and railroad fireman, were operating a passenger train in 1900. The train collided with a stopped freight car. Apparently Casey Jones made a heroic effort to save the train and everyone on board. Casey perished in the crash although everyone else survived.

Good & Plenty, a product of the family-owned Quaker City Confectionery Company of Philadelphia, entered this world around that time, in 1893. The sweet may have gone the way of thousands of Industrial Revolution–era candies were it not for family member Lester Rosskam. In 1946, after serving as a counterintelligence officer in World War II, Rosskam joined his family's business. He realized the power of TV marketing and helped launch the Choo-Choo Charlie advertising campaign in 1950, based on a real-life college football player he knew.[56]

But Charlie's true steam comes from the Good & Plenty jingle. It was based on "The Ballad of Casey Jones," which was written by railroad wiper Wallace Saunders shortly after Jones's death, to the tune of the popular song "Jimmie Jones." The 1950 version was created by advertising executive and copywriter Russ Alben, of Ogilvy and Mather, whose other brainchildren include the Timex tagline: "Takes a licking and keeps on ticking."[57]

The lyrics of the jingle have plenty of memorable repetition, a steady rhythm punctuated by the sound of Good & Plenty irresistibly sliding around in their box, and the wholesome image of Charlie the engineer, who every kid loved and every parent trusted. Once you sing it, it's hard to stop:

> Once upon a time there was an engineer
> Choo-Choo Charlie was his name, we hear.
> He had an engine and he sure had fun
> He used Good & Plenty candy to make his train run.
> Charlie says "Love my Good & Plenty!"
> Charlie says "Really rings my bell!"
> Charlie says "Love my Good & Plenty!"
> Don't know any other candy that I love so well![58]

Two other candymakers stand out among the early licorice pack, and both are still in operation today. One is Young & Smylie, the creator of Twizzlers. Young &

Smylie was founded in 1845 and became Y&S in 1870. The company, now owned by Hershey, made the iconic Twizzler in 1929[59] but no longer uses licorice extract.

The other candymaker is the American Licorice Company, which opened in 1914 in Chicago. The company started making Black Licorice Twists then added licorice cigarettes and cigars during the Depression. At that time, licorice was vastly popular and was being manufactured in every metropolitan city outside of the southern states.

In 1925, around the time that the company moved to San Francisco, it got a call from Charlie Chaplin. He was starring in a film called *Gold Rush* in which his character needed to eat a shoe to avoid starving. The American Licorice Company obliged him, making a black licorice shoe with licorice laces as the shoestrings. The company went on to invent Snaps in the 1930s, and in the 1950s, it introduced a new, non-licorice licorice—aka "red licorice," or Red Vines, which today is a better seller than black licorice.[60]

CHAPTER 6

THEN COMETH THE SUGARCANE

When the sugarcane made its way to North America, the ground didn't shake, but it should have. The plant had a mighty impact on the North American continent that resonates to this day. The backstory of sugarcane is little known or understood—even its origin. In an informal survey of roughly twenty customers at my shop, an overwhelming majority (eighteen) thought the cane originated in Africa, one believed it was from South America, and one had no idea. Researchers agree that India was the likely starting point, although it may have existed in New Guinea nine thousand years ago.[1]

From there it was grown in China, where Buddhist monks either introduced or popularized it. The Chinese were among the first to use cane sugar in food, drink, and even the classic rock candy. People chewed the cane for its sweetness—which is still done today in some countries—and valued what they considered its aphrodisiac qualities.[2]

The Romans and Greeks eventually got hold of cane sugar, and the first-century botanist Dioscorides likened its brittle texture to salt. Its aphrodisiac properties notwithstanding, the ancients used sugar primarily as a medicine.[3] Cane sugar finally reached Europe during the Crusades and gradually became a potent and important part of their diet. Medieval physicians in Europe considered it important for balancing the humors, a concept that originated as far back as Pythagoras in 550 BCE.[4]

The idea goes something like this: people have four properties or "humors," each with its own hot, moist, cold, or dry "quality." If a person's humors are not balanced, disease can take hold. One remedy for imbalance was food. Sugar was "hot" and honey was even hotter. In fact, honey was so hot some people were advised to use it with caution.[5]

Fig. 6.1. Sugarcane. *Image from Wikipedia, user Editor at Large.*

MOLASSES, TAXES, AND RUM

By the time the Colonists in Virginia, Massachusetts Bay, and elsewhere were plotting to liberate themselves from the British, the Portuguese had been using slaves to grow sugarcane for hundreds of years in their colonies. Eventually, the British, Spanish, and French did the same.

The problem for Europeans was simple: they needed a workforce. The Native peoples lacked the necessary skills and were too susceptible to imported diseases to be reliable. Africans, with their knowledge of agriculture, their familiarity with hot climates, and their availability through the system of enslavement, were a valuable resource.

But why sugarcane? In the colonies, the answer was rum, which was made from molasses—the dregs of cane sugar production. For the Colonists, alcohol—whether hard cider, whisky, or rum—served as a replacement for water. It was something they drank to get up, drank to go to sleep, and drank in the time in-between. Alcohol was also considered medicinal and was believed to aid digestion, cure colds, and heal other ailments. Plus, the colonists liked it. As for alcoholism: it existed, it was real, but it took 150 years for the Europeans to realize that it was a health problem and not a personality quirk.[6]

The first still was made in New England in the seventeenth century by Emmanuel Downing, who found that molasses was cheaper than grain and, therefore, rum was more economical than whisky. Within one hundred years, rum, especially rum punch, became the colonists' favorite beverage. As an added bonus, the colonists could produce rum more economically than the British colonists in the West Indies. Rum was more than a useful and delicious drink; it was also a powerful tool. George Washington knew this well when, as a candidate for the House of Burgesses in 1758, he coerced voters with twenty-eight gallons of rum and fifty gallons of rum punch, among other distilled beverages.[7]

Rum was also a moneymaker. Colonists traded such items as fish and lumber for molasses, which they used to make and then sell rum. This deal was good for everyone—seamen, merchants, boat builders, and the universe that supported this profit-making cycle. At the heart of all this activity was the sugarcane, which John Adams considered a major force driving the American Revolution. It was, as he put it, "an essential ingredient in American independence. . . . Many great events have proceeded from much smaller causes."[8]

The two most significant sugar-related issues were the relatively tepid

Molasses Act of 1733 and the ire-inspiring Sugar Act of 1764 that followed. It all started because British molasses was more expensive than the French variety, which the colonists naturally preferred. This put a dent in the economy of the motherland. To recoup their losses and punish the unruly colonists, the British placed a steep tariff of six pence per pound[9] on any molasses, rum, or sugar the colonists bought from British competitors. For many reasons, including the cost of enforcing the act, corruption within the ranks, and the British decision to trade sugar directly with European countries[10] to ease the financial stress, the Act was never enforced.

In 1764, as the Molasses Act was about to expire, Great Britain was feeling the economic pinch due to the costs they had incurred from the Seven Years War. So, where could they get cash? The answer was a new revenue stream compliments of the new Sugar Act. The British figured that the colonists wouldn't really mind since the new tax would only be 3 pence per gallon, less than what it was under the Molasses Act. Except, of course, they didn't pay the tariffs in the first place. Even worse, the British included wines, coffee, and other items under the taxation umbrella and sealed the deal with a strong navy presence.

The economic effect was profound, and the colonists, not exactly happy with the British to begin with, were livid. They held protests in Boston's Faneuil Hall, among other places, and boycotted British goods. The British eventually repealed the law but tightened their taxation authority. The colonists resisted. The standoff ended in 1775 with the beginning of the American Revolution.

MORE ON THE LIFE AND TIMES OF MOLASSES

Molasses was more than a gateway to rum. Throughout the eighteenth, nineteenth, and early twentieth centuries, it was one of America's most conflicted foods whose identity was shaped by whoever was eating it. It appeared in desserts, candy, biscuits, and gingerbread, made hot and delicious in rural kitchens. It was also a cheap substitute for nourishing foods, for slaves, prisoners, and the poor.

African Americans of the south, including those working in Thomas Jefferson's Monticello before and after the Civil War, lived on bread, molasses, and fat,[11] a diet that left them malnourished. Prisoners, who ate molasses as part of their regular diet, loathed it. According to an article in a 1908 Topeka newspaper, several prisoners loathed it to the point that they went on strike, refusing to go to the "rock pile" with only bread and molasses for breakfast. These prisoners were then served bread and water each morning until they "gratefully returned" to molasses.[12]

Later, in 1912, a Congressman underscored the desperate lives of strikers in Lawrence, Massachusetts, saying: "It has been testified that these striking people have to put molasses on their bread because their wages are not sufficient to purchase butter."[13]

Molasses was controversial as a food, but it was most definitely enjoyed as a candy. One of the early, pre–Civil War favorites were molasses pulls, which were among the few luxuries that enslaved people enjoyed on the plantations. In an interview with former slaves through the Depression-era Federal Writer's Project, Josephine Hamilton, who was enslaved in Arkansas, recounted: "At Christmas time, we had . . . cake, molasses candy that you pulled, horse apples that was good, better 'n any apples we get these days."[14]

Lucky Civil War soldiers may have received pulled molasses in packages from home and definitely pulled the molasses themselves. Early on, confederate soldier John S. Jackman wrote in his diary: "Pleasant day for winter. We are living well. Have good fresh beef, good pork, flour, sorghum, rice and so on, issued in abundance. We make the molasses into candy, have candy-pullings among ourselves."

The pulls that soldiers and enslaved people mentioned were like taffy. On the battlefield and plantation, they may have flavored them with whatever was available since early molasses was bitter. In the confectionery, with the addition of vanilla, sugar, or spice, the pulls were literally pulled by hand or pulled from a hook. *The Art of Confection*, written by J. E. Tilton in 1865, reveals other molasses treats still with us today:

> Candy of various kinds is made from molasses, such as stick molasses candy, pulled candy, taffy. . . . The sticks may be single, twisted, braided flattened. Almonds, peanuts, hickory-nuts, &c, are often stirred into molasses candy which is also flavored with different essences, according to taste.[15]

The late 1800s ushered in a new phenomenon to the candy world: the pull party. At these parties, young European American couples—well-dressed and well-to-do—would pull the candy with lightly buttered fingers. The activity was recommended many years later, in 1964, in *Boys' Life*, a magazine for the Boy Scouts of America. The article gives a beautiful description:

It was great fun to watch the bubbling pan of hot liquid and to taste it when it was "tested" in a cup of cold water. The most fun, though, was pulling it. As you worked air into the candy it became lighter and lighter. When it cooled, the pulling became harder and harder. Soon it was a thick twisted rope that could be broken into bite-size pieces to hold in the back of your mouth or under your tongue as it melted.[16]

The molasses pull is also known as the molasses "taffy" or "toffee." Many toffees today are still made with molasses and nuts, as described in Tilton's Civil War–era recipe. Toffee may have originated in England, where a favorite was the Everton Toffee made in the late 1700s.[17] The words "taffy" and "toffee" are often used interchangeably, but the difference is clear: toffee is harder and chewier and typically contains nuts. This was the style of candy Tilton was referring to in 1865. The American toffee took off in the early 1900s during Prohibition, with such delicious molasses treasures as the Mary Jane and the Squirrel Nut Zipper.

By the 1940s, with machinery and industrial production a given, new candies were popping up everywhere, with colors and smells that excited the imagination. One popular new molasses candy was straightforward and simple: sponge candy, also known as sea foam. Today, you're likely to sample these crunchy bits in such places as upstate New York, Vermont, and Massachusetts, but only from October until about February because of the candy's sensitivity to humidity.

There are different styles of sponge candy. The plain version looks like molten chunks of brick of various sizes, with bubbly centers. The texture is amazing; they melt in your mouth, shrinking down to a mere reminder of their original size in seconds. Other sponge candies are bite-sized and enrobed in chocolate. The texture inside is almost like honeycomb—crisp, yellow, and ribbed—and is a delicious contrast to the smooth chocolate coating on the outside.

SUGAR GOES TO NEW YORK WITHOUT THE MOLASSES

North America started edging its way to sugar independence in the early 1700s by establishing its own sugar refineries. The first was opened by Nicholas Bayard in New York, where the ports made receiving and shipping sugar possible. The *New York Gazette* of 1730 contained this advertisement:

Public notice is hereby given that Nicholas Bayard of the City of New York has erected a refining house for refining all sorts of sugar and sugar candy and has produced from Europe an experienced artist in that mystery. At which refining house all persons in city and country may be supplied by Whole-sale and Re-tale with both double and single Refined Loaf-Sugar as also Powder and Shop-Sugar and Sugar-Candy at Reasonable Rates.[18]

More refineries opened in New York and other cities over the years, but one stands out in the annals of sugar history. It began with German-born William Havemeyer who immigrated first to England and then to New York City in 1799. A few years later, his brother Frederick, a sugar boiler, joined him.[19]

The brothers' beginnings were modest: a refinery in a small brick house, trimmed with white tiles. They built an oven on the first floor, where they baked the sugar, and lived on the second. They may have started humbly, but soon the brothers opened a factory, and by 1816, the Havemeyer Company was producing nearly nine million pounds of sugar a year.[20]

At that time, sugar was remarkably expensive, partly because the process of producing it was difficult and time-consuming; it involved boiling the sugar, then straining it through blankets or cleaning it with bull's blood, much like the old maple-sugar-making process. The brothers invested in the newest machinery, including a vacuum pan that replaced the old cast-iron kettle, to speed things up and tested the result for purity.[21]

As fate would have it, both of the brothers had sons, William F. Havemeyer Jr. and Frederick C. Havemeyer Jr., who followed in their fathers' deep footsteps. Frederick helped build the company. Newspapers of the time described him as "the venerable head of the well-known Havemeyer family . . . and the founder of the great sugar-refining industry in this country."[22]

William—energetic, combative, and controversial—become a three-time mayor of New York City. You can imagine that his position was awkward. Here he was, at the dawn of the Civil War, a Northern mayor whose fortune was built on the labor of slaves. Havemeyer was devotedly against slavery. He was a true born-and-bred New York native, as he insisted in his mayoral campaigns. He realized the morally bereft nature of enslavement.[23] But, he believed that "no forcible interference" should occur "in states in which it already existed" and where, he felt, the status quo should remain. In other words, keep the enslaved workforce on Louisiana plantations working.

Over the years, the Havemeyer Company expanded, taking on new workers and more family members. By the late 1800s, it was producing 1,200 tons of sugar each day and was possibly the largest sugar refinery in the world. In 1887, the company renamed itself the American Sugar Refining Company, aka the mighty "Sugar Trust." They absorbed a number of other refineries and appointed Henry Osborne Havemeyer, Frederick's son, as president. They also placed family members and close associates on the board of directors. In other words, they created a deliciously self-serving monopoly, shaping labor costs, sugar prices, and government policy to their desires. Over the next twenty years, they controlled 98 percent of the nation's refined sugar.[24]

In 1901, when Teddy Roosevelt enacted legislation to maximize competi-

Fig. 6.2. An ad for cane sugar.

tion, the American Sugar Refining Company saw the sun setting on their heyday. Competition was eminent. That's when Henry Havemeyer came up with an idea: give the company's sugar a name, trademark it, and market it as a brand that people are sure to love, and the government would leave it alone. They named their brand Domino, after the shape of sugar cubes.[25]

The American Sugar Refining Company soared through the Depression when they created their own identifiable packaging and sailed into World War II. The era of rations was on, and sugar was a prime target. Domino Sugar sputtered but didn't fall. America felt a surge of sugar-love after the war, and Domino was there to satisfy them.

Unfortunately, the public wasn't loyal. About thirty years later, spurred by the health food movement and the public's impression that sugar was not a medicine or a power food, the company began to suffer. Eventually British corporation Tate & Lyle purchased the American Sugar Refining Company. This may have been the American dream: two Germans who left England for a better life, building an empire in the United States. Or it may have been an irony that control of the United States' sugarcane production would, after two hundred years, return to the British. Domino and Tate & Lyle are still around today.

PERSONAL PERSPECTIVE: DABNEY CHAPMAN

Dabney, a former State Department diplomat, was known among friends and neighbors as the last true gentleman: polite, congenial, and considerate. When we met for this interview he had terminal cancer. When I asked how he felt, he smiled and said he was ready. He passed about three months later. It's an honor to share his memories.

My mother was an immigrant from England. She moved to Seattle in 1914 when she was thirteen years old. Her father was a ship's captain who circumnavigated the world. My grandmother's family were well-to-do industrialists but they left my grandmother without means because she married a sea captain.

My parents and my brother, John, and I lived in Rockbridge, Virginia, but Roanoke was our city. It was built after the Civil War. Every two months it would be a major expedition for my mother, my brother, and I to go to the great city of Roanoke. It had shops where you could get English toffee and cigarettes with a Union Jack label on them. My mother had a great fondness for English Toffee . . . it spoke of England to her like Pears soap.

Later, the toffee was rationed out to us, one or two at a time to reward us for weeding a row of cornstalks or some such thing. We didn't stuff it in our mouths indiscriminately. It was chewy and it tended to stick to your teeth and it lasted a long time, maybe twenty minutes of sucking time. It came in a round tin you were reluctant to discard even though you didn't have anything to do with it. They all had a caramel flavor.

My father was born and raised in Greer County at the foot of the Blue Ridge Mountains. He worked as a salesman for a distributor for Gulf Oil. My father's mother died when I was three. She was a paralytic—she couldn't talk but if you sang a hymn she'd join in. She was a great lover of candy. My grandfather came home one time and told my grandmother, "I have bought you a farm down the road and I hereby present it to you." Her response: "I would rather have candy." Candied fruit was her favorite: pears, apples, and peaches.

I learned all this when I went to my father's parents' house near Charlottesville, Virginia. My Uncle Billy was there—he was a farmer and a self-taught veterinarian. A lot of doctors had been practicing without a degree when I was a kid in the '30s. They had a good standard of service and delivered a lot of babies.

Uncle Billy served in the Confederate army when he was fifteen years old. In Petersburg he was lying on his belly looking toward the Union line and saw these boots and he heard a voice behind him say: "Throw down your arms you little rebel son of a bitch. You're my prisoner now." And he was. He was a prisoner at Port Lookout and stayed that way for months after the war ended. He ate rats and worms in the biscuits.

Whenever we'd visit, my brother, John, and I would make rock candy. We'd put a thread in sugared water, suspended with a cardboard lid. Crystals would form under the lid. We presided over what was made ourselves, but I don't recall that it was strictly monitored. We made it whenever the spirit moved us.

NEW YORK LOVES CUBA, LOUISIANA LOATHES FLORIDA, AND HAWAII STANDS ALONE

Before the Civil War, the plantations of Louisiana produced the most sugarcane in the nation. A number of things worked in their favor. First, in the late 1700s, the French colony of Saint-Dominique was the largest sugar producer in the world. The enslaved workers were fighting for their survival against the demands of a Europe that was hungry for more and more sugar. This demand made the dire conditions even worse. Tensions mounted, energy gathered, and the first successful slave revolt, led by Toussaint Louverture, marked the beginning of the Haitian Republic.

It also marked the death of the largest sugar producing plantation in the area and left a hole for American planters to fill. Around then, Louisiana planter Jean Étienne de Boré started using new—literally groundbreaking—methods for processing sugarcane.[26] He brought over Haitian slaves, adept at working with sugarcane, to help,[27] and soon, he achieved remarkable success, earning $12,000 that first year.

In 1803, sugarcane production got another boost: growers identified a new, quick-growing variety of sugarcane called "ribbon cane." Yet another pivotal event occurred when the United States acquired the French territory of Louisiana. Entrepreneurs and investors, largely from the North, seized the moment, and in less than twenty years, there were six hundred sugar plantations and mills, making sugarcane production Louisiana's major industry.[28]

The Civil War put an end to that. The economy was left in tatters, the plantations were wrecked, and the 125,000 previously enslaved workers[29] were off to find better lives. Some eventually returned when they discovered the options for livelihood weren't as bountiful as they had expected. Louisiana slowly recovered, and today it is one of the nation's leading sugarcane producers.[30]

But Louisiana was not the only grower in the race for market share. The sugarcane industry of Florida took off after the Civil War, and the two states were in a tough, competitive race. In 1868, a New York Tribune article proclaimed that Florida's cane sugar was sweeter than Louisiana's,[31] and the New York Weekly Tribune said that "Florida cane sugar grows luxuriantly without fertilizing and the average cost of preparing and planting a sugar crop there is $10 per acre as compared with $18 in Cuba and $24 in Louisiana."[32] In 1943, with the race still on, another journalist pointed out that Louisiana cane sugar must be replaced after two seasonal cuttings, while the Florida cane can be cut almost any time of the year, allowing for twelve seasonal cuttings.[33]

These articles were not reports filed by savvy investigative journalists, but part of a PR and advertising scheme to entice northern investors to "get rich quick" on the fabulous and virtually risk-free opportunities of Florida cane. One full-page ad in 1910 practically shouted in their headlines: "Will you spend 2c to Be Independent for Life?" The ad promised loans that were not too-good-to-be-true, because "We Know Our Land," and told investors: "Stay Home. We'll Do the Work." [34] Eventually, much of this land was bought from disappointed investors by the Southern Sugar Company.[35]

The Florida sugar industry's success depended on one factor: dredging the useless muck of the Everglades. The Southern Sugar Company spent millions of dollars essentially changing the landmass of that part of Florida to make it profitable. In spite of their best efforts, the company was on the brink of bankruptcy when it was rescued by Charles Stewart Mott, who reinvented it as United States Sugar Corporation in 1931. The new company sunk investment money into new machinery and hired sugarcane experts from Louisiana, Cuba, and the West Indies to make the venture a success. Their efforts paid off: United States Sugar Corporation remains one of the nation's largest sugar producers today.[36]

CANE SUGAR IN CUBA: THE OTHER REVOLUTION

Not too far from the Florida coast was the tiny but sugar-rich island of Cuba. For centuries, sugarcane grew on the island, which was a Spanish colony. It never developed into a full-fledged sugar-producing land largely because of Spanish policies on trade with other nations and limits on the number of slaves that could be owned.

French colonists moved their factories—enslaved people and all—to Spanish-controlled Cuba, and investment money from the United States and other places flowed in. The sugar industry was growing, and with it came railroads that moved the sugar from refineries to seaports. The Spanish, who had signed an agreement with England to abolish slavery in Cuba in 1812, brought in new groups of enslaved people—123,000 to work the railroad alone.[37]

A few other international boons affected Cuba's success. One was that the British- and French-controlled sugar-producing islands emancipated their slaves, leaving them without a skilled workforce. The other was the American Civil War, which annihilated one of Cuba's strongest competitors, drove sugar prices up and opened a dynamic new market.

One supporter of the Cuban sugar industry was the Sugar Trust, headed by the Havemeyer family. This was bad news for Hawaii, which had its own sugarcane industry and watched the events nervously from afar. In 1901, the *Hawaiian Star* announced that Americans were making large investments in Cuban sugar and could "produce enough to supply America." The article went on to explain:

"There is certain political significance to the report that certain American capitalists are planning for the consolidation of the Cuban sugar industry under one management. The best known American name connected with this project is that of Theodore Havemeyer of the American Sugar Refining Company."[38]

CANE SUGAR IN HAWAII

The Hawaiians had something to fear. In spite of Cuba's own ups and downs—with revolutions and political mayhem in the late nineteenth century, not to mention the Spanish-American War—the island rose up as a sugar-producing mecca, exporting 3.5 million tons of sugar by 1925. The United States, which controlled 40 percent of that sugar, was a key beneficiary.[39]

As for Hawaii, the series of islands far from the boom of New York's refineries and the depleted swamps of Florida were unique in the sugar-producing kingdom. Sugarcane was already growing freely in Hawaii in 1778 when Captain Cook arrived; it was even planted decoratively around the native peoples' huts.[40]

The Hawaiian natives probably knew how to get cane sugar early on as whalers, missionaries, and explorers landed there with plants and foods from the world over. Of all these travelers, New England whalers and traders made an impressive contribution to the Hawaiian economy. The New England ships shuttling furs and spices between China and the Pacific Northwest would get provisions and rest in Hawaii before their grueling journey around Cape Horn on their way back to New England. Eventually, Hawaii signed the "Articles of Arrangement" with the United States—its first foreign treaty.[41]

Among these many travelers was Charles Brewer, a Massachusetts sea captain. Brewer, born in 1804, was the son of a dry-goods dealer. As a boy he and a friend "borrowed" a neighboring farmer's old horse while the man was off in Boston. As Brewer said in his autobiography: "We had no switch, we began slapping him with our hands on each side. As that didn't have much effect, we gave him an extra-hard slap, when he started off suddenly with great speed and we both slipped off behind."[42] The iron from the horse's hoof caught the boy in the head, and it "badly mangled" his cheek and jawbone and left a scar on his face. He must have grown into a formidable looking man.

Brewer had long been enamored of the sea, possibly influenced by the writings of Captain Cook and the many sea captains in the area. His first trip was a long one—to Calcutta. He must have gained his sea legs quickly because over the next twenty-five years, he traveled to and from Honolulu, primarily collecting and trading sandalwood, and, essentially, cutting a path that would direct other New Englanders to the Hawaiian islands.

PERSONAL PERSPECTIVE: CHARLES BREWER, MOLASSES AT SEA, FROM *REMINISCENCES*, 1884

The sailors use to have an allowance of a glass of grog every day just before dinner, and an extra glass on Saturday night with which to toast sweethearts and wives; we two boys received . . . in lieu of the grog, a bottle of good molasses every week.

When going on deck in my middle watch at night, I most always carried my bottle of molasses and a ship biscuit to eat during my watch. I always kept my bottle of molasses under the lower berth, and would often use some when the watch was over. One dark night during the watch on deck, I took some of the molasses directly from the bottle by tipping it and swallowing it a little at a time; but something seemed to prevent it from flowing freely. I shook it several times before it would run then to my surprise out came a *dead mouse* with but little hair upon him; he was anything but an agreeable sight to look upon. I immediately put the mouse back into the bottle, with the remaining molasses and corked him up tight, so that he might float, and then threw it overboard. No doubt it was picked up by some passing boat crew during a calm, who expected to find letters for some loved one at home, and were probably disappointed enough to see only the remains of a dead mouse. It was a long time before I could relish any molasses after that experience. I had had quite enough of that quality and concluded for the future I would take it *pure* and *unadulterated*, or go without.[43]

• • • • • • • • • • • • • • • • •

On July 27, 1833, the brig *Velocity* landed on the island of Kauai. What transpired was the beginning of a sugarcane operation that would last nearly two hundred years. The passengers were two young men from Maine, their wives and children, and another young man from Boston. With the help of missionaries, who had been pushing the native people into growing sugarcane, they obtained the first lease in Hawaii's history and started the islands' first full-fledged sugarcane plantation.

The plantation, named Ladd & Company, only survived until 1848 when new owners took it over at auction. The new owners knew what they were doing: by 1898, the plantation produced 225,000 tons of sugar a year. A century later, it was spinning out a million tons.[44]

Still, Hawaii's sugar production was always volatile, peaking during the American Civil War when Southern production was at a stand-still and diving once the war ended. In 1898, the Spanish-American War closed down sugar production in Cuba and Puerto Rico, creating a demand for Hawaii's sugar and a justification for US annexation of the islands.[45]

Over the years, others followed Ladd & Company's lead, including the "Big Five" companies that dominated Hawaii's sugarcane production for over a century. Most had ties to missionaries; well into the 1930s, descendants of missionaries were on their boards. The oldest of the Big Five was C. Brewer & Company, named for Charles Brewer, who started a trading company years before.[46]

The boom and bust of the sugarcane industry persisted through the twentieth century—at one point a tenth of all American sugar came from the islands. The company once known as Ladd & Company shut down in 1996 and, under new ownership, produces coffee today. After many changes organizationally, Brewer & Company closed down in 2001—their old building is now a center for the elderly.[47] Hawaii became a US state in 1959, and most of its other sugar plantations have also closed.

PERSONAL PERSPECTIVE: DAVID RAWLS, HUNTING IN THE SUGARCANE

David Rawls stopped by my shop as he was motorcycling with friends from his home in South Carolina. He is originally from Broussard, Louisiana, which is where this childhood memory takes place.

Starting when I was eleven or so, my Dad used to take me quail hunting. He had lots of friends, and they let us use their land. We'd get in the truck, and when we got there we'd start walking with the dog along the edge of the cane field because that's where the quail would go. While we were walking, we'd take a piece of the cane and strip the leaves and bark and suck the sweet sugar juice out of it.

The cane looks like a corn stalk but no corn. It can get tall, taller than a person. When it was good and tall, they would cut it down low, like corn, and lay the stalk down on the ground and burn it. That would get rid of the leafy part and when you'd pick it up just the stalks were there. They'd load them in the truck and take them to the sugar mill. When they cooked it, it would stink. A horrible smell. The remains of the plant would be in a pile, and we could take all we wanted for free. We pulled up the truck, and we took piles of it that we'd use as bedding for the dogs and plants.

I remember being in these little stores near where I lived and getting sugar from the cane just after the processing. It had a brown tint, it was coarser than the white stuff, it had a different taste. More like a flavor you get from molasses. You could get cane syrup, it tasted like maple. You still find it, it's just not as easy to find anymore.

CHAPTER 7
A BAD CASE OF SUGAR BLUES

For all their competitiveness, the major sugar growers had one thing in common before and after the Civil War: workers were underpaid, if paid at all, and the living conditions they provided were deplorable. For example, in Hawaii, native Hawaiians hired by Ladd & Company were housed in near squalor and paid only 12.5 cents per day, which they spent on food and supplies that had to be purchased from the company store.[1]

As the sugar industry grew, so did the demand for workers, and hiring natives was no longer enough. Companies began to recruit immigrants from Japan and other countries. In fact, so many were recruited that Hawaii's indigenous population fell from 97 percent in 1853 to only 23 percent in 1923.[2]

On the plantations, immigrants worked long, exhausting hours overseen by European American managers who severely punished them for such minor infractions as stretching or talking while working. They were beholden to contracts for three to five years in which they had to live in company homes and shop in company stores. If they fled and were caught, they went to jail.[3]

This outsourced labor became even more critical after the bombing of Pearl Harbor and the start of World War II. Able-bodied Americans went off to fight, leaving plantation owners scrambling to find workers. Some used German prisoners that had been sent to the United States, and many used immigrants from poor countries who were searching for seasonal work. The conditions on the plantations were so bad and the pay so poor, even they broke their contracts and, whether secretly or through official channels, headed home.

Among the most prized workers were those who were from such places as Jamaica and already familiar with cane production. Still, this newspaper report sums up the feelings of these "prized" workers: "Ninety-two homesick Jamaican Negros are in jail Saturday awaiting action by immigration authorities because they balked at working in Florida's sugarcane fields and said they wanted to go home."[4]

LIVES OF SLAVES: FROM PLANTATION TO PUBLISHING HOUSE

Slavery made sugarcane production economically viable, sustaining it for hundreds of years.[5] The enslaved people on the plantations were part of the machinery of sugarcane production, and their lives were appalling: mothers were torn from children, rape was commonplace, food was scarce, and work hours were never ending. In her book *Sugar, A Bittersweet History*, Elizabeth Abbot describes the conditions as follows:

> Slaves, many of them women, were then working 18 to 20 hours a day, and often fell asleep or faltered as they fed cane through the huge rollers. The rollers easily caught a careless hand and pulled its owner along through the roller, crushing her to death. This was such a frequent occurrence that many overseers kept a hatchet or saber at the ready so they could chop off the trapped limb to save the slave's life.[6]

The subtext of an ad for a sugarcane plantation in New Orleans *Times-Picayune* in the 1860s explains it differently. Items 1 through 5 describe tracks of land, noting their size and the quality of the terrain. This is followed by a list of slaves categorized by name and age: Vaul, Negro man, aged about 37 years; Noah, Negro man about 30 years, engineer; Caroline, Negro girl, aged about 3 years; Onizeme, Negro girl, aged about seven years; Lucy, Negro Woman aged about 23 years and her two children.[7]

Even three-year-olds taken from their mothers, such as Caroline, old men and women, and young people full of never-to-be-fulfilled promise were part of that sugar machine. These people were mostly born-and-raised Americans, many in the fifth generation, who had been enduring the rigors of slavery for generations.[8] Their role in sugar was not unilateral; they used sugar themselves and contributed to sugar production, candy making, and their own sugar-related destinies in a myriad of ways.

PERSONAL PERSPECTIVE: LENI SORENSON, PhD, ON SLAVES IN THE KITCHEN

To get a more well-rounded view, I contacted Leni Sorenson, PhD, a culinary historian and expert in cookery and rural life skills from Richmond, Virginia. Here is what she said:[9]

Depending on where they lived, the African American community would use sugar differently. On deeply isolated plantations there were deeply isolated people. Maybe they had molasses or some special sugar on Christmas but that was probably about it.

The urban world of the nineteenth century was different: they were consumers of sugar, especially the ones who worked at a professional status such as valets and coachmen and ladies' maids. They had access to tips and other forms of income. These slaves would come into the general store and buy sugar, mainly because it was not part of their rations and it was a highly desired thing. They used it to make alcohol, they used it for cooking, they used it in their tea, and they may have traded it.

Of all the slaves, the cooks were really valuable—the white folks paid a lot of money for cooks. You have to remember that only 20 percent of African Americans were from Africa by the mid-1800s, most of the slaves had been here for generations, and the direct influences on food from Africa were mostly over. They had an understanding of what was good and tasty in their region.

In the kitchen, the cook was working intimately with the wife, not on a friendly basis but a work-based one. There was a dynamic between the cook and the housewife, sometimes they liked each other, sometimes they didn't. If the housewife's family just sold the cook's children that would definitely change things.

The cooks came into the kitchen when they were about eight: they were scullions, they apprenticed, then they learned how to cook over the years. The cookbooks of the time were general because they were written to help the housewife guide her servants. The job of the housewife was to make a menu, buy and store the food, and run the household while she was in their eleventh pregnancy. Most were far too busy to do the actual cooking. . . . The cook had deep experience and the housewife was reliant on her.

SO WHO WERE THESE SLAVES ANYWAY?
FOUR PROFILES OF COURAGE

In our conversation, Leni pointed out that women were cooks, but men were chefs—available only to elite households and for considerably more money. Many were men of style and grace, who could make delicate sugars and smooth comfits emerge from above a molten flame. The most famous chef is probably Hercules, a man who was enslaved by George Washington.

THE LIFE, TIMES, AND ACCOMPLISHMENTS OF AMERICA'S
MOST FAMOUS ENSLAVED CHEF

Hercules was born around 1754 and had been a ferryman for John Posey, George Washington's neighbor. In 1767, he began working as ferryman at the Washington mansion, which is where Martha Washington likely trained him as a cook. Hercules became a man of great style and taste, and above all, a brilliant chef. In 1790, George Washington brought Hercules to Philadelphia to serve as his chef.[10] At that time, George Washington Parke Custis, Martha Washington's grandson, was living at Mount Vernon, where he was raised after his own father passed away.[11] In his memoirs, he writes of Hercules:

> The chief cook would have been termed in modern parlance, a celebrated *artiste*. He was named Hercules, and . . . was, at the period of the first presidency, as highly accomplished a proficient in the culinary arts as could be found in the United States. . . . The chief cook gloried in the cleanliness and nicety of his kitchen. Under his iron discipline, woe to his underlings if speck or spot could be discovered on the tables or dressers, or if the utensils did not shine like polished silver. . . .
>
> It was while preparing the Thursday or Congress dinner that [Hercules] shone in all his splendor. During his labors upon this banquet he required some half dozen aprons, and napkins out of number. It was surprising the order and discipline that was observed in so bustling a scene. His underlings flew in all directions to execute his orders, while he, the great master-spirit, seemed to possess the power of ubiquity, and to be everywhere at the same moment . . .
>
> In the evenings, he would walk along the promenade in Philly, wearing, said Custis, "black silk shorts, waistcoat, stockings, and shoes highly polished, with large buckles covering a considerable part of the foot."[12]

Hercules was what people later called a "dandy." During the day, while shopping at Philadelphia's vast market, people followed him from stall to stall to see what he was buying. Hercules also sold leftover food from the Washington household, sometimes making one or two hundred dollars a year.[13]

In 1797, Washington moved Hercules from the kitchen of Philadelphia to the fields of Mount Vernon where he was forced to work among field slaves in rough woolens, spreading dung, smashing stones, and digging clay for one hundred thousand bricks. Why would Washington do such a thing? There were a few

possible reasons. One was the
Pennsylvania law permitting
slaves to claim their freedom
after living in the state for six
months. Rather than abide
by the law, Washington sent
his slaves back to Mount
Vernon.[14]

Besides, numerous slaves
had tried to escape from the
Washington household over
the years; some were suc-
cessful, but most were not.
Some joined the British during
the Revolutionary War. One
slave, Tom, attempted to run
off but was caught, hand-
cuffed, and sent to live out his
life in the rigors of the West
Indies. Christopher, a literate
slave, was captured when

Fig. 7.1. Hercules,
George Washington's chef.
Image from Wikipedia, user Jan Arkesteijn.

someone in the Washington household found a note to his wife discussing his
plans. Then in 1796, Oney Judge, Martha's maid, escaped from Philly.

Washington was determined that Hercules would not be the next to go[15] and
sent him to do hard labor in Virginia. "That will keep them out of idleness and
mischief," Washington wrote to his field manager.[16] Not too long after, on George
Washington's sixty-fifth birthday, Hercules fled from Mount Vernon.

Washington was devastated. He posted messages to Hercules promising his
freedom if he returned. He sent letters, with increasing urgency, to his contacts
to track Hercules down.[17] But, in the remaining two years of his life, Washington
would never see Hercules again.

On January 1, 1801, Martha Washington freed her husband's slaves. On that
day, Hercules was allegedly spotted. No one knows if Hercules knew he was offi-
cially free.[18] He was living life on his own terms, as a free man anyway, quite possibly in Canada, and probably didn't care.

PERSONAL PERSPECTIVE: RUFUS ESTES,
COOKBOOK AUTHOR AND ATTENDANT

After the Civil War, African American chefs frequently found jobs as professionals, earning decent wages and significant respect. Rufus Estes was one of them. As a preface to his cookbook, Good Things to Eat, As Suggested By Rufus; A Collection of Practical Recipes for Preparing Meats, Game, Fowl, Fish, Puddings, Pastries, Etc.*, he tells readers his remarkable story.*[19]

I was born in Murray County, Tennessee, in 1857, a slave. I was given the name of my master, D. J. Estes, who owned my mother's family, consisting of seven boys and two girls, I being the youngest of the family.

After the war broke out all the male slaves in the neighborhood for miles around ran off and joined the "Yankees." This left us little folks to bear the burdens. At the age of five I had to carry water from the spring about a quarter of a mile from the house, drive the cows to and from the pastures, mind the calves, gather chips, etc.

In 1867 my mother moved to Nashville, Tennessee, my grandmother's home, where I attended one term of school. Two of my brothers were lost in the war, a fact that wrecked my mother's health somewhat and I thought I could be of better service to her and prolong her life by getting work. When summer came I got work milking cows for some neighbors, for which I got two dollars a month. I also carried hot dinners for the laborers in the fields, for which each one paid me twenty-five cents per month. All of this, of course, went to my mother . . .

In 1883 I entered the Pullman service . . . until 1897. During the time I was in their service some of the most prominent people in the world traveled in the car assigned to me, as I was selected to handle all special parties. Among the distinguished people who traveled in my care were Stanley, the African explorer; President Cleveland; President Harrison; Adelina Patti, the noted singer of the world at that time; Booth and Barrett; Modjeski and Paderewski. I also had charge of the car for Princess Eulalie of Spain, when she was the guest of Chicago during the World's Fair.

In 1894 I set sail from Vancouver on the Empress of China with Mr. and Mrs. Nathan A. Baldwin for Japan, visiting the Cherry Blossom Festival at Tokio.

In 1897 Mr. Arthur Stillwell, at that time president of the Kansas City, Pittsburg & Gould Railroad, gave me charge of his magnificent $20,000 private car . . . I [now] have been employed as chef of the subsidiary companies of the United States Steel Corporation in Chicago.

●●●●●●●●●●●●●●●●

SPIES IN THE KITCHEN

The kitchens, bakeries, and confectioneries were gathering places in the nineteenth century for a confluence of people—housewives, professional cooks, and enslaved workers. Mary Bowser was one of the latter, and she likely shaped the course of the Civil War.

Mary Bowser was born into slavery in Richmond, Virginia, on a date unknown, at the plantation of a wealthy hardware merchant, John Van Lew, who lived with his wife and his daughter, Elizabeth. After John Van Lew died, his wife, an abolitionist and part of Richmond's high society, took control of the estate, freeing her slaves, and buying and freeing their relatives.

From the start, Mrs. Van Lew saw in Mary a woman of great intelligence and possibility, and so she sent her to Philadelphia's Quaker School for Negroes. There Mary learned to read and write—skills that would prove instrumental in the events that occurred later. Her education complete, she married Wilson Bowser, a free black man, in 1861, just before the start of the Civil War. The couple moved to Richmond, where they kept in close contact with Mrs. Van Lew and Elizabeth.[20]

As it happened, Elizabeth lived two lives. In one, she wandered among Richmond's high society, daft, muttering, and eccentric, a known but harmless abolitionist nicknamed "crazy Bet." The veneer was Elizabeth's best camouflage. In her other, behind-the-scenes life, she orchestrated a network of spies and regularly brought food, supplies, and information to inmates at Libby prison, a three-story former tobacco factory used to hold Union prisoners, which was later used as an officers-only prison.[21] In the plush walls of her mansion, she also harbored escapees.

It was through the Van Lew's connections that Mary Bowser, now a free, educated African American woman, became the kitchen slave Ellen Bond, who cleaned, cooked, and served none other than Confederate president, Jefferson Davis. As Ellen Bond, Mary was disguised as exactly what the Confederate slaveholders expected her to be: slow-witted, marginally competent, and subservient.

Ellen Bond dusted, cleaned, and served meals, while Mary Bowser, with her quick, photographic mind, listened to conversations, snapped mental pictures of documents lying around desks and tables, and reported in to the Van Lews and a baker, Thomas McNiven. McNiven's bakery was a central meeting ground for the Richmond elite, and he delivered his sugary treats from one established Richmond home to the next, engaging in brief tête-à-têtes as he went.

Richmond society was unaware that McNiven was a spymaster and that among his customers were spies swapping information, including the dim-witted Ellen Bond, who greeted McNiven on his daily rounds. Eventually, Davis realized there was a spy in their midst, but he didn't realize it was Ellen Bond until late in the Civil War. By then, Mary Bowser had escaped.[22]

After the Civil War, spies and others involved in similar activities, burned their correspondences and kept their actions a secret for fear of retribution. Still, Benjamin Butler, Ulysses S. Grant, and George Sharpe acknowledged the Van Lews as an essential part of the Richmond spy network. And Mrs. Van Lew gave full credit to Mary Bowser. She wrote in her war-time diary: "When I open my eyes in the morning, I say to the servant, 'What news, Mary?' and my caterer never fails! Most generally our reliable news is gathered from Negroes, and they certainly show wisdom, discretion and prudence which is wonderful." [23]

In 1995, the US government inducted Mary Elizabeth Bowser into the Military Intelligence Corps Hall of Fame.[24]

RESEARCHERS AND THE RESEARCHED: NORBERT RILLIEUX

No one, black or white, contributed quite as much to the sugar industry as New Orleans native Norbert Rillieux. He was born in 1806 to a well-to-do Creole family; his mother, Constance Vivant, was a free woman of color, and his father, Vincent Rillieux, was a European American plantation owner and inventor. Unlike the rest of the South, 25 percent of African Americans in New Orleans were free, and mixed couples often raised families together, minus legal papers supporting their union.

Being Creole, Rillieux had access to education, and he proved to be so precocious that his father sent him to the famous l'École Centrale in Paris. At twenty-four years of age, he became an instructor of applied mechanics—the youngest to reach this position.[25] Eventually, in 1834, Rillieux returned home to his father's plantation[26] where he worked on developing a multiple effect steam-operated evaporator that, through a series of steam-driven processes, turned raw sugar into sugar crystals. He patented his evaporator in 1843.

At the time, sugarcane production relied on something called the "Jamaica Train": a backbreaking, dangerous process where slaves ladled scorching sugarcane juice from one boiling container to another. Frequently, these workers were scalded to death or endured debilitating burns. The result was a dark, thick syrup.[27] Then came Rillieux's system, which saved lives, quickened the sugarcane production process, and produced a better product. It was renowned as the greatest achievement of nineteenth-century sugar technology and was considered of the same magnitude as Eli Whitney's cotton gin.[28]

Rillieux's success further accentuates the bizarre nature of slavery. His sugar evaporator made him the most respected and sought-after engineer in Louisiana, and, strangely, his

Fig. 7.2. Norbert Rillieux.
Image from Wikipedia,
user Theo's Little Bot.

process was embraced by Judah Benjamin, a lawyer at the center of the sugar circles who later became a Confederate secretary of war. Yet, Rillieux, as a "person of color," could not sleep at the plantation as a guest and, as the Civil War drew near, faced an increasing number of restrictions, such as the loss of his right to walk along the street. As for the machinery, many plantation owners considered the enslaved workers too inept to operate Rillieux's machine, or feared they would master it, become emboldened, and rebel.

Eventually Rillieux moved back to France where he lived with his wife, Emily Cuckow. He died in 1894 and was buried in the famed Paris cemetery of Père Lachaise.

In 1872, French impressionist painter, Edgar Degas visited New Orleans during a bout of artist's block. There he visited the home of American relatives. Louisiana, still recovering from the devastation of the Civil War, somehow inspired Degas and fueled some of his finest paintings. The home once belonged to Vincent Rillieux, whose son, also named Vincent, was Norbert's father. Degas was one of his cousins.

SUGAR STANDS ALONE

As a food, sugar held its own since the early days of the colonists. White sugar ran the spectrum from double-refined to powdered, which was more or less pulverized with a mortar.[29] Sugar was sold in big lumps and ultra-refined cones. Regardless of how they bought it, colonists enjoyed sugar in chunks, which they dropped in their tea and used to make a sugar syrup, or "sugar candy," that was an ingredient for other foods. The whiter and more refined the sugar, the better.

Martha Washington's Booke of Cookery and Booke of Sweetmeats has receipts, aka recipes, that show sugar at work in candy, such as in the sugared orange peels mentioned earlier. "Sweetmeats" refers to candy, preserves, and other treasures involving sugar. Since the book is titled "Martha Washington's Booke" and not "The Washington Household's Booke," and most certainly not "Martha and Hercules's Booke," I was curious about how much cooking Martha Washington actually did.

Leni Sorenson clarified the matter: Martha did not bend over the molten hot fire, careful not to send her skirts up in flames, but likely supervised the kitchen, putting together menus and keeping tabs on George's favorite foods. As for Hercules, he and his staff, among other chefs, were the true talents.

Candied treats included rose and violet petals, ginger, and fruits, all of which required sugar candy to make. Chefs such as Hercules would prepare them by boiling the sugar and letting it sit for three weeks, the syrup dripping out the bottom:

To Make Sugar Candy:

Take refined sugar & boyle it to A Candy height. Then pour it into a deepe earthen pot y is narrow & put into it a stick and stop it up close. Then set it on a warme oven or stove, & soe let it stand 3 weeks. Your pot must have A hole at the bottom stopt with a cork to let out all the sirrup that will run from it. Then let it stand A week longer, allways keeping it warme. The break yr pot and dry yr sugar candy.[30]

Rufus Estes used sugar candy about one hundred years later in his recipes, as well, such as in this deceivingly simple one, cooking the sugar to a "crack" stage, where most of the moisture evaporates:

> **A Simple Way of Sugaring Flowers**: A simple way of sugaring flowers where they are to be used at once consists in making the customary sirup and cooking to the crack degree. Rub the inside of cups with salad oil, put into each cup four tablespoonfuls of the flowers and sugar, let stand until cold, turn out, and serve piled one on top of the other."[31]

Another pure sugar candy that later became a nineteenth-century penny candy classic was rock candy. For confectioners, rock candy must have been deliciously easy; they just added sugar to water and let the crystallization process do what comes naturally—form big lumps of sugar crystals.

No mere sweet-lover's treat, rock candy has served many purposes and won much praise. In the early 1800s, for example, the Massachusetts Charitable Mechanics Association, a group cofounded by Paul Revere, showcased rock candy at a judged exhibition. Revere started the group in the late eighteenth century to address the problem of runaway apprentices, but soon their mission shifted to publicize the mechanical arts, showcase new products of all sorts, and provide funds for members' widows and families.

Among its many uses, rock candy was a medicine for soothing sore throats and was also part of the fermentation process. Many people used rock candy for both, at the same time. For example, older customers tell me their parents gave them rock candy with a shot of whisky and a twist of pure honey when they were sick—a more or less medicinal whisky sour.

No joke: in the late nineteenth century, this same combination was advertised to cure consumption and an array of pulmonary infections. One 1893 ad, disguised as a heartfelt letter, relays a common message of the time:

> Dear Sister,
>
> We were delighted this morning to read in your letter of the sure recovery of Cousin Edith from her recent severe attack of pneumonia. In your last letter, you despaired of her ever leaving her bed.
>
> How thankful I am that you yielded to my entreaties and tried *Clarke's Rock Candy Cordials*. It is such a pity that you did not do so before spending so much

money in doctors' bills and medicines of mysterious compound. . . . Here . . . we look upon it as a sure cure for all throat and lung problems.[32]

The follow-up "article" adds: "Physicians agree that pure rye whiskey is the most efficient as a tonic, and in combination with pure rock candy is unexcelled for pulmonary troubles."[33]

The enslaved people of the nineteenth century used rock candy mixed with whiskey as a medicine, as well. In one interview conducted by the Federal Writer's Project in the 1930s, eighty-year-old Josephine Bacchus recalled the medicine she used, saying: "Oh de people never didn' put much faith to de doctors in dem days. Mostly they would use de herbs in de fields for dey medicine. Dere two herbs I hear talk of. Dey was black snake root and Samson snake root. Say, if a person never had a good appetite de would boil some of dat stuff and mix it wid a little bit of whisky en rock candy and dat would sho give dem a good appetite."[34]

Outside the sickroom, in the more comfortable setting of the saloon, rock candy rested in whisky bottles, coolly fermenting into a nineteenth-century drink known as "Rock 'n' Rye." You can imagine the drink was, more or less, medicine for the spirit, if not the soul.

But no one told that to the temperance crowd. They disparaged rock candy for its role in drink and tried to stop businesses from making it. They almost succeeded, too. Dryden & Palmer, a rock candy company that opened in 1880, claims to be the lone survivor of the Prohibition-era ruckus.[35]

Still, rock candy's greatest role in American history has been as a candy, whether it was served up as little diamond-like bits, in chunks on a string, the old-fashioned way, or dyed and glistening on a stick crafted for cocktails. It's popularity may have been enough to make a Prohibitionist shriek, but the rock candy, and sugar candies overall, were embedded in our culture, at home as a metaphor for all things American in newspapers, magazines, and stories.

For example, in one story in 1859, a rough-and-ready adventurer showed his softer side by carrying sugar candy in his saddlebag to "give to the children as I went along."[36] In another piece protesting tax increases a few years later, the author railed that taxes were so bad, even children sucking on their sugar-sticks were being taxed.[37] Even the *Liberator*, an established Boston-based abolitionist publication (with strong temperance leanings), discussed the controversy over a law regarding slavery as being "like a petulant boy whipped just enough to madden him—then given sugar candy to quiet him!"[38]

By the late 1800s, rock candy was holding its own in penny candy stores and confectioneries. One newspaper nicely describes it this way: "Good rock candy is always sought for. Pure rock candy is crystallized sugar. The best is always on a string, and when held up to the light is clear as glass."[39] Other uses of sugar were to come along, among them the sugar cube, which took off in the United States in the late 1800s. Sugar cubes were delicately formed and perfect for holding between the teeth while sipping a cup of tea. European immigrants at the turn of the century were known to enjoy their tea this way alongside a light confection.

No question, the sugarcane, with its dark history and demanding nature, was the prince of the sugars. And it would stay that way, even with plenty of people pushing for a change.

PERSONAL PERSPECTIVE: EDITH ELIZABETH LOWE HIGDON, HONEY AND SUGAR AT HOME

Much of the sugarcane grown in the United States came from small farms where farmers grew it for their families. Edith Elizabeth Lowe Higdon, who was born in March 1928, recounts her memories of honey and sugarcane on her father's farm when she was a young girl.[40]

About the Honey . . .

I was born on a farm in Belton, South Carolina, in March of 1928. I remember Daddy going down to the pasture when the swarm came in each year. He'd tell us kids to go inside because he was going to rob the beehives. That's how he said it. He was going to rob the bees.

We'd know they were coming because we'd hearing a roaring sound from the pasture. Daddy knew when to go down, maybe from the humming, and he went to the pasture and saw them in the tree and he would build wooden boxes and put them around the tree and they would make a nest and make honey. A few weeks later, when he would rob the bees, he put on a mask with a hood to cover his face and head and shoulders that Mother made out of screen wire so he wouldn't get stung and head for the pasture. He would tell us kids to go in the house and stay because there might be stray bees that would go around the house and sting us.

We would wait and when he came back we'd take the comb and chew the wax like chewing gum. Mother made hot buttered biscuits with honey. We didn't have honey except then. The old swarm would leave and in the spring or summer, we would be playing on the wrap-around porch and we could hear a new swarm of bees in the field and pasture. The honey was delicious, I remember that well.

About the Sugarcane . . .

There were six of us kids and we lived on the farm near the crossroads and Dad and my brothers planted a lot of sugarcane. When they were ready to harvest and cut that cane my two older sisters helped load the wagon and hook up the mules, and they took it to a molasses mill a short distance away. They'd take several loads and come back and load up more. At the mill, they had some kind of a big, what did they call it? The mules would go round and round and the machine would squeeze and crush the cane and the syrup went into a tube that opened into a pot and the mules would go round and round until all the cane was in the pot.

They had a long paddle and they kept stirring the molasses until it got to the right consistency, then they put it in another big tub and took it home, put it in jars and sealed the jars until we were ready to use it. Occasionally Daddy would put a bench on the wagon and Lewis and I would sit on the bench and watch. We were never allowed to get off the bench because it was a big fire. They let that cook for a long time but not so long that it turned to sugar. They didn't want that. Everyone used more molasses than sugar on bread and gingerbread. If it cooked too long we'd bring it to the house and put it in jars where it turned to sugar.

A few years ago, when scrap metal was scarce, someone went to the mill and tore it down to sell for scrap metal. It was very sad.

About Helpers and Strangers . . .

A man lived in a shed on our property and he helped. Daddy hired him and he lived there separately. Mother made food for him but he didn't eat with us, he ate outside. We had a lot of blacks helping around there, they'd come and clean the yards and would prefer food rather than money. Some of the clothes we had outgrown and they would want that rather than money. They just didn't have anything hardly.

We had convicts that would come by the roads in stripes with balls and chains. The guards would ask if they could draw some water from the well to give them. My mother would let them and she would make food for all of them. I don't know if this was legal, but if my mother knew someone was ill, she would ask the mail carrier to carry a pie or cake to those people because he was going that way.

Everything we ate, the sugar, the chickens, the butter, Daddy grew. Even the cornmeal came from the corn Daddy grew and took to the mill. Mother made peanut brittle from the molasses and homegrown peanuts a couple times a year. She made it in a great big pan, put it in a bowl or dish. We always had a lot of company. If they had kids, she made a big pan of brittle so us kids could have some.

Those were the good old days.

They were hard working days but real treasures.

CHAPTER 8

AN ARSENAL OF SUGAR

Abolitionists had strong feelings about sugarcane production given its role in slavery. If you eat cane sugar, you economically support the use of slave labor. Stop eating cane sugar, and you bankrupt the industry, rendering the slaves unneeded. So, the abolitionists launched a boycott of cane sugar. It wasn't exactly successful at first—it took the Civil War to complete the task—but it did draw the public's attention to the issue and dramatically change the sugars we eat today.

Here's why: the abolitionists didn't want to give up sugar, they wanted to give up *cane* sugar. So they needed to find other tasty, useful, easy-to-grow replacements. Their quest broadened in the mid-1800s as Northerners saw, with the Civil War nearing, the waning of their sugar supply. Besides, even if cane sugar production roared along, which was unlikely, they'd be supporting the Southern economy if they bought it.

At first, the most readily available alternative was one they were already using: maple. Its use was first championed by Benjamin Rush, who was a member of the Continental Congress, a signer of the Declaration of Independence, a doctor, a chemistry professor, and, in 1799, the treasurer of the US Mint. He was also an ardent abolitionist in the true style of civil unrest—his father was a gunsmith and slaveholder.[1]

Rush came to this awakening in 1766 when he was heading from Liverpool to Edinburg for his studies. He, "a free-born son of liberty," as he called himself, saw a stunning sight: at a nearby dock were a hundred slave ships bracing for travel. The sight shook him to the core. In that instant, Rush decided to devote his life to combating slavery—a decision he embraced for good.[2]

Rush was close to alone in his mission. But he was supported by Anthony Benezet, a French-born American and Quaker convert who was also one of the nation's first—and pretty much forgotten—abolitionists. To convince the public, including his fellow Quakers, to join his crusade, Benezet wrote abolitionist-related pamphlets. Unlike any other abolitionists, he also worked within the black community, teaching enslaved children in his house at night and running the Negro School at Philadelphia by day with the help of the Society of Friends.[3] When Benezet died, he was mourned by many, including four hundred of the city's black residents.[4]

It was Benezet who encouraged Rush to publish a pamphlet in 1773 entitled "An Address to the Inhabitants of the British Settlements in America, upon Slave-Keeping." The pamphlet was subtitled, "Slavery not forbidden by Scripture; or, A defence of the West-India planters."[5] In other words, it was a response to those who defended using slaves on sugarcane plantations.

Soon after, in 1778, Rush wrote another publication, the "Advantages of the Culture of the Sugar Maple Tree." According to Rush, his purpose was "to lessen or destroy the consumption of West Indian sugar, and thus indirectly to destroy Negro slavery."[6]

Others were more ardent about cane sugar, expressing what Rush definitely believed: that choosing maple sugar over cane sugar was a moral imperative. J. P. Brissot de Warville, an abolitionist originally from France, said that use of maple would "drive out the sugar produced by the tears and blood of slaves," a line that was frequently quoted then and is still used by historians today. Other writers mirrored those feelings, including one who said, "Sugar made at home must possess a sweeter flavor to an independent American of the north than that which is mingled with the groans and tears of slavery."[7]

In 1824, New England agriculturist William Drown published an encompassing volume called the *Compendium of Agriculture or the Farmers Guide in the Most Essential Parts of Husbandry and Gardening*. In it, he provided detailed advice about everything from optimal ways to use manure to the best conditions for growing rutabaga.

Naturally, he devoted an entire section to the maple tree with practical advice. While the text is pretty straight forward, Drown becomes rather eloquent when describing sugar itself:

> As good white sugar can be made of maple as of cane sugar. What a value would not be added to it, by the reflection upon the different manner in which these kinds of sugar are produced? The cane sugar is the result of the forced labor of the most wretched slaves, toiling under the ardent rays of a burning sun, and too often under the cruel lash of a cutting whip. While the maple sugar is made by those who are happy and free.[8]

The availability of maple sugar was only one reason abolitionists touted it. Like the Native Americans, abolitionists knew it was versatile; it could be a candy, a syrup, a drink, or a flavoring. Best of all, it was delicious.

Thomas Jefferson, a passionate agriculturalist and one of the best-known slaveholders in US history, was enamored by maple, largely due to his friend Benjamin Rush. In a letter of July 10, 1794, Rush made a case for using maple sugar, including the cost (ultimately less expensive than sugars involving enslaved people), the quality (considerably better than cane grown in the West Indies), and the flavor (noticeably richer than the cane). He outlined specific ways of harvesting the syrup and provided so many details, Jefferson could hardly resist.[9]

There were two primary reasons why he wouldn't. One was economic: if the United States could rely on its own sugar crop, it would not be dependent on the British for sugarcane from the West Indies.[10] The other reason had to do with slavery. Sure, Jefferson was a slaveholder, but he was the most conflicted slaveholder of his day. For him, another upside of maple was its potential to end slavery. Here's how he described it to Benjamin Vaughan, a British radical and expatriate, in 1790:

> Though large countries within our Union are covered with the Sugar maple as heavily as can be conceived, and that this tree yeilds [*sic*] a sugar equal to the best from the cane, yeilds [*sic*] it in great quantity, with no other labor than what the women and girls can bestow . . . yet the ease with which we had formerly got cane sugar, had prevented our attending to this resource. Late difficulties in the sugar trade have excited attention to our sugar trees, and it seems fully believed by judicious persons, that we can not only supply our own demand, but make for exportation. . . . What a blessing to substitute a sugar which requires only the labour of children, for that which it is said renders the slavery of the blacks necessary.[11]

Jefferson ordered maple trees in near-orchard-size quantities from nurserymen, including William Prince, one of many New Jersey botanists. Prince's nursery started earlier than Elizabeth White's, but his descendants were experimenting with plants at the same time as she was, and it's likely their families knew each other. Later, Prince's son figured into the story of the sorghum grain, another cane sugar substitute.

Eventually, Jefferson's interest in the maple dimmed, probably because he didn't have much luck with it. He did find another interest, however: the sugar beet,[12] yet another abolitionist sugar and a significant player in the sugar market today.

PERSONAL PERSPECTIVE: DAN BOGIE,
ENSLAVED IN KENTUCKY

I read this remembrance years ago when I was just beginning my research about nineteenth-century African American foodways. I can't explain why it impressed me so much. There was something tender about the idea of gathering maple for kids, yet such an ironic tenderness given he was enslaved.

> Old master would call us about 4 o'clock, and everybody had to get up and go to "Stirring." Old Marse had about 30 or 40 sugar trees which were tapped in February. Elder spiles were stuck in the taps for the water to drop out in the wooden troughs, under the spiles. The troughs were hewed out of buckeye. This maple water was gathered up and out in a big kettle, hung on racks, with a big fire under it. It was then taken to the house and finished upon the stove. The skimmings after it got to the syrup stage was boiled down and made into maple sugar for the children.[13]

• • • • • • • • • • • • • • • •

The popularity of maple continued to grow, peaking in 1860 with 8.2 million gallons of maple syrup, some converted into 40 million gallons of maple sugar.[14] Compare that to today, when farmers produce only about 3.25 million gallons of maple syrup a year.[15]

Gradually, sugar beets and sorghum grain were able to compete successfully with maple sugar, although maple remained popular throughout the Civil War. After maple sugar fell from the top spot as the sugar of choice, it was mostly used to make novelty candies shaped like quaint leaves, stars, Pilgrims, and Santas at Christmastime. Maple syrup prevailed in the American kitchen, especially on pancakes, but it had its own problems. In the 1890s, a USDA investigation, under the supervision of Harvey Wiley, showed that the pure maple syrup people were purchasing was hardly pure.[16]

As it happened, with the prices of maple syrup rising, some maple producers started to use cheaper alternate ingredients such as corn or beet syrups. One ad for the tainted maple appeared in the *International Confectioner*. Called "Bush's Maple Flavor No. 1617," the presumably inexpensive vegetable concoction was "so true that expert candy men have refused to believe that syrup flavored with it was not prepared from the sap of the maple tree."[17]

The manufacturers may have told candymakers about the add-ins but didn't bother telling the consumers. So, in 1906, the Food and Drug Administration, another project of Harvey Wiley's, decided to require syrup makers to list the predominate ingredient on the label. A syrup can only be called "maple syrup" if it mainly consists of maple syrup.[18]

Today the labels do quite a bit of fancy foot work, throwing around words like "flavored." Some brands—like Aunt Jemima, every kid's perfect pancake partner—have dispensed with the word "maple" altogether, simply calling their products, "syrup." No problem: with the image of rich golden syrup flowing onto a tempting stack of pancakes on the label, we don't even notice. Here's what it *does* contain: corn syrup, high fructose corn syrup, water, cellulose gum, caramel color, salt, natural and artificial flavor, sodium benzoate, sorbic acid, and sodium hexametaphosphate.[19]

One of these early maple syrup knockoffs was produced by a man named Joshua Dailey who created a syrup made from boiled hickory bark called "Mapleine."

PERSONAL PERSPECTIVE: PAUL PALMER, TAPPING THE TREES

I'd been buying Palmer's maple products for years; they were the only maple sugar makers who produced hard blocks of maple like the Native American had made, as well as softer, molded pieces. It turns out that Paul Palmer has spent his whole life enraptured by maple. Here's why:[20]

I grew up in a small town in Vermont. Across the street, there was a family who made maple syrup and when I got old enough to cross the street by myself, I would go to their sugar house. It was every kid's dream: it smelled sweet, there's wood stacked up, there's fire, and shiny things. What came out of that was syrup beyond comprehension, it tasted extremely good, and ever since then, I was hooked. I first went to their sugar house when I was four.

As I got older, around twelve or thirteen, I was able to venture out in the wood with Fred Allen, my neighbor, gathering sap in two five-gallon pails. It could be a rainy, snowy, sunny day, but you still have to go to the tree, gather the syrup, and dump it in the bed of the truck.

During college, I had the chance to housesit and live for free in a place where the owners were only around in the summer. I was studying mathematics at the time. I knew they had maple trees so I asked them, do you mind if I tap a few trees. They said yes. I started tapping fifty trees, then tapped a hundred the first year. At that point Fred Allen and his family got out of the business and sold me their buckets. That's when I really got started.

Eventually I purchased the property where I was housesitting and now tap about 1,100 trees on thirty-seven acres of land. The trees are anywhere from three feet to fifteen feet apart. We heat with the wood from whatever gets knocked down . . . we always get wood from what falls, about eight cords each year.

The maple sugar process hasn't changed that much over time. The season starts in late February, early March, when there is snow on the ground, and the warm days and cold nights get the tree to wake up. In the spring, in the mud season, you smell the mud, the dirt, the wet leaves. It's a damp, warm kind of smell almost like the smell after a hard rain. Summer is almost too warm: the newness of the leaves has gone away and they have hardened up, not soft and supple as they were, and the smells go away with the crown on the trees.

The fall is a fun time: the leaves are starting to fall, they give a certain scent and it's raining and the rain turns to snow and you can feel the chill in the air. The skies change, everything is very different, and you can almost see the snow coming. Winter is the driest time in Vermont. There's not much happening then.

The process hasn't changed too much, but some things have changed over time. The molds in the early 1900s would have used wood or metal and it would have been difficult getting the hardened candy out of the mold. Now we have blocks so we can take the sides off and the candy pops out easily. Back then, tapping the tree would have been a major operation, every family did it and every family used their own maple as a sweetener. In the early1900s, Vermont produced three times as much sugar as they do today which underscores the number of families who were making the product.

I've been around maple for forty-two years, and it still boggles my mind that this stuff comes from a tree. And it's renewable, you don't have to cut it down, it's wild, and grows naturally. . . . You won't find plantations of maple.

AN ARSENAL OF SWEETNESS: SORGHUM SYRUP

The story of sorghum sounds much like that of sugarcane. Sorghum dates back to the early 1700s; was closely connected to slavery; grows in tall stalks with a plume on top, primarily in the South; and requires a process of milling and boiling. Unlike cane sugar, sorghum has always been the peoples' sugar—homegrown and affordable.

FROM THE BIBLE TO THE US SHORES

The journey of the sorghum plant to North America begins about eight thousand years ago in southern Egypt, Ethiopia, and the Sudan. It traveled throughout Africa and India in the first millennium BCE on ships, where it was used as food, and later moved along the silk trade routes.[21] According to one USDA report:

> It appears that sorghum originally grew wild in all tropical and sub-tropical parts of the Old World. In Beni-Hassan, Egypt, on the tomb of Amenembes, belonging to the dynasty existing 2,200 years before Christ, is frescoed a harvest field which is said to represent sorghum. In the book of the prophet Ezekiel (600 B.C.) is found the word "dochan," translated "millet," which word is still used in Arabic for forms of sorghum.[22]

The first sorghum arrived in the United States aboard ships transporting enslaved Africans in the early eighteenth century. The grain was used in breads and puddings, as a pulled candy, as chicken feed, and to make brooms.[23] As for the taste, sorghum resembles molasses, so much so that it's often called "sorghum molasses." Sorghum syrup entered the American culinary landscape on a large scale in the mid-1800s. It was "discovered" and promoted by abolitionists via Shanghai and Paris, France. The abolitionists didn't seem to notice that it was here in the first place.

Here's what happened: In 1851, the French government asked the French Counsel in Shanghai to send the Geographical Society of Paris plants, seeds, and cuttings that might grow in Europe. The society, like its cousins in such places as Berlin, London, and New York City, had a distinct mission: spread fascinating findings from around the world to anyone who would listen. In 1888, a new geographical society was formed in the United States called the National Geographic Society, which published a magazine under the same name. Both the American Geographical Society of New York and the National Geographic Society still exist today.[24]

The French horticulturists planted only one sorghum seed, but that one was enough to grow and multiply. Soon experiments were underway and the news was good. A letter from a French official extolling the virtues of the sorghum reached J. D. Browne, a US patent office agent in France. *Merchant's Magazine and Commercial Review* of 1855, quoted the letter as saying:

Fig. 8.1. The sorghum plant.

I continue to think the plant is one of the most valuable which exist; that it will yield the greatest advantage not only in Europe, where the climate allows the late maize to grow to perfection, but in the tropics, where it may replace the sugar-cane.[25]

For Browne, this meant the cane could thrive in both warmer and cooler climates in the United States, such as in the North and Midwest, bringing new meaning to sugar production. Browne brought back sorghum seeds from France in 1854, and in the spring of 1857, the patent office distributed 275 bushels to farmers.[26]

Sorghum reached the United States through numerous other sources— among them, Leonard Wray, a British sugar planter in Calcutta, India. In 1857, Wray traveled to Natal, South Africa, where he found numerous varieties of sorghum seed and developed many more.[27] He arrived in the United States in New York but, in a twist of the sorghum saga, shared the plant with Southerners who championed its use, including former South Carolina governor James Henry Hammond, one of the most passionate pro-slavery figures of the antebellum age. After Hammond's death, sorghum was found growing in his garden.[28]

CARETAKERS OF THE SEED

The sorghum seed was also propagated by US nurserymen. One was William Robert Prince, a horticulturist and adventurer—his father, William, was the one who sold maple trees to Thomas Jefferson. According to *The Standard Cyclopedia of Horticulture* of 1919, Prince's nursery in Flushing, New York, was "one of the centers of horticultural and botanic interests in the United States."

William Robert Prince followed in his father's footsteps, but took bigger strides. He branched into livestock, importing the first merino sheep to the United States; introduced a new culture for silkworms; and, on an exploratory and, from what I gather, remarkable trip through Mexico and California, founded the city of Sacramento. Somewhere in the mix, around 1854, he received sorghum seeds at his family nursery in New York. Prince planted the seeds then distributed the plants to nurseries on an experimental basis. The results were promising; the plant grew well in such places as the Midwest, and the production end was relatively easy. But Prince wasn't alone in his pursuits.

Not too far away, in Orange County, New Jersey, Henry Steel Olcott received and distributed some of the sorghum seeds as well. Olcott, who lived on his father's farm at the time, was from an old Puritan family that, among other things, cofounded Hartford, Connecticut. Olcott left college early due to financial issues but was so accomplished that the Greek government asked him, at twenty-three years of age, to be chair of agriculture at the University of Athens. Instead, he founded the Westchester Farm School, near Mount Vernon, New York, which set a standard for today's national agricultural education.[29]

Among Olcott's successes was his work with sorghum, which he described in a definitive book titled *Sorgho and Imphee, the Chinese and African Sugarcanes*. It included a paper by Leonard Wray. The publication was so ground-breaking it enjoyed seven editions and won Olcott an offer to be director of the Agricultural Bureau at Washington. The book also contains a stunning description of the sorghum plant:

> When comparing the appearance of the sorgho with maize or our common Indian corn, we are struck with the superiority of the former in respect to the exceeding grace of appearance which it presents. Like the later, it presents a tall stalk, marked at intervals with marks or nods, and from these at alternate sides of the plant spread long, tapering, drooping and spreading leaves. The stalk very gradually decreases from the base to the top. Its outer coating is smooth and siliceous like the stalks of the maize. . . . The seed grows upon the eight or ten separate stems which group together to form a tuft at the top of the plant; and, unlike the maize, this is the only fruit produced by the plant. . . . When the tassel first emerges from its sheath, the seeds are nothing but a soft green husk, which by degrees, and in like manner to wheat, becomes filled with farinaceous matter, and the grains are plump and hard. The soft green pulp, as the plant approaches maturity, undergoes transitions in color, changing to violet, brown, and finally to a purple, almost black.[30]

Olcott's agricultural life ended when he enlisted in the Union army. He would go on to become a colonel, an investigator for the Navy of fraudulent navy yard activities, and an attorney for the US government. In a dramatic shift, he left this life behind to help found the Theosophical Society, which was devoted to understanding religions worldwide. He moved to India, converted to Buddhism, spent time encouraging Indians to self-rule, and later advocated for a Buddhist revival in Sri Lanka. Two major streets are named for him and statues of him stand in Sri Lanka. The Theosophical Society is still active today.

SORGHUM IN THE CIVIL WAR

The result of these efforts was positive. Sorghum sugar proved to be easy to produce at home, which freed people from expensive sugarcane. Among the rural poor of Appalachia, sorghum syrup was a staple: it appeared in beer; was used in cooking; was a substitute for milk, which children drank with meals; and was used as chicken feed.[31] On a grander scale, the popularity of sorghum added millions of agricultural dollars to cool-weather states. The prestigious American Philosophical Society, founded by Benjamin Franklin, stated that sorghum was the "richest acquisition to our agricultural resources since that of cotton." *Scientific American*, meanwhile, lauded sorghum as the new molasses for the rural community.[32]

The Civil War only increased its popularity. Cane sugar was hard to get and wildly expensive due to a tariff on imported sugar and an embargo on products traveling on the Mississippi River. Sorghum was a choice alternative. In an ironic twist, President Lincoln received some sorghum syrup from St. Louis native Isaac Hedges, who extolled the syrup and emphasized new methods for producing it. Lincoln responded positively, recommending that Hedges send a report to the agricultural wing of the Patent Office.

Actually, Lincoln had intimate knowledge of the sorghum grain. When he was young, Lincoln's mother gave him a special treat of sorghum gingerbread men. One day, Lincoln sat under a hickory tree to eat three of the treats when a boy, whose family was poorer than Lincoln's, snatched up and quickly devoured one of the cookies. The boy then asked for another, saying: "I don't s'pose anybody on earth likes gingerbread better'n I do—and gets less'n I do."[33]

In the first presidential debate in 1858 with Stephen Douglas, and many times after, Lincoln recounted that episode. He often compared the boy's love of sorghum gingerbread with his own love of the equally illusive flattery.[34]

The sorghum also played a bitter role in the Civil War, especially at a Confederate prisoner-of-war camp dubbed "Camp Sorghum," a hastily set up block of land holding Union officers. In a booklet titled "What I Saw in Dixie," Union prisoner Samuel Hawkins Marshall Byers described his experience this way: "We have called our new prison Camp Sorghum from the fact that we receive little for rations, here, but sorghum molasses and cornmeal—the molasses not half boiled and almost green in color."[35]

Mostly, though, sorghum did more or less what Northerners had hoped it would: spared them from living without sugar. It was homegrown, resilient in all climates, and, above all, affordable. In 1862, the Union commissioner of agriculture said: "The new product of sorghum cane has established itself as one of the permanent crops of the country and it enabled the interior states to supply themselves with a home article of molasses, thereby keeping down the prices of other molasses from any great advance over former rates which otherwise would have been a result of war."[36]

THE BOOM-BUST-BOOM-BUST OF SORGHUM SYRUP

Immediately after the war, sorghum production dipped then rebounded with new zeal. States such as Kansas saw themselves as the American frontier of sugar production and focused resources—intellectual, scientific, and financial—on creating new modes of producing sorghum syrup.

William LeDuc, a quartermaster in the Union Army, became commissioner of agriculture in 1877 when the sugar industry was going through a deep depression. He recommended sorghum as the solution. In 1885, President Cleveland named Norman Coleman—a politician, journalist, and editor of the publication *Coleman's Rural World*—the nation's first secretary of agriculture. In his publication, Coleman devoted a front-page column to the sorghum grain.[37]

Perhaps the greatest push for sorghum came from chemist Harvey Wiley. Born in 1844 on an Indiana farm, Wiley spent his boyhood planting and harvesting crops. There was no public school system at this time, but his father was a school teacher and made sure he also received an education. Wiley became a Union army corporal and then, when he was in his thirties, a chemistry professor at Purdue University. In 1883, he left his job for a position as chief chemist at the Bureau of Agriculture, where he threw himself into sorghum experimentation whole-heartedly. At no time in history had the government pushed so many resources toward the study of the grain.[38]

But it was not to be. Despite all the efforts of the researchers, the politicians, and the farmers themselves, sorghum sugar took a hard, sudden fall. Farmers and investors lost money, political allies turned away, and funding went to new and more likely agricultural candidates.

The reason for the sorghum's demise can be whittled down to three factors. First, the sorghum did not produce the amount of sugar everyone expected. The results were erratic, particularly in the cooler states that had championed it. Second, the nation was still enamored with the white, glistening sugar that was tied to the now-defunct institution of slavery. Sorghum wouldn't crystallize into glistening bits—at its best, the hard sugar looks like muddy drops. Third, the competition from other crops was just too great—especially from the sugar beet, which crystallized into amber-colored gems or, with some fiddling, white cane-sugar-looking bits; thrived in cold climates; was cheap to process; and didn't involve messy canes.

It seems that Harvey Wiley took the sorghum's failure in stride. Author A. Hunter Dupree describes it this way:

> The dream of producing sugar in the temperate regions of the Unite States was as old as the dream of producing silk. Sorghum had beguiled the Department since the Civil War days. When Wiley took over in 1883 he extended sugar research to the pilot-plant stage. After sorghum as a sugar . . . proved a pipe-dream, Wiley vigorously pushed sugar beets and determined the belt where maximum results from raising them could be expected.[39]

Besides, Wiley had another passion. In the 1880s, commercial food was often of poor or harmful quality, and few, if any, controls were in place to protect the consumer. Wiley was going to change all that. To do so, he had to combat fierce lobbyists, an unwilling Congress, and a public that was unaware.

Eventually, though savvy PR campaigns and raw determination, Wiley wrote the Pure Food and Drug Act that President Theodore Roosevelt signed into law, giving birth to the FDA. Wiley later established the Bureau of Foods, Sanitation, and Health for the Good Housekeeping Institute, home of *Good Housekeeping* magazine, which was founded in 1885. He also pushed for greater government involvement in meat inspection and helped spur a bill that ultimately reduced the infant mortality rate.

THE STORY CONTINUES . . .

In the end, sorghum sugar became what it had always been: a sugar for those who could not afford others, from the early enslaved people to the rural poor of the nineteenth century. Even in its resurgence during the Depression, it was rural moonshiners who gave sorghum a boost. Many people earned a good living from making the homemade whisky and soon found that sugar helped speed up the fermentation process. What better sugar to use than that from their own, home-grown crop?

Besides, although sorghum never was the panacea to America's ills, it was—and still is—part of the American fabric. The United States is the largest producer of sorghum in the world, though much of it is used as animal feed and in fuel such as ethanol. Sorghum sugar has risen to become a healthy American cottage industry, especially in the South. On a grander scale, Anheuser-Busch of St. Louis is now producing Redbridge, a beer made with sorghum syrup. In doing so, their marketers have found a new, healthy food niche for the historic sugar. Here's what they say:

> Adults who experience wheat allergies or who choose a wheat-free or gluten-free diet, now have a beer that fits their lifestyle. Redbridge is the first nationally available sorghum beer. Beginning today, Redbridge will be sold in stores carrying organic products and restaurants.
>
> Sorghum, the primary ingredient in Redbridge, is a safe grain for those allergic to wheat or gluten. It is grown in the United States, Africa, southern Europe, Central America, and southern Asia. Sorghum beers have been available internationally for years and are popular in many African countries.[40]

On an international level, sorghum upholds its traditional value, growing in every continent in the world except Antarctica. According to the Consultative Group on International Agricultural Research, sorghum "is the world's fifth major cereal in terms of production and acreage. It is a staple food crop for millions of the poorest and most food-insecure people in the semi-arid tropics of Africa, Asia and Central America. The crop is genetically suited to hot and dry agro-ecologies where it is difficult to grow other food grains. These areas are frequently drought-prone and characterized by fragile environments."[41]

Where the sweet, edible sorghum goes from here is anyone's guess—plenty of farmers and investors would like to know, I'm sure. Probably, it will remain a homegrown product, readily available to those who need it, regardless of location or means, and to all those who are fortunate enough to taste it.

PERSONAL PERSPECTIVE: JOHN GUENTHER,
MENNONITE SORGHUM GROWER

I found John Guenther's business, Muddy Pond Sorghum, while I was researching sorghum a few years ago. His family-operated mill and shop are in Tennessee. Being Mennonite, his work is honest and in line with his belief in God.[42]

I was born and raised in Canada. Up there we were isolated; our life was primitive. I grew up in the Tradition and was raised in the Church of the German Mennonite. We believed in the Lord Jesus but we didn't have fellowship. There were a lot of dos and don'ts but nothing about living-making.

In '62, I was twenty-five and me and my sister went to Pennsylvania. The church there had about twenty-five families. I liked the atmosphere very much and realized the salvation we had with Jesus Christ. We had a lot of trials, hard times, disappointments but the Lord led us through. At a church dinner, I tried the sorghum for the first time. I loved it. I don't know what I loved about it, but I loved it. There wasn't much sorghum in Pennsylvania at that time. People there weren't making it.

In '63 we moved to Tennessee where Joe Schock and his family lived. They were born in Indiana then moved south to Mississippi then Tennessee. He and his family knew sorghum from the South: they liked sorghum so they grew it.

When we moved to Tennessee there were about twelve families in the community. It was a wilderness, so we pioneered. No power tools or nothing. Cleared land with an axe and hand saw and by hand. . . . It was primitive. We built our houses from pine wood, just threw up logs, added hardwood.

We had an old time sorghum operation. We cut the cane by hand, with a machete, hooked horses to a mill, put the cane in and squeezed the cane and got the juice from it. Then we boiled it down in pans, big pans.

The first year or two, everyone in the community was involved. We didn't have a market established so we didn't need much land. Most of the family did other things, too. Carpentry. Making bread. I went and picked corn and made $8.00 in one day and that seemed like a lot. . . . We didn't need much money.

In '64, I married Joe's niece. She was a school teacher in the community when I married her and had always been a Servant. We had eight children. When the youngest was born she went back to teaching community children. In the '80s, we started our own family operation.

I've been here for forty-nine years and have made sorghum every year. Making sorghum is a family operation and family is a big part of our operation. We learn about love and humility working together. We believe in honesty and making a living by growing on the land is honest work. The land is in our care. We seek the Lord and believe in the Lord's promise to come; we live in humility and live in the belief we should never despise and forsake.

Things are a lot better now than before. Our operation is more like a factory. It's better set up, it's screened in and inspected. We still use the horses, but that's for show for customers when they come in the fall. In September and October, Tuesday, Thursday, and Saturday are sorghum making days.

You should come see our operation. That's the best way to know about sorghum. There's a sorghum association that has a meeting ever year. Anybody can join in.

AN ARSENAL OF SWEETNESS: BEET SUGAR

In case you think you haven't tried the sugar beet, odds are, you have. Roughly 35 percent of all sugar produced worldwide—and well over half of the sugar produced in the United States—is made from sugar beets.[43] Most of the US crops are grown in Colorado, Utah, and other cooler climates and ultimately end up in your candy bar or chocolate creams.

The story of the sugar beet is similar to the sorghum and other imports; it includes nurserymen, and Americans finding seeds and samples overseas, and even Harvey Wiley makes an appearance. The story of the sugar beet begins in the same way the story of corn syrup began—with Napoleon Bonaparte. The sugar beet reached Napoleon via Andreas Marggraf, a Prussian scientist, who, in 1747, found that the crystals formed from beet roots and sugarcane were identical in nature.[44]

His research was incomplete, and, after he died, a French chemist living in Prussia, Franz Karl Achard, solved the mystery of how to transform beets into usable sugar. He had help from Frederick the Great, King of Prussia. Achard's work ended once his benefactor died. Other scientists continued their investigations, but none with the energy or focus of Napoleon, who recognized the beet as the answer to a problem of his own.[45]

At that time, most French citizens were getting their sugar from the British-ruled West Indies. During the Napoleonic Wars (1803–1815), two events cut off their supply: the British blockade of continental Europe and Napoleon's ban on products from the enemy. Barbados was no-man's-land as far as the French and their allies were concerned, and they needed an alternative.

The sugar beet was it. It was relatively easy to grow and could crystallize, unlike sugars such as honey and sorghum, and unlike the feisty cane sugar, it could grow in temperate climates. Between 1810 and 1815, scientists tested the power of the beet, farmers grew it over 79,000 acres of land, and hundreds of factories throughout France started to produce it.[46]

The news wasn't lost on Americans who, early on, tried growing sugar beets themselves, with varying degrees of success. The *Sandusky Clarion*, of Clarion, Ohio, posted this news on October 30, 1822: "Major Frederick Falley has this season raised a beet, from the seed of the Bonaparte sugar beet, which after trimming off the leaves weighed thirty pounds. It measured in length three feet and four inches, in circumference, two feet, seven inches; which beet Maj. Falley tends to cultivate next season for the purpose of raising seed."[47]

The sugar beet's popularity didn't take off immediately; in fact, Major Falley's efforts were pretty much forgotten. In Europe, its popularity dipped, but only briefly, once Napoleon's reign ended and tropical sugar was available again. By the 1850s, however, as sugar grew more expensive and harder to get, beet sugar regained its importance.

ABOLITIONISTS AGAIN

Abolitionists seized the opportunity that beet sugar presented to break their reliance on the heat-loving sugarcane. In the true tradition of sorghum and so many other plants, their knowledge of the beet, and the seed itself, came from France. In a style typical of the day, the Beet Sugar Society of Philadelphia sent an agriculturist to Europe. He returned with five hundred pounds of French seeds, which he dispersed to nurserymen and farmers across the nation. Sound familiar?

Abolitionists everywhere proclaimed the virtues of beet sugar where it made numerous appearances in the quintessential abolitionist publication, the *Liberator*. In 1836, around the time when the Beet Sugar Society was collecting its seeds, the *Liberator* wrote:

> It is time when all interested in agriculture, or commerce, or politics should direct their attention to the subject of making sugar of beets. . . . If it shall outrun the West India sugar, then our market will be supplied by two competing sugar departments, the Northern and the Southern. This brings Northern and Southern enterprise into competition, and fairly tries the relative values of

slave-labor and free labor. It is said in France that the beet shall hold out acre for acre with the cane: but will slave labor on cane sugar, equal free labor upon beet sugar? If not—if Northern free labor can undersell Southern slave labor and take from her the sugar market, it will cripple the Southwestern states in a very essential degree, and reduce the value of slaves and very strongly tend to make them worthless . . . slave property would then be an enormous taxation, rather than profitable, and would soon go into disuse.[48]

The first sugar beet was grown in earnest in Northampton, Massachusetts, by David Lee Child, an abolitionist, in 1839. Child's efforts won him praise and a silver medal from Paul Revere's prestigious Massachusetts Charitable Association, where rock candy was also honored at that time. Still, Child's efforts ultimately failed. There were many reasons, including what one beet sugar advocate called "crude" machinery, poor quality beets from France, and limited knowledge of how to grow them."[49]

By the early 1840s, the sugar beet seemed doomed.

THE DEATH AND UN-DEATH OF BEET SUGAR

But death was not yet knocking. The beet had a reawakening in Nebraska around 1890,[50] but not without plenty of bumps and bruises. One advocate was sorghum-lover Harvey Wiley, who, as chief chemist for the USDA, received a letter from the Epitomist Publishing Company in 1897 on behalf of small farmers that were eager to get on the beet sugar bandwagon. They wrote:

> The Epitomist appeals to you on the subject of sugar making from sugar beets and asks for such information as you may be willing to furnish for publication in relation to some processes by which farmers may be able to produce beet sugar at home for their own use.
>
> It is hoped that this information, which you are so well equipped to furnish to the public may enable the man with a cider or fruit press and a few pots and kettles do something for himself in this line of work while awaiting the slow development of the beet sugar industry on a larger scale. . . .
>
> We have heard a story of your experiments with sorghum as a boy on your father's farm, and may there not be embryo scientists now to be stimulated by the new sugar movement?

Wiley responded in his inimitable style—honest, blunt, but less-than-assuring—indicating that beet sugar, unless processed in a factory, would be bitter, unlike cane sugar, which is sweet, and, in fact, sweeter when hardly processed at all.[51]

Regardless, farmers large and small persevered, and Wiley continued to give his energetic and hard-to-come-by seal of approval to beet sugar grown on a grand scale. This success was largely due to Thomas Oxnard, a business man who operated cane sugar refineries in Boston, Brooklyn, and St. Mary's Parish, Louisiana in the 1800s. After the Civil War, Oxnard's son Henry went to Europe to learn more about the sugar beet, the rising star of the sugar industry. He returned energized and determined. By 1899, Oxnard owned four beet sugar processing plants, which he eventually consolidated under one roof as the American Beet Sugar Company—the nation's largest beet sugar producing company today.[52]

By 1911, huge processing plants sprung up in Utah, California, Idaho, Colorado, Michigan, and elsewhere, their chimneys rising in peaks to the sky. Vendors were selling seeds from Holland, Germany, and Austria, and confectionery magazines offered help with everything from obtaining beet-related patents to purchasing conveyors, link belts, drains, pipes, and pans so that the modern beet sugar producer could get more sugar, faster.[53]

This was good news for consumers who had an option where sugar was concerned and for Northern farmers who had a new and potentially profitable crop to grow. Investors jumped in to offer support and enjoy the rewards, and everything seemed pretty good for everyone—except, as you can imagine, for the sugarcane producers and, more specifically, the folks at the Sugar Trust. Remember them? One article written in 1913 sums it up best:

> For the first time in the quarter century that the Sugar Trust has been in existence, its domination over the sugar market of the United Sates has been broken this year. . . . This result has been accomplished not by government prosecution or through the competition of other refiners, but by the increase of the market supply of sugars grown by American farmers and manufactured in seventy-three beet sugar factories scattered from Ohio to California.[54]

Yes—the sugar beet was quickly becoming the official sugar of the United States, offering purity and taste from producers right in its own backyards. Meanwhile, the Sugar Trust was mired in lawsuits. One newspaper article reported that the sugar beet was thriving in California, Colorado, and Michigan in spite of unfavorable weather, and that the American Sugar Industry was involved in scandals about business practices, price fixing, and many other unseemly matters.[55]

The beet sugar industry did have troubles of its own and image topped the list. Sure, commercial buyers were happy to use beet sugar, but housewives—a primary target who were making candy and other sweets at home—thought the sugar would smell bad. Besides, they were beets. And beets aren't sugar and they aren't sweet.

The beet sugar industry set to work, more or less knocking the word "beet" out of their marketing altogether.[56] The American Beet Sugar Industry renamed itself American Crystal Sugar in 1934[57] and promised, as it does today, to provide "pure sugar." Its nemesis product, cane sugar, calls itself "pure cane sugar." Who would know the difference? Today, with beet sugar outranking cane in the United States, the cane sugar industry certainly does.

C&H Sugar, for example, compared their pure brown sugar to the beet sugar that those sneaky companies were trying to pass off as the real thing. Here's what they say:

> If cane sugar is not specified on the label, the sugar may be beet sugar. What beet sugar makers call "brown sugar" starts out as white sugar crystals that are then sprayed with a brown coating. Often the center of the crystal remains white and the brown molasses coating can be rubbed off in your hands. Not exactly what you want when you go to the effort of baking something fresh from scratch![58]

In fact, most of us don't know the difference and, most likely, don't really care.

CHAPTER 9
A GIFT FROM THE GODS

Chocolate is popular. You knew that. But just *how* popular? Worldwide, candy falls into three categories: chocolate, non-chocolate, and chewing gum, with chocolate leading the way by 55 percent. Of the chocolates, the most popular is the United States' own M&M's, with worldwide sales of $1.8 billion yearly. After M&M's—made by the family-owned Mars Company—comes Cadbury Dairy Milk, then Milka of Germany.[1] In the United States, on the week before Easter, Americans buy more than 120 million pounds of candy; during Halloween week, 90 million pounds; and around Valentine's Day, 48 million pounds.[2]

That's chocolate. But where can you find the *best* chocolate? A few years back, in a *National Geographic* review of the top ten best chocolates in the world, five were from the United States and the rest come from Switzerland (which holds the number one spot), France, and the Netherlands. The tenth best on the list is Godiva of Belgium.[3]

Next question: Why do millions of people eat billions of dollars' worth of chocolate each year? Aside from the obvious flavor factor, and a few others we'll discuss later, the reasons are ritual and often have close ties to religious holidays such as Christmas, Easter, and Hanukkah. Granted, other holidays, such as Halloween and Valentine's Day, aren't *religious* per se, but their roots started that way. Then there are the celebratory rituals: birthdays, first or second dates, Mother's Day, Father's Day, and so on.

Chocolate, unlike just about every other candy, has been loaded with symbolic meaning and purpose right from the start. The earliest chocolate-eaters had it right: they considered chocolate a power food handed down from the gods.

GODS, CHIEFS, AND COMMERCE

Chocolate originated in Mesoamerica four thousand years ago, more or less, with the Olmec tribe of what is now Mexico. But before we talk about that, and the remarkably circuitous route of chocolate from the jungles to the convenience store, we need to take a quick look at the cacao tree.

A QUICK LOOK AT THE CACAO TREE . . .

Chocolate comes from the cacao tree, with its odd-looking red, purple, or green-yellowish pods. I say "odd" because, unlike other pods, those of the cacao tree grow directly from the trunk. Nestled into the pods are twenty to sixty of the prized cacao beans, set in five rows[4] and surrounded by a white paste-like substance that some cultures use to make juice and jelly. The taste is so delicious it's an enigma of food history that it isn't a prized international dish. The seeds themselves are almost half made up of fat, which is called "cacao butter" and is the main ingredient in white chocolate. And as for pollination: the mighty cacao is not pollinated by hummingbirds or powerful exotic bees, but by tiny flies.[5]

In its purest, rawest form, the cacao tastes strong and bitter with a clear chocolate aftertaste. Today, the cacao has developed a well-earned reputation for being healthy, and some in the health food world enjoy it straight, as is, or in smoothies, on cereal, or atop yogurt.

The name "cacao" reflects the cross-cultural life that would become the reality of this ancient bean. The ancient Olmec, who lived in Mesoamerica thousands of years ago, pronounced the tree's name as "kakawa."[6] Centuries later the Maya, and the Aztecs after them, called it ka'kau and chocol'ha.[7] The tree's formal botanical name is *Theobroma cacao*, given by the Swedish botanist Carl Linnaeus in 1735. Linnaeus joined words from three distinct cultures: the Greek word *Theobroma*, which translates into "food of the gods," and "cacao," the Mayan-based name that was used by the Spanish.[8]

Linnaeus's approach to plants was done for the glory of God; to understand God, he believed, you must understand God's creations. It was also based on sex—in this case of the reproductive organs of the plant—which made Linnaeus logical, limited, and controversial in his time.[9] As for God, Linnaeus's was an entirely different one from his Mesoamerican predecessors, as you'll see in a moment.

BACK TO THE PAST

Not much is known about the Olmecs aside from their sculptures of immense stone gods with broad, well-defined noses, full lips, and enormous, focused eyes, and their use of chocolate.[10] We know they turned cacao into a drink, by first removing the seeds from the pod, then fermenting them for two to eight days. Next, they dried, roasted, and cracked the seeds to release the inner "nibs" from the shells and ground the nibs on a hot stone, adding such spices as allspice, chili, and the delectable vanilla orchid. Last they created a chocolate paste that they cooled and formed into hard cakes.[11]

Later, the Mayas cultivated the cacao tree, moving into the region now known as Guatemala. The Mayas held chocolate in great esteem. In death, the aristocrats were buried with great quantities of it for the afterlife; while living, a spicy, frothy cacao drink was their greatest culinary pleasure. As for the poor—they ate a porridge-like blend of cacao mixed with maize and spices, such as chili pepper or the milder vanilla,[12] and dried flowers.

This delicacy was brought to them by the sun god Hunahpú. As charming as this might seem, the patron of cacao was Ekchuah,[13] the black-eyed war-god with a hanging lower lip and a scorpion tail, who carried off the souls of warriors killed in battle.[14] In his honor, the Maya had a festival each April where they made offerings of cacao, feathers, and incense; exchanged gifts; and sacrificed animals, including a dog with cacao-colored markings.[15] Reflecting the true spirit of the event, an eighth-century Mayan chocolate-making vase was decorated with two masked figures beheading a victim while a woman prepared a frothy cacao drink close by.

Later, the Aztecs engaged cacao in another form of sacrifice. They were extremely superstitious and lived in a constant state of fear that the unpredictable wrath of their many gods might cause their universe to topple.[16] To placate their temperamental gods, the Aztecs sacrificed a human every day.

This unfortunate victim was usually a prisoner of war: as perfect a specimen of human fitness as possible, since he represented the Aztec gods on earth. They treated the prisoner with great reverence until the apex of the sacrificial ritual, when they cut his heart from his body while he was still alert and alive. The prisoner was expected to accept this fate bravely and, remarkably, with joy. If he showed fear, dread, or horror, he was given a concoction—made from chocolate and the blood of other sacrificial prisoners, with additional bewitching ingredients mixed in—that would transform him into a willing participant.[17]

Interestingly, the cacao-loving Aztecs lived in a dry region and were unable to grow the cacao themselves. They obtained it through trade or "tributes"—taxes paid to them in cacao bean currency by provinces they had captured. For the Aztecs, the cacao was also, quite literally, money, hence the expression "money doesn't grow on trees." A large tomato was worth one cacao bean; a turkey egg, three beans; a rabbit, one hundred beans; a slave, one thousand beans; and a prostitute, a paltry eight.[18]

The cacao was made available by Quetzalcóatl, the Aztec's creator god and giver of agriculture, who had been banished in a celestial battle long ago. The loyal Aztecs awaited his return. In 1517, when Spanish explorer Hernán Cortés arrived in Mexico, the Aztecs thought he was Quetzalcóatl returning. This was not the case.[19]

ENTER THE WEST

The Spanish explorers—headed by Hernán Cortés, himself no stranger to violence—landed at the Mexican coast near Veracruz. They soon found their way to the capital city, Tenochtitlán, which was ruled by the near-mythical emperor Montezuma. In his lifetime, Montezuma was renowned for many things, being a warrior chief among them, but today he is remembered for his intestinal revenge, his sex drive, and his love of chocolate.

This legacy was born from the creative talents of Bernal Díaz del Castillo, who traveled with Cortés and recorded their journey many years later in *The True History of the Conquest of New Spain*. His accuracy is unknown, but the spirit of his account is impressive. It was from him that we learned the improbable truth that each day Montezuma drank fifty servings of chocolate from a golden chalice. The chocolate's alleged aphrodisiac powers were boosted by adding chili to the mix, which enhanced, or quite possibly *enabled*, Montezuma's performance for his two hundred wives.[20]

The chocolate drink itself fascinated Cortés. He wrote to Spanish king Carlos I: "A cup of this precious drink permits a man to walk all day without food."[21] In the true spirit of conquistadors, Cortés was not content to merely observe the Aztecs in their rituals; he wanted to conquer them. The Spanish lay siege on their hosts in battles that pitted native people with canoes against crossbows, armor, firearms, cannons, steel swords, horses, and military attack dogs. Montezuma, who had conquered so many lands, tried to appease Cortés, but to no avail. The Spanish were ultimately victorious. Montezuma was dead, the city was conquered, and the powerful Aztec civilization was at its end.

THE NEW TASTE OF CACAO

The cacao bean edged its way into the European-style we know today, each change absorbing the tastes of the next culture. The Spanish colonists made Mexico their home and took native women as wives, concubines, or lovers. Similarly, they comingled the Mesoamerican cacao with European flavors, many adopted from spice traders who brought such remarkable flavorings as cinnamon, anise, and black pepper.[22]

Back in Spain, the cacao took some time to develop a following. But, by the late 1500s, it became all the rage among royalty and religious orders. Monks and nuns, in their respective monasteries and nunneries, made chocolate, adding spices such as nutmeg and sugar. They even had an idea so innovative that it's lasted to this day: serve the cold drink hot.

Some in the Church objected to chocolate for pretty much the same reasons it has panache today: they considered it an aphrodisiac from a lush pagan land. Pope Pius V held the drink in high contempt. In fact, it was so contemptible it went beyond the sphere of moral harm. Worshippers could indulge freely.

For almost a century, the Spanish kept their new favorite drink a secret. English and Dutch sailors who captured Spanish ships returning from the West threw the cacao beans overboard, thinking they were sheep droppings. Nearby, a group of chocolatiers was developing the first French chocolates. These were Jews who had been expelled from Spain, then Portugal, and had few places left to go. So, they lived a more-or-less isolated existence in the French Basque country, creating chocolate that the Parisians, later known for their sumptuous turn-of-the-century truffles, knew nothing about.[23]

GO WEST, YOUNG CHOCOLATE, GO WEST

In the early 1600s, two big events happened. One was that an Italian named Antonio Carletti discovered chocolate while in Spain. He liberated the bean from its Spanish keepers and, in the process, made it available to the rest of Europe. In addition, in 1615, the daughter of Philip II of Spain gave her French husband, Louis XIII, a chocolate drink. This ignited a wildfire of interest throughout Europe, as chocolate jumped from royal family to royal family and into the diets of wealthy Europeans.

Later, Spanish princess Maria Theresa gave Louis XIV of France an engagement present of an elegant box filled with chocolate. Louis was a renowned lover who, in the alleged Montezuma-style, made love to his wife by night and sullied away hours with some lover, concubine, or mistress by day, all while ruling a relatively stable government. Louis loved the gift and soon chocolate became a favorite at the Court of Versailles.[24] Chocolate also spread to Germany, Belgium, and other parts of Europe. In 1657, the first chocolate house opened in London, serving a drink that competed with coffee and tea.

The love of chocolate took hold of Europe for reasons that went beyond the taste. One reason was that people believed chocolate was good for health and virility. Louis Lémery, a renowned French physician of the seventeenth and eighteenth centuries, described chocolate this way: "It is strengthening, restorative, and apt to repair decayed Strength and make People strong; it helps Digestion, allays the sharp Humours that fall upon the Lungs; It keeps Down the fumes of the wine, promotes Venery, and resists the Malignity of the Humours."[25]

The snob factor, always a plus in promoting anything, also helped. In Mesoamerica, cacao was a food for the entitled and the Europeans kept it that way. The Spanish hoarded their Mesoamerican prize and once released, it resided in the homes of the privileged few. Louis XIV, the king of many desires, appointed baker David Chaillou as the grand master of chocolate, giving him a monopoly over the Parisian chocolate-drink trade and the chocolates of the French Royal Court.[26]

Undoubtedly, at the top of chocolate's most esteemed qualities was its power as an aphrodisiac. The legendary Casanova allegedly drank chocolate to enhance his sexual stamina instead of the alluringly traditional champagne. Englishman Dr. Henry Stubbe wrote in the seventeenth century that: "The great Use of chocolate in Venery, and for Supplying the Testicles with a Balsam, or a Sap, is so ingenuously made out by one of our countrymen, that I do not presume to add anything after so accomplished a Pen."[27] How could Europeans, how could *anyone*, resist?

The answer, of course, is they didn't.

CHOCOLATE FROM THEN TO NOW

Today, Americans indulge in chocolate for the same reasons as chocolate lovers early on. The exclusivity aspect is a given. Even though M&M's—the people's chocolate—are popular, chocolate remains a deliciously luxurious item, especially when packaged in a box or bag with gold trim. Godiva has mastered the art of high-end positioning. "Our iconic Gold Ballotins are the gold standard in chocolate. Presented in our instantly identifiable, luxe gold box," they say on their website.[28]

But even the biggest health-food lovers, or should I say *especially* health-food lovers, believe in the powers of chocolate today. This is a dramatic shift in thinking from the late twentieth century, when chocolate was single-handedly responsible for acne, caused nearly instant weight gain, and had unrivaled powers to rot teeth.

Experts have now reversed their thinking about chocolate, claiming that it contains properties that can help lower cholesterol, improve blood pressure,[29] lessen the odds of having a stroke, and limit the effects of a stroke, should you have one.[30] Other findings are simply baffling: researchers recently found that teens who eat a lot of chocolate tend to have lower levels of fat[31] and that an antioxidant in cacao may prevent two health problems—obesity and diabetes.[32] Just imagine the generations who squandered their eating time by avoiding chocolate or by feeling guilt rather than sheer, sumptuous pleasure, when they did partake in it.

Naturally, business is seizing the moment, and I must admit, it's a little embarrassing. Chocolate was once an overtly guilty addition to breakfast foods made for kids, such as Cocoa Puffs and Pop-Tarts. (The relationship between this chocolate and anything Montezuma, or even the Spanish, touched, was unflinchingly nonexistent.) Now, however, food makers are adding chocolate bits to crunchy granola cereal, health food bars, and energy drinks targeting health-conscious consumers.

One excellent example is Cascadian Farm, which is owned by General Mills, the makers of Cocoa Puffs and Count Chocula cereals. Cascadian Farm offers organic and natural granola bars in a variety of flavors such as peanut-butter chocolate, chocolate chip, dark-chocolate almond, and, with a nod to Elizabeth White and the many Native Americans before her, dark-chocolate cranberry trail mix.[33]

We cannot end this section without delving into the last and most fetching reason people enjoy chocolate. But, spoiler alert, it might be disappointing. That reason is its aphrodisiac qualities. Granted, people don't take the aphrodisiac aspect of chocolate too seriously, but the *idea* of chocolate being an aphrodisiac

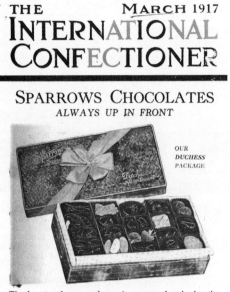
Fig. 9.1. Truffles ad in the
International Confectioner.

gives a box of truffles or other suitably spectacular chocolate special significance.

Is chocolate actually an aphrodisiac? Many sources say "*no.*" Well, sort of no. Chocolate *does* contain phenylethylamine, which *can* activate a feeling of giddy warmth, and it *does* contain serotonin, which *can* excite the senses,[34] but neither chemical is present in significant amounts. But, if its sexiness you're after, don't give up. Many of the fillings and flavorings in chocolate, such as vanilla, ginger, and nutmeg, have been used as aphrodisiacs for centuries. Nutmeg, a Thanksgiving favorite of grandmothers everywhere, is also a hallucinogen if you eat enough of it—eat too much and it can kill you.[35]

All these reasons for loving, if not worshipping, chocolate go right back to Montezuma, the fierce leader of Tenochtitlán. Bedecked in feathers and jewels, Montezuma had exclusive hold on the cacao, in his own kingdom and in those he conquered. Consuming it gave him health, vitality, and enough sexual stamina for one with an untold number of wives. In spite of his fall at the feet of the conquering Spanish, Montezuma, in spirit and in legend, lives on.

CHAPTER 10
CHOCOLATE OVER WATER

I t's strange to research something on your own ancestral stomping grounds. I say this because chocolate manufacturing was born in Massachusetts—just like me, my son, my parents, and even my grandparents (all thanks to my great-grandparents, who left their European enclaves for the uncertainties of Boston). When the cacao bean first arrived in North America isn't entirely clear, but it was definitely earlier than my kin.

Most likely the Native Americans of the Southwest used cacao early on, being close to Mesoamerica. But cacao didn't move around the country much until the 1600s. Its route was circuitous, to say the least, having left Mesoamerica for Spain, then Europe, where it headed back on British ships to North America.

The first historic sighting of the cacao bean was in a petition that Dorothy Jones and Jane Barnard drafted in 1670 "to keepe a house of publique Entertainment for the selling of Coffee and Chucalettoe [sic]."[1] The officials approved the women's request, although chocolate had its normal detractors in those who considered it a sin.[2]

This early chocolate was no granola bar you could snack on at leisure. It was a drinking chocolate, vaguely reminiscent of the Mesoamerican's, which wealthy New Englanders enjoyed at various times, particularly at breakfast or, possibly, instead of breakfast. Preparing the drink was quite a chore. They had to boil the water then pour it over a cake of chocolate which they stirred constantly until the chocolate was dissolved, and, at last, the liquid was rich and frothy. Depending on the hour and purpose, they may have added sugar, spices, milk, or even wine, which they probably needed after all that effort.

The beverage was usually made in a tin, copper, or silver chocolate pot, which looked like a cross between a tea pot and a lemonade pitcher, with a long slender neck. At the top of the pitcher was a perfectly round hole where they placed a stirring rod that resembled a bamboo skewer. They typically served the drink in matching cups.[3]

Fig. 10.1. Chocolate pots.

One of the many fascinating chocolate drinkers was Samuel Sewall, an important but all-but-forgotten man of early US history. From 1674 through 1729, Sewall kept a journal aptly named "The Diary of Samuel Sewall." [4] In it, he recorded remarkably commonplace goings-on, giving historians unique access into the lives of the Puritans, and candy enthusiasts a glimpse into the early life of chocolate.

Sewall, the son of a minister, was born in England in 1652 and moved to Newbury, Massachusetts, in 1661 to what is now known as the North Shore. In 1671, he graduated from the nation's first college, which was started thirty-one years earlier by a young minister to educate ministers-to-be. The founder's name was John Harvard and the school became known as Harvard College.

Sewall went on to become many things: a prominent merchant, a member of the Governor's Council, and a justice of the Superior Court of Judicature. Actually, he was one of the judges who presided over the notorious Salem witch trials. Why these non-witches were turned in by their neighbors and subjected to trial and death by burning is unknown. Was the rye in the local bread bad, inducing hallucinations? Was a conspiracy at work? The theories abound. What we do know is that Sewall, a pretty smart man and a Harvard graduate, bestowed the tortuous sentences.

Within five years, the tide of sentiment changed, and Sewall changed, too. He publically apologized and engaged in a yearly fast as atonement. His redemption may have also sparked an empathy for others quite unlike himself. He became an ardent abolitionist and wrote the nation's first anti-slavery publication in 1700, entitled, *The Selling of Joseph: A Memorial*. In it he condemned those who "hold their neighbors and brethren under the rigor of perpetual bondage," and said, "There is no proportion between Twenty Pieces of Silver and LIBERTY."[5]

Being a man of wealth and refined taste, Sewall was well-acquainted with chocolate. In his diary of 1697 he wrote about serving "chockalett": "I wait upon the Lieut Governour at Dorchester and there meet with Mr. Torry, breakfast together on Venison and Chockalett; I said Massachuset and Mixco met at his Honour's Table." In 1702, he records bringing "2 balls of Chockalett and a pound of figs" for Samuel Whiting, a New England minister, and "two half pounds of chockalett" for Mrs. Stoddard.[6]

He brought Samuel Whiting the chocolate because he was "languishing," possibly from something as commonplace as a cold, while he gave Mrs. Stoddard chocolate instead of "commencement cake." Samuel Sewall's remains are entombed in Boston's elite Granary Burying Ground, across from Paul Revere's marker.

But Sewall lives among us, or anyway, among me. After I finished researching Sewall, I realized that the neighborhood where my grandmother lived when I was growing up was once the Sewall family's farm. A few days later, it occurred to me why my parent's street is called Sewall Avenue. Maybe this speaks to the connectivity of things. I know that sounds corny, but when it comes to chocolate, you'll see what I mean.

BEN FRANKLIN: A QUICK CHECK-IN

Another, more celebrated, chocolate enthusiast was Benjamin Franklin. He admired the exotic bean for its health and medicinal value to the extreme. He believed it was a remedy for smallpox and included "6 lbs. of chocolate" (plus sugar, tea, coffee, vinegar, cheese, Madeira, Jamaican spirits, and mustard) in shipments to officers in the French and Indian War.[7] He ran ads for chocolate in his publication, the *Pennsylvania Gazette,* and sold chocolate at his Pennsylvania print shop.[8]

As chocolate became more and more popular, in apothecaries and elsewhere, tensions between the colonies and their motherland became more and more intense. As with the sugarcane, the colonists were reliant on Britain for cacao that enslaved people grew and processed in the West Indies. Soon, though, the colonists took chocolate matters into their own hands and processed the bean themselves. In 1765, Hannon's Best Chocolate was born.

HANNON'S BEST: THE FIRST AMERICAN-MADE CHOCOLATE

The Lower Mills of Boston, Massachusetts, home to the powerful Neponset River, was once a fishing and trading land for the Algonquin Indians whose tribal chief, Massachuset Sachem Kutchamakin, was the namesake of the future state. The energy brought by the river made it a perfect location for the Puritans who, in 1665, started the first gun-powder mill in the nation.[9] One hundred years later, the first chocolate processing company opened its doors.

It all started with John Hannon, a broke, unemployed Irish immigrant, who was in all ways down on his luck. A former chocolate maker's apprentice in England, he knew one thing: the wealthy colonists loved their chocolate. They had to work hard to prepare it themselves, grinding the bean with a mortar and pestle or using "hand mills," which were expensive, difficult little gadgets. Still, their love and loyalty to chocolate remained steadfast as did the price they were willing to pay for it.[10] For Hannon, chocolate was the ticket to a brighter, more palatable future.

At that time, chocolate could only be processed in cold weather. This was bad news for a chocolate maker who wants to go it alone: the cost of buying and maintaining a mill for part-time use was prohibitively costly. But for Hannon it offered an opportunity: he could rent space in other mills during the cold season then move on, expense free, when the weather turned hot.[11]

In 1764, Hannon made an arrangement with three businessmen—James Boies, Henry Stone, and Edward Wentworth—to use their saw mill to process chocolate. For start-up money, Hannon approached James Baker, a Harvard College graduate who practiced medicine at one point and operated a small general store from his house. Whether they were friends, business associates, neighbors, or, as some speculate, strangers who met on the road, no one knows. No matter, Baker agreed to fund the operation.

A year later, Hannon had rigged two enormous millstones together—the top set at the speed used for grinding corn, while the bottom whirled furiously with the untamed energy of the Neponset. Cacao beans were dumped into a hole in the middle, where the rapidly turning wheels pulverized them into a syrup. This mixture was poured into a kettle, then into a mold, where it cooled to form coarse, dense chocolate bricks. The colonists clearly appreciated this homemade effort: in 1773, Hannon produced and sold about nine hundred pounds of chocolate.

Things got tough during the Revolutionary War when Hannon and Baker couldn't get cacao beans through the usual channels. Their solution was to illegally smuggle cacao through their contacts on the Royal Navy ships that patrolled the Massachusetts shores.[12] After the war, the popularity of chocolate continued to flourish. In a letter that Thomas Jefferson sent to John Adams in 1785, Jefferson said, "The superiority of chocolate, both for health and nourishment, will soon give it the preference over tea and coffee in America, which it has in Spain."[13]

Although successful, Hannon and Baker eventually went separate ways. They may have had a falling-out or wanted to take the company in different directions. Whatever the reason, they drifted apart. Baker went on to start his own chocolate-making operation in an old paper mill. Eventually, his son Edmund joined him, and they grew their business in various rented mills until, in 1806, they bought their own. The name of their company was "Baker's Chocolate."[14]

As for John Hannon: The man who introduced chocolate processing to the nation went on a trip to the West Indies in 1779. He may have gone to buy cacao beans or, just as likely, to escape his wife. One thing is certain: John Hannon never returned. After some haggling, James Baker bought the business from Hannon's wife.

BAKER AND FAMILY: WHAT'S NEXT FOR CHOCOLATE

Baker's made three grades of chocolate—all were unsweetened and each was geared to the social class that could pay for it. The "No. 1 Premium," or "Best Chocolate," was for the well-to-do. It was pure, carefully produced, and appropriately expensive. The "Common Chocolate," at number two, was a grade below that, and the woefully inadequate "No. 3," did little to disguise its true self. Called "Inferior Chocolate," it was intended for enslaved people of the South and West Indies. This version contained ground-up rice and was more a gelatinous brew than a satisfying drink.[15]

Baker's son Edmund took over the company in 1795. Ever eager to expand the business, he started shipping their chocolate to Baltimore, Philadelphia, Norfolk, Richmond, and New York. Ten years later, he bought a grist mill and a fulling mill soon after. That decision saved the business from certain death. Here's why: During the War of 1812, Baker's once again couldn't get cacao. This time the Royal Navy wouldn't help, and the company's cacao supply ran out. Baker's ceased making chocolate—but it didn't die. With the multipurpose mill Edmund invested in years before, they were able to produce other products until the cacao bean returned at the end of the war.[16]

Once Edmund retired, his formidable son Walter took over, renaming the company "Walter Baker's." He expanded the business further, bringing on new employees and relatives, including an even more formidable step-nephew, Henry L. Pierce. Without question, Pierce was the powerhouse behind the Baker legacy, although he didn't start out that way. The powerful Baker and equally powerful Pierce were at odds, especially about the fiery subject of slavery. Baker thought slavery should be contained but not abolished. Pierce was a die-hard abolitionist. The two parted ways. Eventually, Pierce returned to the company and, a few years after Walter Baker died, took command.

Under Pierce's control, the company jumped from being a local business to an international player. All the while, Pierce pursued his political ambitions rising from Boston alderman to mayor to congressman. In 1895, Pierce incorporated the company as Walter Baker Company, Ltd., and the family ownership that began in the eighteenth century ended. Pierce died the following year.[17]

In 1896, the Forbes Syndicate bought the company, which was purchased by Postum Cereal Company, aka General Foods in 1927, who moved the company to Delaware in 1965. In 1985, Phillip Morris bought General Foods, and with it Baker's. Phillip Morris later bought Kraft and merged it with General Foods, which eventually became known, simply, as Kraft, included Baker's all of which merged with H. J. Heinz Co, which is currently owned by 3G Capital and Berkshire Hathaway Inc.

Did you follow that? No matter—you don't need to. What *does* matter is that Baker's Chocolate is still around, sandwiched among other companies. And given the thousands and thousands of well-known companies and the millions of smaller, unknown ones that lit up like a blaze of stars only to perish soon after, this is quite a feat.

BAKER'S SECRET TO SUCCESS

What was Baker's secret recipe for success? They had stealth. John Hannon couldn't afford a mill, so he rented one. They couldn't get cacao during the American Revolution, so they smuggled it. When they couldn't smuggle it during the War of 1812, they made something else. They had loyal customers and a product that promised health, vitality, and delicious flavor.

But that's all beside the point. What matters most is the company had Pierce, and Pierce was a marketing powerhouse. He made Baker's into more than a company: it was a force of purity, values, and ultimate good. In *The World's Work: A History of Our Time*, published in 1903, author Herbert S. Houston reflects this honed image into a somber truth:

> The principle was laid down in the beginning that there should be unflinching honesty in every stage of chocolate making, to the end that the product should be of perfect purity. . . . This fidelity to an ethical idea has produced an inheritance and a tradition similar to those perpetuated in the craftsmen's guilds of the Middle Ages. And this growth of character is really of more vital significance after all than any mechanical invention or business system.[18]

Granted, Pierce wasn't alone. Baker's had posted the nation's first chocolate advertisement in 1770, stating: "To be Sold By John Baker, at his Store in Back Street a few Bags of the best Cocoa; also choice Chocolate by the Hundred or Smaller Quantity."[19] From there, each generation, in step with the changing demands of the times, brought their advertising efforts to new levels. Pierce orchestrated the crescendo. Here's how Houston describes it:

There was little change . . . in the processes of manufacture and absolutely none in the fixed principle below those processes; but there was marvelous growth in the consumption of chocolate. . . . Herein lay Mr. Pierce's power as a constructive businessman. He not only made a product, but he literally created a larger market for it. He was one of the first American businessmen to perceive the creative force in advertising. . . . Nearly all other food producers sold their product to grocers and they in turn gained buyers after the stereotyped method of retailing. But Mr. Pierce changed all that by appealing first to the consumer. He believed here would be his ultimate market and it would be large or small in proportion to the convincing knowledge that could be spread among the people concerning the Walter Baker cacao and chocolate.[20]

For Pierce, the venue of choice for his ads were the magazines and newspapers circulated to nearly every American household. There, as Houston points out, consumers saw one of Pierce's greatest brainstorms: La Belle Chocolatière or "The Chocolate Girl," Baker's logo, which still graces their packaging today.

The image is based on the pastel portrait of a serving-maid holding a glass of water and cup of chocolate, composed by French artist Jean-Étienne Liotard in the 1740s.[21] After spending almost a century among those who appreciate art most, the Chocolate Girl appeared for the public to behold on Baker ads and packaging. And she personifies everything the Baker brand should be: clean lines, few shadows—a clear, crisp image. In short, she's fetching. She's trustworthy. She's so pure, you just know she's a virgin. But buyer beware! Not all companies are quite as noble.

In their turn-of-the-century ads, Baker alerts readers about underhanded competitors, saying: "Imitations on the market! Housekeepers should examine what they buy and make sure every packet bears our well-known . . . YELLOW LABEL. Trade-mark on every

Fig. 10.2. The Original Chocolate Girl.

package. TAKE ONLY THE GENUINE." Beside the text stands the eighteenth-century Chocolate Girl, vigilantly ready to serve.[22]

Another ad in 1905 calls on the full force of the law to drive their point. Beside the Chocolate Girl, patiently prepared to serve, the text reads: "There are many imitations of Baker's Cocoa and Baker's Chocolate. *Don't be misled by them.* Our trade-mark is on every package of genuine goods. Under the decisions of several United States Courts, no other chocolate or cacao than Walter Baker & Co.'s is entitled to be sold as 'Baker's Cacao' or 'Baker's Chocolate.'"[23]

Many ads gave readers ample health-related reasons to use Baker's Chocolate, a common message throughout the nineteenth and early twentieth centuries. One ad from 1919 claimed that Baker's Chocolate "is particularly adapted for elderly people, as it contains considerable fatty matter . . . yet it is easily digested and pure and delicious. 'It is a real food containing all the nutritive principles.'"[24]

Other ads focused on money: "Economical Housekeepers use Walter Baker's Cocoa and Chocolate because they yield the MOST and BEST FOR THE MONEY." [25] Others such as this convincing announcement in 1907: "47 Highest Awards in Europe and America"[26] emphasize Baker's acclaim.

Baker, along with Knox, Jell-O, and other companies, published pamphlets for homemakers, featuring colorful covers and boundless recipes. Baker's also published books, complete with photos, biographies, and facts that were interesting, predictably one-sided, and remarkably accurate.

EPILOGUE

So, whatever happened to the Native Americans who lived in Lower Mills? In short, they vanished. Their tribe was small to begin with, having only about five hundred members in 1631. Like other Native American

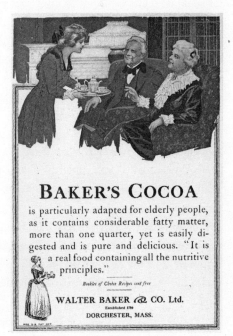

BAKER'S COCOA

is particularly adapted for elderly people, as it contains considerable fatty matter, more than one quarter, yet is easily digested and is pure and delicious. "It is a real food containing all the nutritive principles."

Booklet of Choice Recipes sent free

WALTER BAKER & CO. Ltd.
Established 1780
DORCHESTER, MASS.

Fig. 10.3. Baker's Cocoa.

nations, they suffered through wars and sickness, such as smallpox delivered by the settlers. The Puritans also embarked on a mission that would become the European American's passion for hundreds of years: to convert the native populations to their religion, customs, and dietary ways. Only a handful of decedents from Massachusetts Bay's native population are alive today—their customs and history have been decimated.[27]

HOW A PHARMACIST, A CANDLEMAKER, AND A LITTLE BABY CHANGED THE WORLD

While the Bakers were busily at work in mid-1800s, the young Swiss Daniel Peter was an apprentice in candle making at Madame Clement's candle store. He caught on quickly and soon opened Freres Peter Candle Company with his brother.[28] Life was predictable and bright, except for one problem bubbling up a continent away.

There, in the United States, a Yale University scientist discovered that rock oil could be refined and put to numerous uses, including lubrication and illumination. The findings were groundbreaking. The breakthrough interested New Haven speculator James Townsend, and he sent Edwin Drake, a railroad conductor, to Titusville, Pennsylvania, where oil deposits were constantly showing up. Drake's mission was this: tap into the oil that lay beneath the ground and make sure it keeps flowing.

Drake first tried the usual methods such as digging trenches. No luck. He then hired borers to dig holes. Still no luck. One failure followed another, but Drake pressed on with such veracity that the locals nicknamed him "Crazy Drake." Eventually Drake hired a blacksmith, William "Uncle Billy" Smith, who built a pinewood derrick and, with his men, began drilling steadily, six days a week, with Sunday off.

Unfortunately, their efforts were hampered when water filled the hole. But the entrepreneurial and tenacious Crazy Drake came up with an idea: drive an iron pipe into the bedrock and put the drill inside. This would keep the water out of the shaft and enable them to drill deeper and deeper. The idea worked. On August 28, 1859, seventy feet later, they struck oil, and the petroleum industry was born.[29]

So what did this mean to Daniel Peter? In three words: the kerosene lantern.

Candles might be pleasant, romantic, and atmospheric, but with this new invention, they were no longer necessary. The candle-making business was slowly sinking and Peter knew the Freres Peter Candle Company could not sustain them both.[30]

As it happened, Madame Clement had introduced Peter to the Cailler family. He fell in love with Fanny Cailler and married her in 1863. Her father happened to be the renowned confectioner Francois Louis Cailler, who mechanized the process of grinding cacao beans and became Switzerland's first chocolate manufacturer.[31]

With Fanny's father as inspiration, Fanny as support, and his own personal drive and intelligence as fuel, Peter established a small chocolate company using an empty section of the candle factory. He worked by day and studied everything from chocolate manufacturing to methods of harvesting and transporting the cacao bean by night.

Then tragedy struck. Daniel and Fanny's newborn baby, Rose, was unable to accept her mother's milk. In short, she was dying. At this time, there was a one-in-five mortality rate for babies under a year old and plenty of solutions were in the works. Up the road, a German-born pharmacist was developing one of them. In addition to his work with medicines, he manufactured liquid gas as well as fertilizer, and had a developing interest in the new food-manufacturing business.

The pharmacist had recently developed a milk formula mixed with cereal, but it was still in the trial stage. When Daniel showed up with a malnourished baby Rose, the pharmacist agreed, with some apprehension, to give him the formula. The baby took the nourishment and survived. The name of the pharmacist was Henri Nestlé.[32]

At this time, Daniel Peter's business was floundering. The chocolate industry was dominated by a few families, the Colliers being one of them, and he couldn't compete. According to his grandson, Francois Auguste Peter Sr., Peter had said:

> It did not take me long to convince myself that if I wanted to place myself and my product within the already existing factories, I must try for a specialty. Therefore, it appeared that if I could unite the milk and the chocolate in a state which would assure conservation and satisfactory transportation, I would make useful work for many, while being sure at the same time that the ownership of this industry would be difficult to exploit by anyone.[33]

Once Peter got hold of Nestlé's formula, a lightning bolt of inspiration hit him and hit him hard. He became consumed with a drive to achieve something entirely new—mix milk with chocolate for a smooth instant drink. Even better, why not turn the chocolate into a milky, melt-in-your-mouth sweet. But here was one glitch: the water in the milk and the cacao bean fat wouldn't blend.

Peter spent the next five or so years working out a solution. He tried numerous methods of perfecting his chocolate, including evaporating the milk. Then, at last, he achieved success. At least that's what he thought. Here's how he explained it:[34]

> My first tests did not give or produce the milk chocolate as we know it today. Much work took place and after having found the proper mixture of cocoa and milk—a mixture I was told was impossible to obtain—my tests, I thought, were successful. I was happy, but a few weeks later, as I examined the contents, an odor of bad cheese or rancid butter came to my nose. I was desperate, but what was I do? Go back and try a different procedure? Being as it was, I did not lose courage, but I continued to work as long as circumstances allowed.

Peter then tried using condensed milk. This effort paid off—for about a week. When he sold the candy to vendors, he promised: "If you don't like my chocolate, I will buy it back." Soon, unhappy customers were lining up to return the product with highly uncomplimentary comments. It seemed the chocolate had gone rancid.

Later that same year, Daniel Peter had a brainstorm. He made what he called a "drying room," where he turned the chocolate and milk mixture into flakes, spread it on trays, then further heated it to ensure the moisture had properly evaporated. He called it "Gala Peter": "gala" for the Greek word meaning "milk." Finally and for real, Peter reached his goal; he had created milk chocolate.

Around that time, Peter's neighbor, friend, and advisor, Henri Nestlé, was building an empire. His infant formula was wildly successful but also demanded packing, shipping, selling, and relentless managing, all things that required more effort than Nestlé cared to give. By 1875, he sold the business to a Swiss businessman and with it, the rights to his name. The company was called Nestlé.[35]

NESTLÉ POST NESTLÉ

When Nestlé died in 1890, he was wealthy, respected, and above all, retired. His name continued on without him, spreading to the United States and throughout the world. Thanks to increasingly savvy marketers, with plenty of savvy business dollars fueling their campaigns, Nestlé's formula, once made to stem the mortality rate of sick infants, became a household requirement for babies who didn't nurse *and* for those who did. One ad for the product, referred to as "Nestlé's Food," appeared in the *Evening Star* (Washington, DC) of September 25, 1910, and gave mothers this advice:

> From the Seventh to the Twelfth Month Protect Your Baby for those are the critical months when baby must be weaned. Don't wean the baby suddenly. Give it three or four feedings of mother's milk and one feeding of NESTLÉ'S FOOD at first; then later more Nestlé's and less mother's milk; until finally you use Nestlé's altogether.

The ad didn't indicate why mother's milk was no longer suitable for the healthy, growing baby, but it did have quite a bit to say about cow's milk:

> Cow's milk contains many elements in mother's milk but it doesn't mix them right. For instance, cow's milk has too many indigestibly curds and too little sugar. Besides, cow's milk is full of germs. Every Board of Health tells you that.[36]

Another ad a year later in the *New-York Tribune* made the case more dire. The headline read: "Help Your Baby Fight the Summer Heat." But they're not referring to mere comfort. The ad goes on to say: "It isn't the heat, it's our food that kills our babies in the summertime. And alas, more of them die in these three summer months than all the rest of the year together. Yet, it is all so unnecessary." The reason, according to the ad, boils down to this: "More babies die from summer diarrhea than any other cause. Nestlé's formula, made in the sanitary conditions of a lab, impersonates the cleaner, healthier mother's milk." Further, they say, the formula "suits the baby stomach so well . . . the baby won't notice the difference."[37]

Jump ahead to 1920, and Nestlé's Food is no longer used just for weaning infants or, for that matter, as a safety measure. As a testimonial from a Mrs. Annie Reeve Baker of Bristol, Tennessee, explains, it's for babies of all ages, all the time. According to Mrs. Baker, her eighteen-month-old baby drank Nestlé's formula from the first feeding in the morning to the last one at night. The result: "He is strong and active and always on the go."[38] The company repeated the "on the go" theme in a series of ads.

Daniel Peter's hard work had paid off. He entered his new chocolate in the Universal Exposition of Paris of 1889, which celebrated the end of the Franco-

Prussian War. The event, held between May 1 and November 10, attracted thirteen million visitors, and showcased the finest achievements of businesspeople, inventors, architects, and many others. Daniel Peter's milk chocolate received a coveted silver medal.

Even better for Peter, his chocolate shop in Switzerland was close to the railroad station at Vevey, a destination of the famed Orient Express. There, tourists and other travelers bought his chocolate, carrying it to distant, welcoming lands. Switzerland was also a prime tourist spot for appreciative and well-to-do Europeans, including a British pharmacist who was so enamored with Peter's chocolate that he ordered 110 pounds of it per year, for two years.

This got Peter thinking: if a town of eight thousand people buys 110 pounds of chocolate a year, then a city the size of London would likely buy 88,200 pounds, at least! This realization, among others, propelled Peter to expand his business and become a major player in the confectionery kingdom. In 1904, Peter's company, merged with several others, including the F. L. Cailler Company. They, in turn, merged with another, larger company whose name was Nestlé.[39]

CHAPTER 11
THE MYSTERY OF THE MARVELOUS WILBUR BUDS

There comes a time in every candy researcher's life when she knows she must hit the road, yet again. This is not a bad thing. Candy history seems to lie in sophisticated cities and quaint rural towns, so no matter what, the trip is bound to be good. This time, my destination was Pennsylvania dairy country—home of the marvelous Wilbur Buds.[1]

Before I go further, let me describe these sumptuous little treats. Wilbur Buds are shaped a bit like nonpareils, with a delightful flourish instead of sprinkles on top. The name "Wilbur" is embedded on the bottom of the unwrapped—*naked*—treats.

As I drove along Route 30, I felt something resembling melancholy. I expected the road to be rural or rural-*ish*, with farm stands and antique shops in aged buildings, and maybe an old fashioned ice cream shack. I saw plenty of those but the road was congested, and the air, filled with exhaust from cars and trucks,

Fig. 11.1. Wilbur Buds.

weighed down on everything like a fog. The ride grew even worse as I headed north: seething industrial buildings alongside abandoned farms, majestic silos stretching upward into the filthy sky. I thought this might be a metaphor, a candy metaphor, but I couldn't think of any.

At long last, I reached the town of Lititz, the home of Wilbur Chocolate. The town had a railroad track, a pond with a stream running into it, a few restaurants, a few small shops, and the Wilbur "factory." I say "factory" because the real factory is located some ten minutes away in Mount Joy, Pennsylvania. This was the original—one of those turn-of-the-century factories with evenly laid red brick and "WILBUR CHOCOLATE CO." in movie-set large letters stenciled on the side. I must say, after all the years of eating, selling, and talking about the Buds, I felt a chill of delight.

Inside, the company shop was stuffed with customers: a group of Mennonite students on what looked like a school trip, middle-aged tourists clutching bags of Buds, and families with kids. I was greeted by Kathy Blankenbiller, who multitasked as a greeter, tour guide, and chocolatier. We stepped through a nondescript door to a nondescript stockroom stacked with cardboard boxes on either side. I definitely had the feeling I was in a turn-of-the-century manufacturing plant and not a modern chocolate company. As I soon learned, that was a lot like thinking you're in a run-down shopping mall when you're really in the bowels of the CIA.

Kathy worked in a partially glass-walled, windowless cubicle that faced the stockroom. We needed to wait for Ann Charles, a twenty-something-year employee and the prime knowledge holder. Seizing the opportunity after a long car ride, I asked to use the bathroom. Kathy walked me to a water closet—that really was the size of a closet—just a few yards away, then waited outside the door. That's right, she waited.

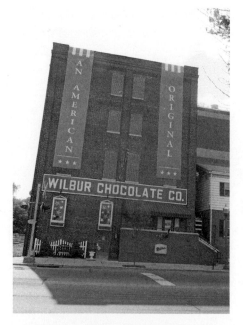

Fig. 11.2. Wilbur Chocolate Co. in Mount Joy, Pennsylvania.

Why did she wait? "So you won't get lost," she told me once I was done. Get lost? I could spit into her office it was so close. How could I get lost?

A few minutes later, Ann arrived and the interview began. I told her about the book, my fondness for Buds, and how eager I was to hear all about Wilbur. "Actually," said Ann, "there isn't much to tell." Isn't much to tell? I had already done preliminary research on the company, which opened in 1865 in Philadelphia, and knew it competed with Hershey's company, moved to Lititz in the early 1900s and continued to grow, and that now, 150 years later, it had two manufacturing plants.[2]

I guess I looked surprised, because Ann explained that the company always kept their records in the basement. Years ago, the stream that flowed so gently into the pond had flooded into the basement, destroying the archives. *All* the archives? Yes, all of them.

What Ann did know, she found in the brief, typed document held securely in her hands. I asked questions, and she searched the pages for answers. When I suggested she give me a copy, making things easier for all of us, she refused. She couldn't even *show* it to me let alone *give* it to me. As it happened, I found what I believe, based on my calculated glances in Ann's direction, is that very document. I found it on the Wilbur website, actually, and the information corresponds exactly to what Ann told me.

INFORMATION FROM THE "SECRET" DOCUMENT

In 1865, Henry Oscar Wilbur operated a hardware and stove business in New Jersey. For reasons unknown, he decided to switch careers and open a confectionery business with Samuel Croft in Philadelphia. The pair made molasses and hard candies using only a kettle, a coal or coke fire, some buckets, and a marble slab. A little like Daniel Peter and the Orient Express, Wilbur and Croft sold these treats to the railroad companies whose "train boys" then sold them to passengers. The pair did pretty well and eventually moved to a bigger facility on Market Street where they began manufacturing chocolate.

Apparently, all went well for twenty years. At that point, the partners had what seems like an agreeable breakup. Croft went on to make hard candies, and Wilbur and his sons took the chocolate-making route. Over the years, the chocolate did well, and Wilbur expanded to larger quarters in Philadelphia. Among their many innovations were the renowned "Stirring Cupid" advertising campaign, featuring a cupid stirring a cup of chocolate (I'd never heard of it), and, in 1894, the bud-shaped chocolate. And—get this—while in Philadelphia, Milton Hershey became their neighbor.

So, let's pause to consider. Wilbur made a bud-shaped chocolate that resembles a nonpareil with a swirl on top. Then, in 1905, one of H. O. Wilbur's grandsons invented a machine to foil wrap—*silver* foil wrap—the above mentioned candy. And in 1907, Hershey "invented" the silver-foil wrapped Hershey Kiss. Coincidence?

At that point, I asked Ann and Kathy the most salient question I could muster: Was there any truth to the rumor that Hershey stole the Wilbur Bud and turned it into the Kiss? As it happened, I heard this rumor from their receptionist the first time I called to place an order. Kathy and Ann looked uncomfortable. They exchanged glances. Then Kathy said, "Let's just say that Wilbur made the first Kiss." I pressed, eager to get to the root of this, but the most I could get was from Ann, who said: "They were supposed to have a gentleman's agreement."

Was this the reason for their secrecy? The much-publicized fact that Hershey stole Wilbur's chocolate idea? Actually, all was about to be revealed, without Ann ever flipping through the secret document.

MORE REVELATIONS *PLUS* THE CONNECTIVITY OF THINGS IN THE CHOCOLATE UNIVERSE

In 1927, as the Depression was about to shatter the nation, Wilbur Chocolate began negotiations with Suchard Societe Anonyme of Switzerland and, within a year, won the right to produce and distribute Suchard chocolates. For whatever reason, this spurred a new direction for the company; it started manufacturing chocolate for other companies and left behind all of their own confections except one of the cacaos and the Wilbur Bud.

Gradually, Wilbur's grew into this new line of work, moving, in 1928 to Lititz, Pennsylvania, close to the new facility operated by one Milton Hershey. And the reason? Simply put: dairy farms. The plethora of dairy farms made it possible for them to easily receive the vast amount of milk necessary for their chocolate. Wilbur's new line of business was so successful, the company has been sticking to it for almost one hundred years. But Wilbur's business was not a simple matter of whipping up a chocolate bar or powder and throwing someone else's label on it.

Each customer had their own written "formula," as Ann called it, which determined the amount of cacao fat and sugar needed and the length of time required to process the blend. Upscale brands spend more money on the chocolate-making process, while waxier, inexpensive brands spend less. The formula could be printed or even written down, most likely filling less than a piece of paper. As Kathy and Ann pointed out, each of these formulas was highly secretive—you might say "classified"—the secret text containing precisely the taste, color, and texture of multimillion dollar brands.

As a result, each requires considerable strategy on behalf of scientists and researchers Here's why: each batch of a particular candy must look, feel, and taste exactly the same as the one before it. However, not all the cacao, sugar, or other ingredients they receive are the same. Some chocolate is blonder. Some is sweeter. Some is stronger or coarser. It is the researchers' job to navigate the differing sets of ingredients so, for the customer, the end products all look and taste the same. Today, Wilbur manufactures candy for roughly seven hundred companies, and 60 percent of the cake mixes on supermarket shelves contain chocolate made by Wilbur.

So who are these remarkable researchers? Kathy and Ann have never met them; in fact, no one in the Lititz plant seems to have. And where are these formulas kept? Kathy claimed they didn't know, but my guess is at the company's Mt. Joy facility. I'm pretty sure Kathy and Ann did know, but they would never divulge the whereabouts of these multimillion-dollar secrets. What Kathy did say is that some of the candies are prepared right there in Lititz, and the candymakers receive recipes prepared from the formulas, in tiny little print—print far smaller than what the passing eye, returning from the bathroom, separated by walls and stacks of candy-filled cardboard boxes, could ever see.

Next question: Since the facilities are so close and all, does Wilbur make Hershey's chocolate? One of the women let it slip—yes, they do—but the other cut in quickly: "We did, but I don't think we do now, do we?" After a nervous moment, I promised I would never tell anyone they made chocolate for the one-time competitor, Hershey. But they did, and still do. I can tell you now, without being considered a liar, for reasons that will be revealed before the end of this chapter.

Here's another fascinating fact about the connectivity of the chocolate universe. In 1992, Wilbur Chocolate was bought by Cargill, which started as a grain storage operation in 1865, the same year H. O. Wilbur opened his shop. And, Wilbur Chocolate, through their parent corporation, purchased a masterpiece in candy history from Nestlé: Peter's Chocolate.[3] Yes, Wilbur is now the exclusive manufacturer of the chocolate made by the one-time candlemaker with a sick baby.

According to the Peter's website, Wilbur still uses whole milk crumb according to Daniel Peter's original method.[4] This got me thinking: If the difference between chocolates depends on written formulas, what about Peter's? When Cargill/Wilbur bought Nestlé, what exactly did they buy? My hosts confirmed that Nestlé kept the machinery, and no special beans, flavorings, or equipment were exchanged. So basically, Cargill/Wilbur bought a piece of paper with a formula on it. Granted, they bought the name, the logo, the distribution channels, and the related legal rights and entities, too. But all of this means nothing without the formula.

Kathy, Ann, and I joked that Wilbur purchased a pretty expensive piece of paper. We laughed because I knew all along why Kathy had waited for me outside the bathroom. Then we all laughed when Kathy told us that her father had been in military intelligence when she was growing up, and she is *really* good at keeping secrets.

As for Ann, she grew up just outside of Lititz in a community of Moravians who originally settled there in 1757. Ann herself was Moravian, which, she said, is the oldest denomination of Protestantism in the world. They value hard work, leading by example, and being ethical in all things. She said the locals never used the name "Wilbur's." They called it "The Chocolate." The Chocolate fragranced the air and gave them jobs—many, many jobs. And they loved it.

When it was time to go, I felt that Kathy, Ann, and I were great friends. Though it was a work-meeting kind of friendship: pleasant, revealing, then over.

When I left, my GPS sent me in a different direction, along roads bordered by sprawling dairy farms and green hills speckled by roaming cows. I stopped at a few farm stands and bought some springtime asparagus and strawberries. I even went to a place called Candyland, which was crowded with customers on that early spring day. I found some Lucky Charms there that was just the pastel bits of marshmallow, no cereal. I ate some on the way home; it tasted like toasted marshmallow. I made a mental note to buy some for my store. I drove on, not really caring about very much and feeling pretty good.

Deep in my heart, I knew it was time for Hershey's.

Fig. 11.3. A Pennsylvania dairy farm.

SIDENOTE: WHO IS CARGILL TODAY?

This could be one of the great questions of the modern age. Here's what it says on the Wilbur website:

> Cargill is a company focused on providing food, agricultural, financial, and industrial products to the world. Together with farmers, customers, governments, and communities, the company helps people thrive by applying experience and insight that span 150 years. Cargill works in 67 countries and celebrates the diversity of 145,000 employees.

Cargill is every one and everywhere, apparently. What they really do I can't say because, in the parlance of secret-keepers worldwide, if I told you, I'd have to kill you.

HERSHEY'S HERSHEY

A week or so later, I was heading to Hershey, Pennsylvania. The drive there was much better than the one to Wilbur's: plenty of farms, fields, and dairy cows on a gorgeous spring day. I passed a factory on the way, which was making the air smell of what? Popcorn? Roasted seeds? I soon found myself in Hershey's own Hershey, Pennsylvania. The town, which Hershey started in 1906, named for himself and his product, is an odd little place with a street named "Chocolate Avenue" and street lights topped with enormous fake Hershey Kisses. Otherwise, it's an ordinary town with your basic service station, convenience stores, and restaurants.

After a few turns of the wheel, I saw my destination: the Hershey Story Museum. I parked in the lot next door and was startled by a wave of screams as I got out of my car. It took me a few moments to realize the screams came from Hershey's amusement park, the uppermost part of a roller coaster and a Ferris wheel vaguely glistening behind a fence.

To be perfectly honest, I had some trepidation about going to Hershey in the first place. After researching the Wilburs and Bakers, I dreaded finding a chocolatier who doubled as a caricature with his own amusement park. And seeing the Hershey Story Museum, even seeing the *name* "Hershey Story Museum," didn't help.

Immediately inside the glassy museum was a vast portrait of Hershey surrounded by five children, one handing him a flower. The colors were pure Hershey, with plenty of that particular shade of brown. I went to the front desk and asked for Jan, the archivist, whom I was scheduled to meet. It turned out Jan was at lunch; she had expected me the day before, but thankfully she would be able to meet me in half an hour. This gave me a chance to visit the Hershey Museum, just upstairs.

The Hershey Museum wasn't exactly a museum. It vaguely reminded me of the New York World's Fair, which I attended when I was very young. It was filled with "exhibits" that were meant to amuse and amaze, although they were more entertainment than fact. As it happened, the Hershey Story Museum actually had an ornamental streetlight from the Chicago World's Fair in 1893, which held special significance to Hershey and, by default, the chocolate world.

The first room I entered confirmed my fears. It focused on Milton Hershey's life, with voice-overs of what was supposed to be Milton, his father (Henry), and his mother (Fanny). There were a lot of lighthearted comments like "Now Henry, leave the boy alone," and "Now Milton, finish your diner," from Fanny and the appropriate responses from Milton and his father, as if scripted by writers of *The Waltons*.

In reality, Milton Hershey was born in central Pennsylvania to Mennonite parents. His mother, Fanny, was the daughter of a Mennonite clergyman and believed in the disciplines of hard work, self-denial, and obedience. His father did not. Henry Hershey was a dreamer; he dreamed of big businesses, big schemes, big money, and interesting places. As a result, the family moved quite a bit, running to the next big thing in the next town or city, after enduring yet another one of Henry's failures. Eventually, Hershey's parents split up,[5] possibly precipitated by the death of Hershey's younger sister.[6]

As for Hershey, he was a terrible student who had trouble reading—a problem he never overcame—and he quit school after only eight years of education.[7] His mother tried pushing him into farming but he disliked it, so she arranged for him to apprentice at an ice cream and candy store. There he learned how to transform the moody and demanding cane sugar into a universe of lollipops, boiled sugars, and other sweets.

The candy business suited Hershey's tastes, if not his ability. By the time he was twenty-nine, he had a series of failed candy stores behind him in Denver, Philadelphia, and New York.[8] One reason for these failures was Hershey's father: while Fanny Hershey gave her son stalwart support, from finding start-up money to wrapping candy, Henry kept appearing, giving bad advice, steering Milton into loans he shouldn't take, and more or less ruining everything.[9]

By 1886, Milton Hershey was at the end of his rope. He was broke. He was living with his mother. And his candy business was going nowhere. It was then that Hershey had his first break. Granted it was a small break—metaphorically speaking, it was the size of a seed—but this seed grew into a towering empire. It happened because Hershey did what he spent a lifetime doing best: taking other people's ideas and building on them.

In this case, Hershey made caramel from a recipe belonging to a caramel maker he worked for in Denver who replaced the standard paraffin wax with milk. The result was a creamy, delicious treat. This jump-started Milton's first success, the Lancaster Caramel Company, and the new Milton Hershey, the man who would become the "Hershey" behind Hershey, Pennsylvania, was born.

THEN CAME JAN

I cruised through the museum then met Jan back at the reception desk. She took me to a basement meeting room where I sat, facing a wall with books about chocolate. Jan opened the conversation unenthusiastically saying something she probably said thousands of times before: "You know how people are always saying this person or that person was just plain good? Well, Milton Hershey really was."[10] Uh-oh.

After a few questions about the nature of Hershey's early home life, which Jan more or less dismissed, we talked about Hershey's trip to the Chicago World's Fair of 1893. That was where Hershey saw a wonder to behold: a German chocolate-making machine. At that point, Hershey employed one thousand people at the Lancaster Caramel Company and had several factories and a shop in New York.[11] He was rich, he was successful, and he bought the chocolate machine when the fair closed. That purchase changed the course of Hershey's life and America's chocolate experience forever.

Hershey was not content, however, with the dark chocolate people were eating in those days. Being an insightful businessman, he could see the future, and the future was milk chocolate. There was only one problem, the very problem Daniel Peter faced decades earlier: How could he make it? Hershey needed ideas.

It was then that Hershey went on his many trips to Europe. What happened there, Jan told me, no one exactly knows. There was plenty of espionage going on in chocolate factories, even among the most accomplished chocolate makers. Was Hershey really a spy hoping to steal his competitor's methods? Did he pretend to be an expatriate American looking for work, who slipped away during lunch breaks to scribble notes about ingredients and processes in the men's room? Jan admitted that he often traveled under an assumed name, but, she quickly added, not necessarily to spy. Someone as famous as Hershey needed to protect his privacy.

When Hershey returned to the United States, he devoted the next few years to figuring out how to make, or remake, milk chocolate. And, as we all know, he was successful. That year, Hershey also met Catherine "Kitty" Sweeney, the sprightly daughter of Irish immigrants. He and his good friend William Murrie (who would later become the president of the Hershey enterprise) saw her chatting with a group of girls at the candy store where she worked. Hershey was enchanted and evidently so was Kitty; they married about a year later. Hershey was happy. Kitty was happy. But Hershey's mother, with her strict Mennonite background, couldn't accept her whimsical new daughter-in-law. To resolve the situation, Hershey bought his mother a separate home in nearby Lancaster.[12]

In 1900, Hershey sold the Lancaster Caramel Company[13] for a cool $1 million,[14] a remarkable sum in those days, and started Hershey's Chocolate. According to the *Lebanon (PA) Daily News* in 1900, Hershey sold the "machinery, stock, fixtures and goodwill of the company" and left his employees to retain their positions.[15] In leaps and bounds, Hershey's empire surged, riding on the distribution channels and sales force he acquired through the Lancaster Caramel Company. Within twenty years, Hershey, now known as the "Chocolate King," became the largest milk-chocolate manufacturer in the world.[16]

During this time, Hershey continued building on other people's ideas. He may have based the Kiss on Wilbur's Bud, but he also created a machine that would spit the fully formed Kiss onto a conveyor belt, creating a Kiss-making assembly line for quick, cost-effective production.[17] As for the wrapper: Wilbur invented a wrapping machine in 1905. Hershey made his own version in 1921.[18] And the delightfully fanciful name "Kiss" was the name of a family of sweets.

Fig. 11.4. An ad for Hershey's Kisses.

Hershey didn't invent the candy bar, either; that was Frye of England, although his bar was gritty. The smooth texture of the chocolate was developed by Lindt, who in 1879 invented a process known as "conching" that essentially massaged the chocolate into soft-and-supple submission. What Hershey *did* do was add almonds to the chocolate in 1909 for a delicious crunch and inexpensive filler that kept the cost of the candy bar down.

Like a long line of industrialists, Hershey built a town around his factory, including a full-fledged school to replace the existing one-room schoolhouse, homes for his workforce, and the accoutrements they needed such as a self-service laundry, an electric company, a department store, a cemetery, a greenhouse, and a streetcar that would transport employees from their homes and milk from Hershey's dairy farms to the factory. He also established the Hershey Improvement Company to oversee the whole operation. But Hershey added a twist to his town: he turned it into a destination, with a zoo, a rose garden, a swimming pool, a dance hall, and an amusement park.[19] By 1909, he was advertising the park in postcards tucked inside candy-bar wrappers, the perfect marketing concept. The consumer unknowingly pays for the advertisement and reviews it in the perfect conditions—while eating a deliciously gratifying candy bar.

It's likely that Hershey had a model for his town. In England, in 1879, the chocolate-making Cadbury family opened a factory in Bourneville. The Cadburys had a long and prestigious presence in England's chocolate world, starting in 1824 when John Cadbury set up a chocolate house in Birmingham. For Cadbury, a Quaker who valued honesty, purity, and hard work, the chocolate drink was a perfect fit. It tasted good, was good for you, and was an excellent alternative to alcohol.

By 1879, the Cadburys built a state-of-the-art factory. Unlike the dark, fire traps of other candymakers, their workspace was light, clean, and roomy. In 1893, they bought the surrounding fields and a 118-acre estate nearby to make room for Bourneville Village—a community where employees could buy their own homes, with room for a garden and enough space to raise a family. The houses were nestled between village greens with parks, tennis courts, and playgrounds. The tenant-workers were able to purchase their homes through low-interest loans that were cheaper than the average rent, enabling them to own their homes outright in twelve years.[20]

Bourneville was a success and a model that Hershey probably witnessed on his trips to Europe. In 1903, *Cosmopolitan* (New York) columnist Annie Diggs wrote: "The very streets of Bourneville laugh in the place of crude conventionalism. The monotony of capitalistic housing . . . with rows of all a-like houses is prohibited."[21] So, it's no surprise that Hershey's homes were uniformly different.[22]

Hershey's town, set in the green hills of Pennsylvania's dairy country, were a welcome addition to the community. An article in the *Harrisburg Telegraph* of 1911 reflects the excitement: "During the past year, the greatest building boom in the history of the town was realized. The average visitor to the town is astonished at its rapid growth." The sub-headline underscores the fact, announcing, "Demand is great!"[23]

CHILDREN, LOTS OF CHILDREN

You'd think that Hershey, the man who transcended his own limitations to create an empire, would have been happy. And he may have been, except for two problems. One was that he and Kitty couldn't conceive children. So, at her prompting, in 1909, Hershey opened the Hershey Industrial School, an orphanage for boys.

The school was a success and its all-male alumna lived healthy, substantive lives. The headline of one article published in 1915 when the sixtieth student was enrolled, describes it best: "Hershey Industrial School, Making Real Men of Boys within Its Doors." The subtitle read: "Bids Fair to Become One of Most Important Asylums for Boys in the United States; Lads Taught to Do Things which Will Profit Them in Actual Life; Now 60 Lads Being Cared for." [24]

The second problem was Kitty herself. She began to grow weak about three years into their marriage and continued to decline with an unidentified illness. Eventually, she was confined to a wheelchair. She continued traveling abroad with Hershey, hoping the trips would somehow make her better. After one particularly long trip, she decided the sea air would improve her health and headed for Atlantic City. One evening, while sick with pneumonia, she asked Hershey to get her a glass of champagne to lift her spirits. When he came back, she was dead.[25] The grief-stricken Hershey never married again.

Once Kitty died, Hershey fled to Cuba, joining other sweets makers, such as Charles Hires and the fat cats at the Sugar Trust, who were eager to fill a hole that Spain had left behind. For Hershey, Cuba represented an opportunity to secure sugar for his business on his own plantation and more or less bulletproof the company against problems such as the impending First World War.[26] This decision became helpful during the Great Depression. While other companies struggled with sugar shortages, Hershey kept all his employees and stayed solvent, thanks in part to the sugar he produced on the island.

Eventually, Hershey turned his Cuban effort into another Hershey town. He constructed a railroad, built homes for rent, and opened a public school. To his credit, he also opened a school for orphans; the first enrollees were the children of workers killed in a Hershey Cuban Railway wreck. In 1946, Hershey sold his operations to the Cuban Atlantic Sugar Company and donated the orphanage in 1957.[27]

Throughout this time, Hershey continued traveling, which, given his fame, became a news item. "Chocolate King Sails for Europe with Murrie,"[28] announced one paper in 1931. In some ways, Hershey resembled his father, always traveling in search of the next big thing. But, unlike his father, Hershey actually found it.

QUICK PIECES OF REESE'S

My talk with Jan lasted a good two hours and gave me plenty to think about. Then I returned the way I came, past the factory with the nutty scent, only this time I checked for the name. Of course: Reese's of peanut butter fame. As it happens, Harry Reese started out as a dairyman for Milton Hershey in 1916. Before then, he moved from job to job, taking his family of sixteen kids with him. Reese farmed, managed a fishing operation for his father-in-law, and farmed again, until he became a dairy farmer for Hershey.

He apparently did well, because he was promoted, but luck was still not on his side. In 1919, Hershey closed down the farm where Reese worked for financial reasons, and Reese went back to job-hopping. This time, one of his stops was owning a candy store. No success story yet, though. It failed. Finally, Reese landed back at Hershey, this time in the factory shipping room.

Working for Hershey evidently taught him something besides milking cows. At home, in the privacy of his basement, Reese began making candy again. He figured if Hershey could do it, so could he. He sold a variety of hard candies and chocolate-covered raisins and nuts, making and probably saving money until he could leave Hershey for good.

At long last, Reese was a success. Business took off and he moved his operations to the basement of a building on Chocolate Avenue for more room. Reese's business continued to grow, and in 1925, he built his own factory. In 1928, when assorted chocolates and truffles were all the rage, Reese came out with a selection of his own. The peanut butter cup was one of them.

Then came the Depression. The weather was too hot for Reese to make chocolate, but money was too tight for him to stop. So, Reese did what Hannon and Baker did years before: he improvised. He made candy in the winter and ran a farm and a canning operation in the summer. As the economy improved, so did Reese's candy, and he returned to making candy full time. Eventually, peanut butter cups, dressed in their own packaging and available in three different sizes, rose above the rest . Affected by war-time shortages of the forties, Reese cut back to selling only one size.

After the war, business picked up and Reese, the most flexible man in the candy universe, could rest easy. His business was an unequivocal success. After Reese died in 1956, his six sons took over the business and ran it until the Hershey Company bought it from them in 1963. The legendary peanut butter cup, with its offspring, Reese's Pieces, lived a long healthy life in Pennsylvania. Given the smell, it still does.[29]

BACK TO MILTON: THE AUTHOR'S OPINION

As I was heading south to West Virginia, thoughts about Hershey kept bubbling in my head. I was really troubled by the too-good life that was projected onto Milton Hershey. Then, as I approached the long stretch of dairy land, I got it. Hershey's life wasn't easy. He grew up with a renegade father and a learning problem that forced him to leave school. He never learned to read. He had countless flops. He struggled with money and just when opportunity knocked, he struggled some more.

And that, I realized, is Hershey's glory. The Hershey story is about trying and failing and trying again. He didn't live by the book, but he had a remarkable sense of self. Hershey, the real Hershey, is an inspiration to kids who could never ace exams or get along with their parents.

So now let me tell you the end of the Hershey story: Hershey liked to visit the school, which eventually swelled to one thousand students. On one particular visit, when he was quite old, Hershey showed up at an assembly where he planned to give a talk. He rose but was silenced by thunderous applause and cheering. He stood in silence, tears streaming down his face, then left.[30]

PERSONAL PERSPECTIVE: SHELLI DRONSFIELD,
GROWING UP IN HERSHEY

I met Shelli Dronsfield when she was chief of staff at Shepherd University, a few blocks from my house. When we met, one of the first things she told me was that she grew up in Hershey, Pennsylvania, and her father and grandparents had worked at the school. Years later, we met at a diner, and she told me her story.[31]

There was always a connection between my life and what Milton Hershey did with his fortune. Hershey's was a family business in a larger sense; the business was the factory, and the school was a huge piece of the Hershey culture. The boys at the school were being cared for by wealth amassed by sales of candy. Many of them became Hershey employees later.

My grandparents were houseparents for the orphans at Hershey's school in the early '60s. My father was already in college at that time, at the University of Pittsburg. He graduated in '62 and went there, to Hershey's school, and got a job as a reading specialist. Later, he developed the first television station, which he set up in a central room and would broadcast to student homes. Our family had six girls and I was the oldest. Dad would take the oldest girls and would park the car at the base of a hill behind a hotel. Then we'd go to a coffee shop and he'd get us milkshakes.

My mother was a homemaker, and she was a very good one. We never had store bought bread. She cooked, sewed all our clothes; it was cheaper to do back then with six kids to clothe. We never had enough clothes to go to camp so my mom would be up all night making them before we left. Things were sparse, but we got what we needed. Later, she went to college and got her degree.

In town, Hershey was everything. We had a Hershey department store, Hershey Drug store, Hershey bank, Hershey electric company. The town reminded me of a college town. We had access to things like a community center and indoor swimming pool. Our house was one of the ones Hershey built for mid-level managers at the factory. He had the factory workers further out in smaller houses and the smallest homes were for line workers. When we moved there, the neighborhood was mainly elderly—grandparents and older.

Our backyard had an alley that separated the house from a pasture with a barn at the end. Two blocks away there was an area where the cows would go to birth their calves. We saw the calves' births and knew this was what went into Hershey's candy—it was all connected. When we smelled chocolate, we knew it would rain or snow because the winds would shift and we would smell it.

We grew up going to factory tours; we always went when we had company.

I remember it being loud and hot and industrial. There was a bright sun that came in the windows of the conching room. . . . I remember the conching machines and seeing them turn. My neighbor, Henry, worked in the factory his whole life; he lost some of his fingers working there. There is a famous picture of Hershey sitting on the steps of the "Homestead"—his house—with a little boy with a bowl-shaped haircut beside him. That was Henry. He was like a grandfather to me.

The student homes were attached to dairy farms, and the students worked on the farms after school and probably in the early mornings. They always had gratitude and a strong work ethic that was instilled in them as products of the school. All the kids had passes to the amusement park all year long. They could walk about on their own, get sodas, and they had allowances. They would put on a talent show in the spring in an auditorium in Founders Hall. It was as good as anything on Broadway. It's odd because you never knew who was a student and who wasn't unless you asked.

The Hershey School had always been trade-based, but they started seeing that the students had potential for college so they did an overhaul of the curriculum. My father was named director of curriculum and he was the architect of that.

Today I always eat Hershey Kisses. They're always there, in the candy bowl in my office. For me, there's no other chocolate.

ONE LAST TRIP . . . PEPPERMINT PATTIES: AN AFTERWORD

You can hardly head north from West Virginia without seeing signs for York, Pennsylvania, as I realized on my trips to Wilbur and Hershey. And this brings me to another marvelous candy, known affectionately as the Peppermint Pattie.

THE STORY OF THE PEPPERMINT PATTIE: VIA THE ICE CREAM CONE PLUS JUNIOR MINTS AND THE JOHN BIRCH SOCIETY

Henry C. Kessler opened the York Cone Company in the 1920s. Ice cream cones were relatively new in the United States, although their origins date back to the 1700s in Europe. When exactly the ice cream cone made its American debut isn't entirely clear, but it was certainly broadcast at the St. Louis World's Fair in 1904 and became a classic American treat thereafter.[32] Henry Kessler joined in, adding confections to his list of offerings.

At that time, chocolate-covered caramels, bonbons, and others along that line were old staples for candy lovers: suitors had been giving their intendeds chocolates for decades. But the chocolate-covered peppermint was substandard since the peppermint was soft and gummy. In 1940, Kessler figured out a way to make the center crisp, firm, and delicious. He named the new creation the "York Peppermint Pattie."[33] Soon, Kessler was selling the treat throughout the Northeast, Florida, and places in-between. In fact, the Pattie became so popular Kessler gave up his ice cream cone business and focused exclusively on that.

But Kessler was not alone. Plenty of candy companies jumped onto the Peppermint Pattie bandwagon, including James O. Welch. In 1949, in Cambridge, Massachusetts, he developed a smaller version of the iconic sweet called Junior Mints. Welch was no lightweight in the candy world; a native of North Carolina, he started his company in 1927 and went on to manufacture such iconic candies as Milk Duds, Sugar Babies, and Sugar Daddies. His brother, Robert, started his own company called the Oxford Candy Company. After it went belly up in the Depression, Robert joined his brother only to leave in 1956 and cofound the John Birch Society.[34]

As for the Junior Mints: the candy was named for *Junior Miss,* a popular book written by Sally Benson in the1940s. It was serialized in the *New Yorker* and went on to become a Broadway hit and a Shirley Temple radio production. The Junior Mints, which were bite-size and easy to navigate in the dark, became a movie theater favorite.[35]

The Junior Mints stayed in the family, more or less. Welch's company was bought out by Nabisco in 1963; Welch remained director until 1978. His son, who had joined his father's business after completing Harvard and serving in the Navy, became president and chief operating officer of Nabisco Inc. In 1981, Nabisco Inc. merged with R. J. Reynolds Industries, to form Nabisco Brands, Inc. Welch Junior became president of the parent company, according to an AP newswire announcement at the time.[36] Today, current owner Tootsie Roll Industries produces more than fifteen million Junior Mints a day in Cambridge.[37]

And as for Kessler's York Peppermint Pattie? After a number of corporate owners, it is now manufactured by Hershey.

CHAPTER 12

CANDY BAR BLITZ

I f ever there was a reason for candy haters to lower their collective voice, it would be candy's service to our nation. Soldiers have relied on candy for nourishment and comfort since the Revolutionary War, when they received sweets from home.[1] During the Civil War, soldiers made molasses pulls in the field and were sent homemade peanut brittle in packages from their families and sweethearts. In 1908, one New York newspaper article, with obvious temperance tendencies, put it this way:

> Nowadays every battleship leaving the Brooklyn Navy Yard has on board a lot of candy for the men—Brooklyn candy. "Why, in the navy, when a man is handed a pound of tobacco now he is also given a certain amount of candy, and it is believed that the drinking habit will be lessened in that way," said a manufacturer. "The sailors like the plan immensely, but if they knew it was done for that, they would probably chuck the candy overboard. But aside from that, it is a good food for them; men can fight better on chocolate than on meat—that has been proved in the German army."[2]

Candy first appeared in rations in the First World War when the military recognized the value of "countline" chocolate. These types of chocolates, which we now refer to as "chocolate bars," were not weighed and sold by the pound, but sold by the piece. There were many advantages to the countline candy bars; the distinctly substantial chocolates were meant to satisfy hunger, unlike than the thinner variety, which were made to satisfy taste. Also, the chocolate coating on the bars preserved and held the contents inside, much like an edible protective wrapper.[3]

For the military, this meant added nutrients and calories. For candy bar makers, it meant the opportunity to fill their expensive chocolate with deliciously cheap fillers, such as caramel, peanuts, and marshmallow—all relatively new, post–Civil War ingredients that the consumer loved. The first American-made countline bar, or "combination candy bar" in the parlance of the consumer, was the Goo Goo Cluster. First made in 1912 in Nashville, Tennessee, it is often referred to as a "mound of chocolate-covered marshmallow, caramel and nuts."[4]

There were plenty of other reasons to give service men and women chocolate and other candy. An important one was discussed in a 1918 article filed from Camp Lewis, Washington. It said:

> That the government recognizes the usefulness in the diet of soldiers is shown in the immense order for $200,000 worth of candy which has just been placed for the men at Camp Lewis. . . . It is the largest candy order ever placed in the Northwest and probably the largest yet authorized by the government for the soldiers. . . .
>
> This war has done more than anything else to demonstrate that candy is of tremendous food value. A soldier after a hard day's work needs candy; his system craves it. Likewise, shipyard workers, loggers, men and women doing all kinds of heavy work, crave candy because it supplies the need for something sweet to supply bodily fuel. . . .
>
> The candy which is being made today is being manufactured with the sugar that is being authorized for this purpose by the food administration.[5]

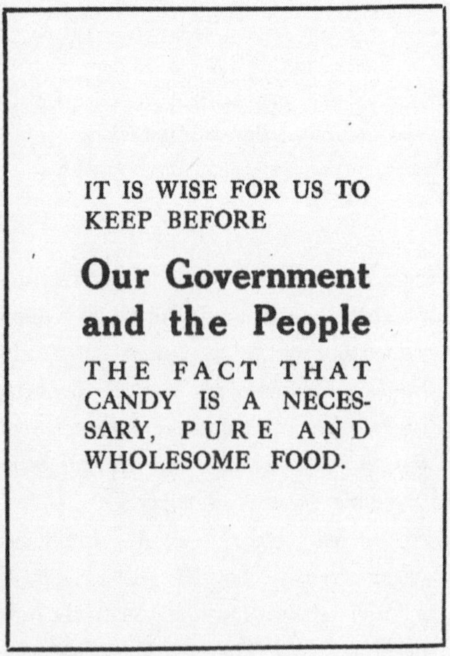

There were different kinds of rations—trench rations, emergency rations, and so on—depending on the whereabouts of the soldiers eating them. Some contained chocolate bars, others didn't. After the war, when the quartermaster general asked veterans what would improve their mealtime experience, they recommended chocolate bars for everyone. Believing candy boasted morale and energy, the military agreed, and candy has been military fare ever since.

IT IS WISE FOR US TO KEEP BEFORE

Our Government and the People

THE FACT THAT CANDY IS A NECESSARY, PURE AND WHOLESOME FOOD.

Fig.12.1. An industry ad to promote the use of candy as a food during World War II.

HENRY AND WILLIAM GO TO WAR

C'est la soupe qui fait le soldat." (It's the soup that makes the soldier.)
                                                —Napoleon Bonaparte

One of Hershey's most publicized accomplishments was the Field Ration D, also known as the D ration bar, the famously thick brick of chocolate that World War II soldiers were *not* supposed to eat—bizarrely not even *want* to eat—until the situation was dire. And, in its own way, the D ration truly was an accomplishment. Through all of industrial history, candymakers focused on making their products taste good: Hershey purposefully made this bar to taste perfectly bad.

The D ration story actually began in 1937. That's when Captain Paul Logan, from the US Army Quartermaster General's office, contacted William Murrie, Milton Hershey's close friend and president of the Hershey Company. Logan wanted Hershey to develop a chocolate bar specifically suited for the requirements of a global war: a bar that weighed about four ounces, could endure high temperatures without melting, was high-energy and high-calorie, and tasted only slightly better than a plain boiled potato.

Somehow the company pulled it off, using ingredients that sound pretty good to an unknowing outsider: chocolate liquor, sugar, skim-milk powder, cocoa butter, oat flour, and vanillin. Hershey chemist Sam Hinkle used his magic to reach the military's low-taste, high-calorie requirements by using more chocolate liquor and less sugar to create a heavy paste that was pressed into the molds rather than a smooth, silken liquid that was poured. In the process, six hundred calories were crammed into a mere four ounces of chocolate. Without question, it was a chocolate bar soldiers hated.[6]

In fact, they hated it a lot. These men were battling malaria, bullets, and bombs, and the possibility of death, captivity, starvation, and torture, but they still found time to protest Field Ration D loud enough for Washington to hear. Enter Hershey's Tropical Chocolate Bar, the company's new and improved version of Field Ration D. While the name indicates a creamy blend of milk chocolate with shaved coconut and diced pineapple, it was still the Field Ration D, although better tasting.[7]

The chocolate bar, like other rations, offered some slight comfort to families waiting at home. A newspaper article in August of 1942, tells the public: "Carried in the pocket, these chocolate bars offer real nourishment and prevent loss of energy to the soldier who suddenly finds himself 'on his own.'"[8]

All told, Field Ration D led an interesting life. It was tested in Panama, on the Texas border, in the Philippines, and in Antarctica, on the last expedition of Admiral Byrd. Hershey was producing one hundred thousand bars per day in 1939 and around twenty-four million per week in 1945. From 1940 to1945, over three billion chocolate bars reached soldiers around the world. In 1971, Apollo 15, landed on the moon and in its very distinctive cargo was Hershey's Tropical Bar.[9]

MARS WITHOUT M&M'S

To understand the story of the M&M's you have to understand the story of Mars. If you can compare the Hershey family to the Waltons, then the Mars family is right up there with the TV show *Dallas*. In the interests of full disclosure, I really like Mars, in spite of the company's somewhat riotous past. It makes the delicious and authentic eighteenth century American Heritage chocolate, a hard feat given it's mass producing it on modern machines. Mars even gives free talks about how the colonists made chocolate. Years ago, my husband knew Pam Mars; he either dated her, worked with her, or she was his boss. The story seems to change or maybe I remember it incorrectly, but his opinion of her has always been good.

Frank Mars, the father of the Mars empire, had spent a good deal of his child-hood indoors watching his mother cook, since he was sick from polio. Among other things, she taught him how to hand dip chocolate.[10] He learned his lessons well and developed a knack for making confections. At nineteen years of age, he started selling candies door-to-door to shopkeepers. A few years later, he opened a company and married the first Ethel Mars.[11]

Frank and Ethel had a child, Forrest, but when the candy company failed, the stress shattered their marriage and they divorced. Frank was supposed to send $20 a month in alimony but often missed payments. Ethel was forced to send her son, then six, to live with her parents in a remote mining town in Canada.

Frank, meanwhile, married a second Ethel, and, after a few false tries, they started a successful candy-making business from their house. Frank made the candies, and Ethel sold them to passengers on the trolley. Eventually, their candy found homes in Woolworths and other retail stores, and, soon enough, Frank had hired 125 people and was living more than comfortably in Minnesota.[12] The name of his business was the Mar-O-Bar Company.[13]

In the meantime, Forrest, sent to the northern reaches of Canada, grew up and went to school at the University of California in Berkeley and, later, Yale. And guess who he bumped into while earning money as a traveling salesman one summer? His long lost father, Frank. The two talked over malts at a five and dime, and a spark, albeit an uneasy spark, was lit that would eventually set the candy world on fire.[14]

Around that time, revealing the family gumption and nerve, the young Mars salesman posted ads for Camel cigarettes around the streets of Chicago without proper permits, fees, or permissions. The ad strategy got him a prompt and thorough response from the police, who threw him in jail. A surprise visitor—Frank—bailed him out.[15]

While estranged for most of Forrest's life, Frank found in his long lost son a confectionery ally who helped him lift his business from a Minnesota-based candy company to a national concern. One of Forrest's truly great ideas was to make a solid countline bar that could be mass produced, which consumers would purchase in droves. The result was the Milky Way.

Allegedly, the concept for that particular bar arose when Forrest and his father were drinking malts at the soda shop, and Forrest said something like, "Gee Dad, why don't we add malted milk flavor to a candy bar? The people will love it!"[16] A bit simplistic, I know, but soon they had devised a relatively inexpensive nougat and caramel filling, held and protected by a loving layer of chocolate.

Within three years, the father-son team had opened a new factory in Chicago and was selling millions of candy bars. In 1922, the company was down $6,000; in 1924, sales exceeded $700,000; and in 1930, just as the Depression revealed itself to bleary-eyed Americans, Mars produced Snickers, named for the family horse, and 3 Musketeers.[17] The company dropped the name Mar-O-Bar and picked up Mars, Inc. instead, and then it relocated to Chicago, where the railway system could transport their candy all over.[18]

During the Depression, hungry and anxious Americans continued to eat Mars bars. As other companies were downsizing or closing their doors, Mars's sales quadrupled. Even Frank Mars's largest rival, Milton Hershey, with sugar from his Cuban plantations and an expensive initiative to develop his community (and provide jobs), felt the pinch.

The father-son team may have been good for business, but it was bad for family. In 1933, Forrest and Frank had a battle that goes down in the annals of candy history. Frank yet again cast Forrest from his life, with some cash, the rights to a foreign Milky Way, and the command to never contact him again. Forrest hightailed it to Europe full of energy and ambition. The Europeans, even the candy-makers so finely attuned to sabotage and competition, had no idea what hit them.

FORREST ALONE

> The company's objective is the manufacture and distribution of food products in such manner as to promote a mutuality of services and benefits among all stakeholders.
>
> —Forrest E. Mars Sr., 1947

Alone in Europe, Forrest decided to start from scratch, beginning the same way that launched other seasoned confectionery makers, such as Milton Hershey, into new directions: with education. The education was entirely hands-on, of course, and in Mars's case it meant learning from the best—the chocolate-loving Swiss. Mars found work at Tobler and Nestlé, picking up their secrets as well as a few paychecks, then he left for England.

There he set up shop in the town of Slough, equipped with second-hand machinery and his own remarkable problem-solving abilities. A steady supply of sugar and chocolate was a challenge for the best of candymakers and more so for Forrest who had limited funding. He asked the Cadburys for chocolate to coat his candy, and the company's coating department, ignorant of exactly who was asking, agreed. The candy was an improved remake of the Milky Way, which, in the spirit of true celestial branding, Forrest named the Mars Bar. In one year, Mars sold a remarkable two million bars, becoming a major European player.[19]

The European chocolate makers were no slouches, and they shot out round after round of confectionery treasures, such as Roundtree's whimsical sensation known as the Kit Kat, possibly named for the famous 1920s KitKat Club.[20] Eventually, recognizing the competition he faced from his European counterparts, Mars bought a dog food company whose profits could fund his candy, just in case.[21] His success was even greater than that of the father who had abandoned him twice.

Eventually, Forrest returned home, where he started the M&M Company. Later, after his father's death, he bought out the American Mars and merged the two Mars giants into one—Forrest's final triumph over Frank.

M&M'S: WHEN MARS MEETS MURRIE

The concept of the M&M was ignited, so it seems, in the 1930s in Spain, where Forrest Mars was spending time during the Civil War. What he was doing isn't exactly clear: he was living in Europe at the time, had a successful business, and didn't seem to have any political affiliations. But there he was, in the midst of a battle between an array of left-wing factions: anarchists, communists, socialists, and a powerful Fascist, Francisco Franco. The Fascist won.

Apparently, while there, Mars hooked up with someone from the Roundtree family, one of the Quaker, candy-making giants of England. Together, they seemed to have discovered a chocolate candy with an intriguing sugar shell that soldiers carried for energy. The two men, who were competitors at the time, agreed to try their separate hands at making the candy: Roundtree in England, and Mars in the United States, where he, the prodigal son, planned on returning.[22]

The story is a little confusing since the Roundtrees began making candy-coated chocolates in 1882 that were first called Chocolate Beans and later, Smarties.[23] Either way, Forrest upheld his end of the deal, calling his candy M&M's.

But why "M&M"? That part of the story started when Forrest returned home in 1939. He saw opportunity and was eager to make a go of the new candy for a few reasons. One was that people stopped buying chocolate in the summer because it melted. The candy shell would protect the inner chocolate and get people buying again. Another was the likelihood of war. Wartime brought on two conflicting realities. One was a new distribution channel: the US military whose soldiers needed all the chocolate and sugar they could get. The other was the inevitable shortages of both these ingredients. Mars needed a steady flow of product, and he knew exactly where to get it.

The *where* was Hershey's Chocolate Company, the nation's largest chocolate producer and the chocolate source for Frank Mars's candy bars. That was obvious. The bigger question was *how?* In Forrest's inimitable style, he found an in: Bruce Murrie, son of William. To get to the father (Hershey's president), go to the son.

Bruce Murrie was working on Wall Street when Mars made his offer: a limited partnership, an executive position in the company, and his name on the candy. In return, Mars wanted an investment of 20 percent (Mars would add the rest), a steady stream of chocolate, and *his* name on the label. They split the difference on that point and called the candy M&M, for Mars and Murrie. It was an offer no father could refuse, and William convinced Bruce to jump in.

About a year later, M&M's were hitting the shelves in tubes, in brown, yellow, green, red, violet, and later, tan colors. The famous "M&M" logo had yet to be stamped on the top, but the shape, color, and flavor were unmistakable, although quite like the British Smarties, which were also packaged in tubes. In any case, M&M's were a hit!

Whatever hunches called Forrest to action, the reward was great. During government rationing in 1942, his Hershey connection kept the chocolate flowing, all the way to their biggest customer, the US military. They bought millions to send to bomber pilots in Africa and the Pacific, Army soldiers in Guam and the Philippines, and others around the world. The military men and women were enthusiastic about the candy and carried their enthusiasm when they came home.

In spite of the wartime boost, sales were lackluster. And Forrest knew why. It was Murrie; he was no good at sales. Forrest more or less cast out Bruce Murrie, buying his minority share for what, even then, was a paltry $1 million. M&M's, with their black, and later white, lettering, have been the Mars family's shining star ever since.[24]

BACK TO MARS

There's no question that Forrest was a difficult man: loud, abrasive, and demanding. But, he was also brilliant—a blinding and irrepressible brilliance. But then, so was his father. Frank, like his enterprising son, added other products to his portfolio, including Uncle Ben's Rice. Today, their collective brilliance, and that of their descendants who still own the company, shines around the world.

Mars is the third-largest private company in the United States, with Wilbur's parent Cargill wavering above it. Mars is worth about $33 billion in global revenue, putting it ahead of Starbucks, McDonalds, and General Mills. The company handles about two hundred million consumer transactions a day of its many products, which have expanded to include Wrigley's, Juicy Fruit, Life Savers, Pedigree, and Whiskas.[25]

Mars is still family-owned, under the leadership of Forrest's three elderly children. So, what is the next generation like? It's hard to explain, mainly because the company is notoriously secretive, bringing its neighbor, the CIA, almost to shame. You *can* get a glimpse of human life from its 72,000 employees worldwide, although you have to go pretty far if you live in DC; only eighty employees work at the nearby Virginia headquarters. According to *Fortune* magazine, when the Nestlé chairman once paid a visit, the place was so small, so discrete and inconspicuous, he thought he was lost.[26]

Generally speaking, the employees, who call themselves "Martians," seem happy there. The company has a ridiculously low turnover rate of 5 percent, with some staying for generations, and the employee makeup is diverse. Employees are able to contribute ideas and train for their positions, so they're prepared to succeed and move ahead within the company. The vending machines are free, and chewing gum is allowed, even at meetings.

In 2013, *Fortune* magazine ranked Mars as one of the top 100 best places to work.[27]

CHAPTER 13

CANDY FOR FUN AND FLAVOR

They had in Salem two kinds of candies called Black Jack and
Gibraltar, the latter "the aristocrat of Salem confectionery." It (the
Gibraltar) gazes upon chocolate and sherbet and says "before you were,
I was. After you are not, I shall be." You never soiled your fingers
when you ate Gibraltar, but you might smear yourself with Black Jack.
Gibraltar was not precisely conservative; it changed as to its flavors, so
once a charming old Salem Dame said: "I known I must be growing
old, because a peppermint Gibraltar is so comforting to me." We are
to believe that these two confections are still Salem Institutions, for
Mrs. Bates intimates that Witch Hall, the Museum, and Chart-street
burying ground might all go, but while there was a house left in Salem
village Black Jack and Gibraltar would stick.
—from "By-Gone Days," *New York Times*, June 13, 1886, p. 5

I had enjoyed my travels to New York City, Pennsylvania, and elsewhere in
pursuit of candy history so, I figured, why not go to Boston. I thought I
might peek at the former site of Baker's Chocolate, but that had been "renovated"
into an office building. Besides, given the amount of traffic, the trip would be
disturbingly close to the one I took to Wilbur.

But, Salem, Massachusetts, is the home of the nation's first commercial
candy company, *and* the first commercial candy. Besides, plenty of nearby towns,
including Boston, offer fascinating candy-related sites to see and people to interview, not the least being my dad, the man who once ate Marshmallow Peeps in his
car, and my mother, who hates candy.

So, on a warm day in early June, my husband, Dan, and I set off on a slightly
torturous nine-hour drive to New England. We brought our dog, Moses, an end-
lessly happy hound mix, whose disposition checked our shock and horror as trailer

trucks careened past us, taking the mountainous hairpin turns as if all eighteen tires were made of ice. My dear husband mentioned something, as he so often does, about drivers taking uppers to make better time. Gradually, the eighty-degree temperature in West Virginia became the forty-seven-degree spring chill of New England. Naturally, my husband and I were still dressed in shorts and sandals.

The next day, decked in layers of spring and summer clothes, we set out to see Bob Burkinshaw, owner of the nation's first candy company, Ye Olde Pepper Companie. As you can imagine, I felt a bit like a British tourist who sets off to Kensington Palace, eager and prematurely in awe.

The factory was just outside Salem, in Lawrence, Massachusetts, the famed site of the International Workers of the World's "Bread and Roses" strike. The strikers, largely immigrant women, were protesting work conditions in the Lawrence mills. No one expected them to hold out for more than a few days, but they held out considerably longer. The ordeal turned violent at times but ended more or less positively: the horrid working conditions were exposed, including the use of child labor, the workers received a 20 percent higher pay raise, and conditions gradually improved.[1]

And there, tucked in-between factories and brawny, nondescript don't-mess-with-me buildings, was Ye Olde Pepper Companie. Dan and Moses settled in for a mid-morning nap in the car as I entered the factory. An employee paused from eating her lunch to greet me and, after a moment's conversation, inform me that everyone knew *her* favorite candy was brittle. Then she picked up a phone, spoke to someone, and escorted me up a short stairway.

In an unremarkable room, cluttered with paper, desks, chairs, and a playpen (for Bob's grandchild, it turns out), I met Bob, a delightfully spry man in his mid-sixties with an impressively full head of white hair. His daughter, Jackie, owner of the playpen, sat at the desk beside his. Bob had a stack of papers ready for me, which included information about the company and pictures of the early owners. As Bob and I talked, Jackie filled in details and looked up related facts online. The conversation was relaxed, friendly, and altogether pleasant, as befits the first candy company in the country.

THE STORY OF THE FIRST COMMERCIAL CANDY COMPANY IN THE UNITED STATES[2]

The year was 1800, and the Revolutionary War had ended. In nearby Boston Paul Revere had started the Massachusetts Charitable Association, the Bakers were firmly rooted in Lower Mills, John Adams of nearby Quincy had lost his presidential bid to his friend Thomas Jefferson, and Mrs. Mary Spencer and her son Thomas were shipwrecked in Salem, Massachusetts, after sailing over from England.

As you can imagine, Mary Spencer was destitute, having lost all her worldly possessions in the wreck. The town's women felt bad for her, and upon learning she was an excellent cook, they raised money to buy her a barrel of sugar. Mary Spencer used the sugar to make what she called "Gibraltar," which was named for a British style of confection.[3] The ingredients—cream of tartar, sugar, lemon or peppermint flavoring, and corn starch—were standard components of many candies and medicines, and the result tasted much like an after-dinner mint.

Mrs. Spencer sat on the steps of the First Church in Salem, selling the candy from a pail. She must have had a compelling personality and an extraordinary product, because people bought it. They bought it and bought it and bought it, making Mrs. Spencer relatively well-to-do.

What did she do with her money? At a time when women couldn't vote, rarely owned property, and certainly weren't entrepreneurs, Mary Spencer bought

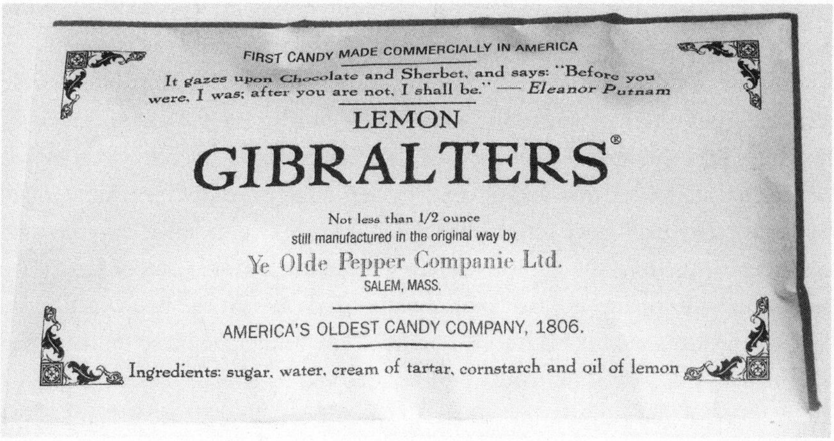

FIRST CANDY MADE COMMERCIALLY IN AMERICA

It gazes upon Chocolate and Sherbet, and says: "Before you were, I was; after you are not, I shall be." — *Eleanor Putnam*

LEMON

GIBRALTERS®

Not less than 1/2 ounce
still manufactured in the original way by
Ye Olde Pepper Companie Ltd.
SALEM, MASS.

AMERICA'S OLDEST CANDY COMPANY, 1806.

Ingredients: sugar, water, cream of tartar, cornstarch and oil of lemon

Fig. 13.1. Gibraltar.

a horse and buggy and went from town to town selling the Gibraltar. She made so much money on her travels that, in 1806, she bought a house on Buffum Street in Salem. She lived on the second floor of the house and, as was the custom of the time, opened a shop on the ground floor. Unlike other shops, this was the nation's first commercial candy company, and it never closed.

Mrs. Spencer's success was partly due to her shop's seaside location and the steady flow of seafaring customers: in war time, sailors and seamen; in peacetime, seamen, traders, merchants, and possibly pirates. Gibraltar was sturdy enough to withstand humidity from the sea and was cut and wrapped in triangular pieces that easily fit in small spaces on board, where it was carried to China, the Far East, Africa, and the East Indies. But something else was at hand.

Mary Spencer's son Thomas grew up to be an ardent abolitionist, known for standing on a soap box on a busy Salem street railing against slavery. His mother was part of the Underground Railroad. As she went from town to town selling the nation's first commercial candy, she secretly transported escaped slaves in a false bottom in her buggy. The buggy now rests in the privacy of the nearby Peabody Essex Museum.

When Mary Spencer died around 1828, Thomas put her body in an easily transportable copper coffin. After running the company for a few years, he returned to England, where a large sum of money and possibly a royal title, awaited him. He buried his mother there. Bob pointed out a photocopied picture, tucked in the stack of papers he handed me early on, of a well-to-do Thomas and his wife standing before an impressive home in England. I asked Bob the next obvious question: "Were they part of *the* Spencer family? The Princess Diana Spencer family?" Bob shrugged. "Everyone asks me that."

Before leaving for England, Thomas sold the shop to his neighbor, George Pepper, a businessman and confectioner whose brother owned a sweets shop in Boston. Pepper wanted to make a candy to balance the Gibraltar, which he felt was feminine. He wanted something stronger. He obviously didn't know Mary Spencer. With help from his brother, John Pepper, George made a stunningly delicious molasses candy that was smooth with subtle hints of Cracker Jack. They made the confection from black strap molasses and called it the Black Jack Stick.

George expanded the company's product line to include horse liniment and shoe polish and also began to distribute tobacco and other goods, turning the first candy store in the nation into a thriving, multifaceted business. When George Pepper retired in the late 1800s, he sold the shop to an employee named George

Burkinshaw, Bob's grandfather. It's
been in Bob's family ever since.

Today "Ye Olde Pepper
Companie" has gone back to its strict
candy-only origins. The company is
named for George Pepper, and the
logo is a sketch of Mary Spencer
in her buggy. The retail shop is on
the ground floor of an eighteenth
century home, across the street from
the House of the Seven Gables (of
Nathaniel Hawthorne fame) and
a mile or so from Buffum Street
where Mary Spencer started out.
Given the success of Ye Olde Pepper
Companie, Bob couldn't make all
their products on site, so he opened
the factory in Lawrence.

Fig. 13.2. Black Jack Sticks.

PERSONAL PERSPECTIVE: BOB BURKINSHAW, CANDYMAKER, OWNER OF YE OLDE PEPPER COMPANIE

*Bob Burkinshaw is a third-generation confectioner. He described his grandfather's time
working for George Pepper and his own life growing up with candy. You'll notice that he
must manage inconsistent ingredients, as does the mega-company, Wilbur.*[4]

I grew up in the candy business going back to my grandfather George
Berkinshaw. He went to work in the Pepper Company when he was only twelve
years old. It was a big, big company in those days. They didn't have child labor
laws, and he started working scrubbing floors and that kind of thing, then manufacturing candy. That's where he met his wife, Alice, my grandmother, who was
also working there. George made his way straight up the company ladder until
he bought the company from George Pepper around the turn of the century.

I think they did pretty well until the Great Depression. The company was
hit hard, and they lost almost everything. But my grandfather kept making the
candy and moving around to different locations, whatever he could manage.

They eventually lived on Buffum Street, the same street where Mrs. Spencer opened her store, which is where my father was raised.

During the Second World War, my father was in the service in the Pacific. While he was overseas, his father, and another candy company, kept a position open for him when he returned. But my father didn't want to go into the candy business. He worked in the Navy Yard, instead. He knew how to make candy, but he didn't want to do it.

One of the reasons I think the company endured and my father eventually helped out is this: in 1950, when my grandfather was dying, he was distraught, not because he was dying but because he thought the company would die with him. Just before my grandfather died, my father went to the shop and stayed up all night making the Gibraltar and the Black Jack Stick. He gave it to my grandfather the next morning to show him the tradition would live on.

After my grandfather died, my grandmother took over the store and my father helped out after work. Eventually, he couldn't keep up the hours, going to the Navy Yard during the day then to the shop to make candy at night. Besides, I was a baby, and he didn't get to see me. So, he moved the whole company into the basement of our house. It was all wholesale, no retail. He would come home, see me, rest for an hour or two, then make candy. Eventually, my mother made the candy by day with a woman she hired as her assistant, and my father made it by night, until he retired from his job at the Navy Yard to made candy full-time.

And this is how I grew up, with a candy company in the basement. All the kids in the neighborhood wanted to be my best friend. There was a big window in my cellar and the kids would stand around and watch my father making the candy. After he was done, my father would take the leftover pieces and hand it out to them. About five or six years ago, I got a letter from a newsman who was one of my friends when we were kids. He said, "I remember those days . . . the crowd around that window was huge. When he was making candy you could smell it all around the neighborhood. Peppermint and lemon."

At the time it wasn't weird, having a candy company in the basement. It was what we did. I started helping out when I was a kid and worked there through high school. I never did anything else. My father used the recipes he got from his father who got them from George Pepper. The Gibraltar is made exactly the way Mrs. Spencer made them and the Black Jack the same way as Pepper. The Black Jacks are still rolled by hand and cut with a pair of scissors and the Gibraltars are pulled on a hook.

We use the same ingredients but it's not the same if you know what I mean. When you're with a chocolate it almost becomes a signature of your candy. My father only used Bakers chocolate. But now the quality has changed. Besides the shipments come in different so you never know what you're getting. Sometimes the sugar is almost like a powder. Sometimes it's coarse and sometimes it's too fine so the batches won't stand up. We have to switch things around to make the candy consistent.

My granddaughters are ten and seven and they come down at Christmas time and make Christmas candy. Megan hooks the candy canes. She is so serious. Very official. Reminds me of me being around it.

But I remember when my father made the candy in the basement. The smells were pervasive. The peppermint from the Gibraltars went all through the house. What kind of candy do I like? I like all of them. But my favorite is the peppermint. I love peppermint.

THE SECRET LIFE OF PAUL REVERE

After a quick lunch, Dan, Moses, and I headed north to Boston, the home of innumerable other candy and, I must add, my ancestral family. In the mid-1800s, my great-grandparents on both sides fled the old country and traveled, in steerage no doubt, to Boston.

One of them was my great-grandfather Joseph Greene. At the age of fourteen, my great-grandfather Joseph Greene arrived in Boston alone. He stayed with relatives he'd never met and immediately got to work on the railroad. Eventually, he became a builder who, being patriotic, named his buildings for governors, carving their names above the front doors. My family history is literally carved in stone.

Some of his buildings survived but others didn't, such as the ones in Scollay Square, an eighteenth- and nineteenth-century fishing port turned market that eventually became a theater district, with saloons, dance halls, burlesque shows, and other attractions, enjoyed equally by sailors and senators. Later, the city of Boston bulldozed Scollay Square to erect Government Center, a brick and concrete wasteland that, according to my sources, the city now regrets.

So, on that June day, we headed to Government Center, enduring the famously traumatic experience of driving in Boston traffic and the shock of paying the exorbitant parking fee. Once there, we saw that some sort of event was in mid-swing right in front of City Hall. As we got closer, I saw it was a marketing effort that shook me to the soles of my feet. It had nothing to do with Paul Revere or the city of Boston, but like most things, it still somehow related to candy. I am speaking of bugs.

Fig. 13.3. Scollay Square. *Image from Wikipedia, user BPL (Boston Public Library).*

CANDY GOES OFF TOPIC

All around, tourists, office workers, and students were eating free samples of fried rice with crickets, cookies with worms, and other variations of cooked bugs. Some visitors shrieked in fascination and disgust, some ate stoically, and others (including Dan) sat the whole thing out.

At first I thought a more gastronomically eclectic nation hoping to enter the US food market was sponsoring the event. That would make sense given that the United Nations reports that roughly two billion people worldwide consume 1,900 varieties of insects.[5] Then I noticed the sponsor was Elkins, the pest-control company who poisons bugs for a living. Why serve people a dish made with the creatures you annihilate? The ones you and your paying customers disdain? I asked one of the workers. He smiled, shrugged, and said: "I guess it's marketing."

No matter, Americans have a long history of bug eating. The Native Americans ate a variety of insects. The Civil War soldiers ate bugs, too, lodged in hardtack or crawling around prison cells where they were the only option. Bugs as food seemed to disappear once the war ended, then returned in the 1950s, with ants enrobed in chocolate.

While the treat was more of a joke or dare, it was startling enough for both the *New York Times*[6] and the *Wall Street Journal*[7] to cover it. These ants were as small as ice cream sprinkles, floating midway between the past and the present. Recently, Hotlix brought them back in a white chocolate disc a little larger than a NECCO wafer. These ants are so discrete, kids think they're actually sprinkles.

Perhaps the true indication of American culinary, and in particular *confec-*

Fig. 13.4. Edible worms.

tionery, desires is the more common insect-related sweet: the gummy worm. Fruit flavored, steroid-colored, and with a texture that defies nature, this gooey bug treat somehow takes us back to Paul Revere.

A QUICK RETURN TO THE SUGAR ACT, THEN THE MASSACHUSETTS CHARITABLE MECHANICS ASSOCIATION AND SUGAR STICKS

After the edible-bug festivities, we headed to nearby Faneuil Hall, built in 1742 by a wealthy merchant, Peter Faneuil. Today Faneuil Hall has polished floors and nicely tended shops and pushcarts where properly sneakered and camera-carrying tourists wander about. In the eighteenth and nineteenth centuries, though, it was a panoply of sounds and smells, with pushcarts loaded with fish, produce, and meat. Orators stood on soapboxes raising their voices against the Sugar Act, and proclaiming the doctrine of "no taxation without representation." By the mid-to-late 1800s the so-called candy butchers likely showed up, hawking candy from pushcarts where they scooped, weighed, and wrapped the goods into newspapers.

It was also here, and in the neighboring Quincy Market, built in 1826, that the Massachusetts Charitable Mechanics Association held some of their exhibitions, whose entries included rock candy. Their publication "First Exhibition and Fair of the Massachusetts Charitable Mechanic Association, at Faneuil and Quincy Halls, in the City of Boston, September 18, 1837,"[8] also noted another entry into the exhibition—the sugar stick, which was likely sold in Faneuil Hall and Scollay Square.

THE MIGHTY STICK CANDY

You know those old-timey shops with wicker baskets, nineteenth-century aprons, and old-fashioned candles with a really, really sweet smell? There, you will find "old-time" candy sticks: brightly colored, hard-textured, and as industrial as a sledge hammer but with greater appeal to kids.

The original stick was made of ingredients that were close, if not identical, to the ones in Gibraltar: sugar, cream of tartar, and flavoring. The sticks were porous, with enough air space for young revelers at festivals, fairs, and seaside resorts to use them as straws in lemonade or simply in halved lemons. You can still find versions of the candy sticks in shops today, although most are made by machines, not by hand. Still lost? If you cut off the end of a sugar stick, that bit would be an after-dinner mint.

Scientific American described the components of making a sugar stick in an interesting article published in 1868:

> The ordinary hard stick candy is an example of the amorphous condition produced in sugar by working it in a plastic state. In order to aid in this condition of producing sugar, a little cream of tartar is added which has the effect to prevent crystallization. The sugar, while in a plastic mass is pulled, a portion of it being taken in the hands of the workman, is drawn out partially by the hands. The middle of the mass is thrown over a hook provided for the purpose and the ends being still grasped the workman steps backwards thus drawing the mass into a sort of rope. This rope is doubled and the process repeated until the proper consistency is obtained when the sugar is divided into sticks and allowed to be cool and hard.[9]

This process is precisely the one Bob described his granddaughter doing at Ye Olde Pepper Companie. As for the stripe on the candy stick, the article explains it this way: "Stripes are made by laying upon a plastic roll of sugar while still hot colored bars of cold sugar which becoming soft when in contact with the hot sugar, are drawn out with it to the proper size."[10]

As for the color? While many people nowadays are concerned with anything that starts with letters such as "FDA" and numbers, such as "red #2," and pine for the good old days of fresh, healthy foods, they shouldn't bother. Things are much better now than they used to be. Here's proof, from *Scientific American*:

> The use of poisonous colors is not so frequent as formally. Red and yellow candies are very rarely colored with poisonous matter. The greens are most liable to be poisonous, especially the light shade called apple green which sometimes consists of arsenate of copper, a very poisonous substance.[11]

AT HOME WITH STICK CANDY

The candy stick originated well before the Massachusetts Charitable Mechanics Association or Paul Revere, for the matter. Europeans in the seventh century were using pulled sugars as medicine and, eventually, as treats.[12] Some sticks in 1837 had been downsized to three inches, most likely because of machinery allowing them to do so, but some held their original candy-cane-size length.

The candy cane, as it happens, is an old form of the candy stick. And, with all the varieties, from the skinny, plastic-looking mini canes in bowls at the bank to the large, glistening versions at high-end shops, the candy cane is where Americans of all religions and ages unknowingly sample their first stick candy.

So, how did the candy stick with a hook, aka the candy cane, get its start? There are several stories. Some say candy canes served as a secret code among persecuted Christians in Germany or England in the seventeenth century (both countries were Christian at the time). Others believe they held a secret language among the Christian faithful depending on the stripe (three stripes represented the trinity, one represented Jesus's sacrifice), and handing someone a candy cane was some kind of secret message, although what exactly, I'm not sure; There was also the more general role of the stripe as representing the blood of Jesus.[13]

The stories are certainly fascinating, but they are unfortunately untrue. Everyone agrees that the candy cane dates back to seventeenth-century Germany. Some think a choirmaster gave the sticks to fidgety choirboys to placate them in lieu of the more common enticement of the times—whacking them with a switch. He added a hook so the stick resembled a staff, a religious reference that would also placate the stern church board. Seeing that the plain, white candy sticks were popular back then, the story does have credibility, but it's just as likely Germans added the hook so it, like cookies, fruits and other treats, could hang festively from their tree.[14]

Just about everyone also agrees that the candy cane first appeared in the United States around 1847 in Wooster, Ohio. This fits with the German-origin story since the Ohio candy cane maker was August Imgard, a German-Swedish immigrant. The stripeless, white candy cane's popularity spread, and soon Christmas lovers were eating them.

There was one problem, though. The canes tended to break when candy-makers added the crook; Bob McCormack, a candymaker who started his business in the 1920s, reportedly lost 22 percent of his candy canes, the shattered pieces sent to their death in the waste basket. At this point, another Catholic priest got involved, Gregory Keller. He invented a machine that would automatically put a hook in the candy cane, leaving the stick intact. Keller was also Bob McCormack's brother-in-law. So, with this divine intervention, Bob's Candies has become one of the world's largest candy cane makers in the world.[15]

Maybe, just maybe, Bob would have been spared the breakage if he followed this advice from the book *Rigby's Reliable Candy Teacher*, published in 1919:

Candy Canes for Christmas

Run out a batch of any flavor stick candy, usually peppermint and lemon are the best sellers, spin these sticks any size you wish and in cutting these cut off at angles. Now have your helper roll them so as to keep them round and when they begin to get cold crook the angle, then set them to one side to harden. Your helper's rolling them until they become cold keeps them from getting flat on one side which affects the sale of them greatly. It is best when spinning these out to make one end of the stick smaller than the other, then place the crook on the large end and have the small end of the end of the cane. Candy canes can be made in any flavor or color, or any size desired.[16]

STICK CANDY GOES TO THE BUTCHERS

In the eighteenth and early nineteenth centuries, candy was sold in apothecaries, in confectionery shops, and by a particular class of merchants called "candy butchers." The name "candy butchers" probably sounds more nefarious than it actually is. These vendors didn't kill or butcher anyone, and they weren't armed, necessarily. Basically, they cut, bagged, and, above all, sold sweets.

The candy butchers peddled their candies from concession stands, pushcarts, or hand-held baskets at fairs, theaters, and movie theaters. When young, Thomas Edison worked as a candy butcher selling his wares to passengers on trains.[17] Faneuil Hall and Scollay Square, with their crowds and pushcarts, were other typical venues as were the traveling circuses.

In his turn-of-the century autobiography, *The Ways of the Circus: Being the Memories and Adventures of George Conklin Tamer of Lions*, Conklin describes the candy butchers' method of selling stick candy this way:

As long ago as when I first went on the road with the circus, the privilege of selling candy in and around the show often brought as much as five thousand dollars for one season. The holder of the privilege employed several men to go along with the show and do the actual selling. They were known as candy butchers and traveled with the managerial. The most of their sales in those days were "barber poles"—long, large sticks of white candy with winding red strands that made them resemble a barber's sign. Pieces that had become dirty from handling and broken pieces were cut up into small bits and put into paper "cornies." These the candy butchers had a trick of selling to "rubes" and their girls for 25-cents each and represented them as being something "extra fine." [18]

Not all candy butchers were deceitful, but you'd never know it from their reputation. In 1880, one traveling circus leveraged the candy butchers' bad reputation in their own advertising. Apparently, their show was "The Scientific Marvel of the Ages," and promised "for the First Time Presented Here in all its Perfected Splendor, [a] $200,000 herd of elephant, [the] only 18,000 drove of six performing Colorado Cattle. . . . [and] the only $22,000 two-horned hair rhinoceroses." To cinch the deal of this remarkable event, it was "the only show that does not permit candy butchers."[19]

The candy butchers attempted to uphold their reputation. In his 1915 article, P. Sapertos of the National Theater in Chicago says: "I am writing you on behalf of the candy butchers in theaters who are judged wrong by the public who believe them to be loafers. I have been in the business 12 years. I have averaged over $40 a week. I am my own boss and more independent than anybody in any line of business." Sapertos added: "I also wish to state that candy butchers in Chicago are organized and have their own Union."[20]

The candy butchers eventually disappeared but the stick candy remained. Today, most kids get the packaged, shiny, industrial kind. It tastes sweet, but it's a chemical sweet, void of flavor or character. And a little bit—a tiny little bit of Faneuil Hall, Paul Revere, and even the candy butcher—is lost.

FOOTNOTE ON PAUL REVERE'S HOUSE

> *Something Chewy!*
> *Something Sweet!*
> *Something Good*
> *For folks to Eat*!
> —Mary Jane candy tag line, 1920[21]

We spent a brief time in Faneuil Hall then headed to the North End, a five-minute walk away. The North End is now Italian, with a subtle, almost invisible blend of multi-ethnic yuppies. We passed Italian cafes, Italian restaurants, and Italian social halls, all so closely resembling Mother Italy herself, you'd never know the area was originally home to Irish then Jewish immigrants, including a few of my own great-grandparents.

The shops offering cannolis once sold herring and rugalach, and the signs, saying in clear, crisp English such things as "Mike's Bakery," were once in indecipherable Yiddish. My family left the North End as they grew more prosperous, heading to East Boston in one direction, Beacon Hill, in another, and branching out across the hills to Worcester.

Before the arrival of any of my relatives, the North End was settled by English Puritans, including the minister Increase Mather and his son, the outspoken Puritan Cotton Mather. Their house burned down in the devastating Great Fire of 1670,

Fig.13.5. The home of Paul Revere.

but a wealthy merchant quickly built a new one in its place and moved in. Each subsequent resident added a little of this and that, expanding the house with their expanding number of children. One such resident, in 1770, was Paul Revere, who lived in the house along with his wife, his five children, and his mother.[22]

After stopping for some sorbet refreshment, we found Revere's home: a two-story blue-gray building surrounded by a picket fence. A gaggle of adolescents were clustered around a uniformed park-service docent who was cheerfully chatting away about the colonists and the American Revolution. The kids couldn't care less. They were fidgety. They were distracted. They'd heard enough. But I knew the one bit of information that would perk them up.

This story starts in 1884, roughly one hundred years after Paul Revere moved out of his home. That's when a man named Charles H. Miller moved in. His family lived upstairs, and he opened a confectionery downstairs, where he made candies of all sorts. In 1914, Miller's son, Charles N. Miller, made a candy that endures to this day. It's called the Mary Jane.[23]

In case you haven't tried one, the Mary Jane is a nut- and molasses-flavored toffee much like its twentieth-century counterparts, Chicago's Bit-O-Honey and Cambridge's Squirrel Nut Zipper. It was created in Paul Revere's former home and allegedly named for Charles N. Miller's favorite aunt, Mary Jane. But the

Fig. 13.6. Charles N. Miller's Mary Jane.

name may have had another source: Richard Felton Outcault's classic comic strip, "Buster Brown."

The strip ran nationwide from 1902 to 1921. Buster was a well-to-do urban kid, with a tagalong American pit bull terrier. Buster is continually up to mischief, and constantly getting caught, and then punished by his mother who spanks him or hits him with a stick. Buster Brown's sweetheart is a little girl named "Mary Jane."

Apparently Outcault was selling rites to use his Mary Jane. Miller, as it happened, had his own vaguely similar Mary Jane, without getting permissions or paying fees.[24] Some were skeptical, but Miller insisted *his* Mary Jane was based on his older aunt. Why did his Mary Jane wear ankle socks, a sunbonnet, and a high, tutu-ish skirt? No one knows. Miller's toffee survived the debate and is now made by the New England Confectionery Company, home of the 1847 sensation, the NECCO Wafer.

I took a few pictures of Paul Revere's house; then it was time for Dan, Moses, and me to return to Judge Sewall's ancestral property and the home of my parents, Joan and Dick Benjamin, in Brookline, Massachusetts.

CHAPTER 14

JUST A SPOONFUL OF *WHAT?*

W e were heading to Brookline because my father bought Red Sox tickets for himself and Dan. I was invited, but I had one more iconic candy site to visit. First, though, we picked up my father and left Moses with my mother where he would eat, thoroughly enjoying whatever she gave him, then fall into a deep sleep, exhausted after a long and exciting day.

Dan, my father, and I went to a Spanish restaurant near Fenway Park. My father had trouble walking because of his knees and was perpetually tired, possibly from diabetes and possibly because of the tension that forms when a candy hater and candy lover don't get along.

But as we sat at the restaurant, drinking wine, eating dessert, and talking and laughing over things that hardly mattered, his old self seemed to rise up from under his skin. When I dropped them off at the side street across from Fenway Park, my father jumped out with the gait of someone who means business, but in slow motion.

OVER THE BRIDGE

It was early, only 7:00 a.m., as I headed over the "Salt and Pepper" Bridge connecting Boston to Cambridge, the former site of the New England Confectionery Company. The building was the grand dame of factories, with yellow brick walls and a narrow chimney reaching above nearby Harvard and MIT. On one side was a rag shop, whose goods included used clothing sold by the pound on Thursdays. On the other side were more factories.

The company, actually a merger of three nineteenth-century firms, formed in 1901 as NECCO Sweets, the acronym standing for New England Confectionery Company. Just a year later, they moved into a new facility in Boston and became the largest factory exclusively producing candy in the nation. The company relocated to Cambridge in 1927 where it chugged out Sky Bars, NECCO Wafers, peppermint patties, and other sweets that filled the air deliciously in what was then a working class neighborhood. My mother's side of the family, including Joseph Greene, lived nearby through the 1950s: the NECCO factory smell was undoubtedly part of their lives.

Throughout the late 1970s and '80s the city started "renovations," which, as we saw with Scollay Square, is frequently a code word for demolishing history. In this case it was primarily MIT that was replacing old buildings with glassy, very science-like structures. As the old factories came tumbling down, I worried that the NECCO factory would be next. But it remained, chugging out an array of candies, until 2003 when the company moved north, in the direction of Salem, Ye Olde Pepper Companie, and the seaside town of Revere.[1]

The old factory remains, albeit in a slicker, glassier form, as an office building. I parked across the street then sat on a bench and looked at the building while a few students strolled by. After a few minutes, I started taking notes.

THE POPPINS CONNECTION

NECCO offers numerous fascinating sweets, but only one changed the history of candy—and possibly the history of medicine as well. In the process, this candy formed a bridge connecting medicine to candy, and traditional candy making to industrialized methods. This candy is the humble yet illustrious Chase Lozenge, later to be known as the NECCO wafer. The NECCO wafer had its start in the 1840s when pharmacist Oliver Chase immigrated to Boston from England. By 1847, he and his brothers, Daniel and Silas, opened an apothecary that was, by definition, a bastion of sugar. Sugar was medicinal in its own right, often used as a sore throat remedy, and was also used to disguise the flavors of other medicines, making Mary Poppins's "a spoonful of sugar" historically sage advice.

At that time, there were numerous styles of sugar-based medicines, such as the naked rock candy we explored before, the hard candy, and the chewy version we call "gums." The earliest gums go back to 226–652 AD when the ruling Sasanids enjoyed a sweet called *abhisa*,[1] made of honey, fruit syrups, and starch. By the ninth century, it was being made in Arabic apothecaries as a remedy for sore throats. Its new name, *rahat ul-hulkūm*, was later shortened to the modern *lokum*, meaning "throats ease."[2]

Many people still use some variation of the word "lokum" today, but not Americans. We, like the British and a handful of other Europeans, call it "Turkish delight." The exotic-sounding name change was probably a British marketing move based on a true lokum lover, Sultan Abdul Hamid, who reigned in 1750. Sultan Abdul Hamid fell in love with the treat and, according to legend, had his chefs prepare daily batches to satiate his many wives. Trade being what it was at the time, word spread and folks in England started enjoying it, too.

There, in the mid-1800s, it took on a literary life as "lumps of delight" in Charles Dickens's *The Mystery of Edwin Drood,* in which character Rosa Bud announces: "I want to go to the Lumps-of-Delight shop."[3] By the late 1800s, the candy was called "Turkish delight," probably because of Sultan Abdul Hamid, and the name has endured in the English-speaking world ever since. Most notably, Turkish delight appeared in C. S. Lewis's classic book *The Lion, the Witch, and the Wardrobe*, in which it reigned as young Edmund Pevensie's greatest passion. Thanks to the book and the movie most Americans know about Turkish delight, although few have likely tried it.

An early American producer of Turkish delight was Daniel Fobes, who advertised his sweet in the mid-1850s. Fobes's business was among those who merged

Fig. 14.1. Turkish delight.

with the Chase Candy Company in 1901 to form the New England Confectionery Company.[4] The ingredients in the gummy Turkish delight are the same as Mrs. Spencer's Gibraltar, the stick candy, and the candy cane. The quantities and cooking time were all that changed.

Many of the medicine candies were hard candies: sugar boiled in water with medicinal herbs and spices mixed in. These were the parent to such delicious and time-honored sweets as Life Savers, sour balls, and sparkling mints. Throughout the late nineteenth and early twentieth centuries, these treats straddled the candy-medicine line. In 1921, for example, Traxel's House of Sweets advertised their cough drops, which came in horehound, anise, and menthol flavors and were basically interchangeable with their other hard candies.

Traxel's also carried two popular brands that were considered "old timey" even then; both are still available today.[5] One is Smith Brothers Cough Drops, which started when William and Andrew Smith's father, James, moved to Poughkeepsie, New York, from Quebec in 1847 and started a restaurant. Somehow James got hold of a recipe for "cough candy," as it was called, possibly from a traveler passing through. James made the candy in his kitchen and a new "cough candy" called the "cough drop" was born.[6] By 1852, James's company was advertising widely in Poughkeepsie papers.

It had plenty of competition including Hayes's Cough Candy, with an aggressive advertising campaign, and Butler's Cough Syrup. In 1859, these essentially candy companies promised their products could "cure" whooping cough, asthma, bronchitis, and diseases of the throat and lung and also bring relief to sufferers of consumption, a fact which is lost on modern medicine manufacturers today.

Cough candy was sold all over the country, its medicinal value renowned and deliciously exaggerated. In 1887, this piece appeared in a Missouri newspaper on behalf of Maynard's Cough Candy:

> We take pleasure in making known to the public this valuable candy as a medicine. It is best made with a view of combining the best known remedies for Bronchial troubles with pure candy in such a manner to make a medicine yet very effective in its work. . . . Mr. Maynard has been manufacturing and using this candy for many years, and has hundreds of testimonials from physicians and patients.[7]

The article has a few of these physician's testimonials, such as Dr. T. W. Shaw, a "prominent physician," who said, "The prescription from which Maynard's Cough Candy is made is a better remedy for throat or bronchial troubles than the many troches and lung balms now in the market."[8] Even better, Dr. T. S. Ruby spoke from personal experience: "This candy undoubtedly saved me and my son from a spell of pneumonia."

Regardless of their claims, the James Smith's drops endured the longest, remaining in the Smith family until 1964. It's hard to say if his candy was superior to the others, but his marketing sure was. In 1866, after James Smith died, the sons named the company "Smith Brothers." They must have been doing right because competitors bubbled up, using Smith-sounding names such as the "Schmitt Brothers" and "Smythe Sisters." So, the brothers developed a label with their handsome, bearded faces on it, clearly distinguishing themselves from the Smythe Sisters and anyone else who dared be imposters.

At the time, most cough drop makers were selling their products in bulk for the pharmacist to weigh and pour in their own bags. The Smith Brothers sold theirs in labeled packages, making them among the first "factory filled" products. They were also among the first to use the trademark notation, which they placed directly by their bearded images—"trade" under William and "mark" under Andrew. Since it was new, people had no idea what "trademark" meant and assumed it referred to Mr. Trade and Mr. Mark, a mistake customers still make today. The company added menthol cough drops in 1922 and cherry in 1948.[9]

Traxel's also sold Luden's cough drops. Like the Smith Brothers, Luden's story is rags to riches with a big dash of savvy marketing. William Luden's father was a jeweler who emigrated from the Netherlands and died soon after. At fifteen, Luden left school to apprentice with a candymaker and, in 1879, began selling candies that he made in the back of the jewelry shop. His innovations included the menthol cough drop, which the Smith Brothers later made, that allowed cold sufferers to put away their menthol vials and suck on pleasant sugar candy.

Like Wilbur, Hershey, Mars, and the ever-growing list of confectioners, Luden also leveraged the possibilities of the railroad. Instead of selling candy to passengers, he gave it to railroad workers for free. Their throats suitably soothed and freshened, they sang Luden's praises nationwide. The result was extraordinary. After Luden retired in the early 1930s, his cough drops were easing sore throats and tasting delicious in twenty-six countries.[10] Today, they're still around, now owned by Johnson & Johnson who, like Warner-Lambert, owner of the Smith Brothers, refers to their product in curative terms omitting the equally accurate word "candy." Here's what the Smith Brothers website has to say:

As cough and cold experts for over 160 years, Smith Brothers is known for making great-tasting cough and cold relief products, and the famous trademark continues to stand for pioneering innovation in over-the-counter family wellness.[11]

Amen to that.

BRIDGING MEDICINE, MAKING CANDY

The Oliver Chase story is different. Chase was a genuine pharmacist who emigrated from England in the 1840s and set up an apothecary in Boston with his brothers Silas and Daniel. He was making "soft paste" lozenges consisting of sugar, gum arabic, a flavoring, and possibly gelatin. The ingredients are pretty much like those of stick candy or Turkish delight, but the texture is both smooth and chalky. Customers report that they used NECCOs as a practice communion wafer and that their grandmothers used them as a sugary sedative to keep the grandchildren quiet at church.

Fig. 14.2. An ad for NECCO Wafers.

As a medicine, the pharmacist would mix in peppermint for stomach problems, rhubarb for constipation, ginger for nausea, and opium for just about everything else. Making the lozenges was tedious, exact work. According to *Scientific American* of 1868, the "plastic" sugar was rolled into a sheet then cut, lozenge after lozenge, like crackers from dough.[12] The batter was temperamental; it had to be just the right consistency, measured and pressed to make close-to-exact doses, with as little handling as possible.[13]

Chase's success created a problem. His lozenges, both medicated and unmedicated as candy, were exceptionally popular but the production process was so slow, he got further and further behind on filling the orders. So, in 1847, Oliver Chase developed a lozenge-cutting machine that cranked dough onto plates with lozenge-size indentations. The lozenges tumbled out in uniform sizes as quickly as his hand could turn.[14]

Chase called the result the "Chase Lozenge" or "Hub Wafer"—one with a glazed wrapper and the other with a transparent wrapper. "Hub," by the way, was a nickname for Boston. Later, the confection was called the NECCO wafer. For the first time, candymakers could quickly produce consistent pieces, and medicine makers could create predictable doses. Chase's machine was revolutionary.

Oliver soon partnered with his brother Silas to make a sugar-pulverizing machine that, according to the patent application of 1850, "consists of a cylindrical vessel or mortar made of caste iron or other suitable material and of such thickness and dimensions as circumstances may require."[15]

Almost twenty years later, another Chase-inspired change was on the way, this one by Daniel Chase. During the nineteenth century "conversation lozenges" were popular in England, where little sayings were hand-printed on the candy. Some were romantic, such as "Love me," while others inspired precisely the opposite sentiments. The temperance movement was behind many of those, with such sobering comments as: "Drink is the Ruin of Man," and "Sobriety is the way to riches."[16] In the United States, Daniel invented a "motto-making" machine that printed sayings quickly and directly onto heart-shaped candies. The phrases focused entirely on matters of the heart, not the liver. The resulting candies were called "Conversation Hearts."

As the candy industry grew, the confectioner's role seemed to have taken on greater stature. In 1912, the *Americana*, an encyclopedia, wrote:

Of course, we know that in the early days, the art of manufacturing confectionery was confined almost exclusively to the apothecaries and physicians, both of whom made use of these sweets in their attempts to disguise the unpleasant characteristic of their medicines. . . . During the 19th century the confectionery trade has experienced its greatest development for it is since the dawn of that century that it has become what it is to-day, one of the world's great business enterprises. In the making of this transition, the druggist has not ceased to be a factor in the trade. He still requires his medicated candies but in this respect he has become a purchaser.[17]

The *Americana* also noted that:

> Candy usually was confined to such ordinary products as the old fashion stick
> candy, sugar plums, and the ordinary molasses candy. . . . In 1846, Oliver R.
> Chase, who with his brother, formed the firm Chase & Company, invented a
> machine for the making of lozenges. . . . In 1866, a further innovation in the
> lozenges innovation was produced by Daniel G. Chase. This was a machine for
> printing on candies and it was to those invention that the well-remembered con-
> versation lozenges owe its existence.[18]

Since that day, the history of the confectionery trade has been a constant
record of development.

The Chases may have ushered in the industrialization of candy, but there's
more. It's possible, and I emphasize *possible*, that the Chase Brothers sent Oliver's
lozenge to the Union soldiers. This distinction is relevant because many in-the-
know people such as reenactors, historic websites, and NPR's quiz show *Wait,
Wait Don't Tell Me* indicate this exchange of sweets definitely happened. I called
the New England Confectionery Company for confirmation after I failed to find
original sourcing. A young, chipper-sounding employee from their outsourced
PR department merrily informed me that the NECCO was *not* in the war.

Here's my opinion. Seeing how friends, family, and businesses sent candy to
Civil War soldiers during the war, why wouldn't Oliver Chase and his popular
lozenge be among them? So, did they send or didn't they? My vote is yes. Either
way, Admiral Byrd definitely took two and a half tons of the lozenges on his
expedition to the South Pole, and during World War II, when Hershey was busy
with Field Ration D, the United States sent NECCOs to troops because they were
"practically indestructible."[19]

Over the years, the company underwent many changes. After building
a factory on Melcher Street in Boston, the Chase brothers opened a "western"
branch in Chicago. It was destroyed in the Great Chicago Fire of 1871, and, in
1872, the Boston factory burned down as well. The company rebounded, and, in
1901, joined the other companies to rise up as the New England Confectionery
Company.

Today, the company produces approximately eight billion of Daniel Chase's
Conversation Hearts a year. As for the NECCO wafer, the company still uses the
original sugar paste ingredients, including vegetable dyes and the original flavors,
and uses pre–World War II style machinery. They now produce 680 million

wafers a year. According to their website, if placed edge to edge they would circle the world twice. The company has expanded over the years and now makes such venerable products as the Squirrel Nut Zipper, the Clark Bar, and Paul Revere's very indirect favorite, the Mary Jane.[20]

TAKE ME BACK TO THE BALL GAME

After visiting the former home of NECCO and having a quick stop for a cup of coffee, I headed back to the chaos of Fenway Park to pick up Dan and my father. Since they were at the ball game—and seeing how the time periods of this chapter match up—a word about the quintessential baseball-game treat, Cracker Jack.

In 1869, around the time that British immigrant Daniel Chase was inventing his motto-maker in Boston, German immigrant Frederick William Rueckheim arrived in Chicago. He started his career selling popcorn made using a steam-operated machine, earning enough money to send for his brother Louis in 1872.[21] Together, they opened a popcorn shop called F. W. Rueckheim & Bro. Skip a few years ahead, and they had moved their popcorn-making operation to a three-story plant.[22]

Entrepreneurship was one thing, but creating a legacy was another. That happened in 1896 when Louis discovered a method for sugar-coating the popcorn, While the secret to their success has yet to be fully disclosed, insiders reveal that the brothers added a dash of oil.[23] Their confection was a hit.

But oil did not do it alone; advertising helped. In the early twentieth century, people were concerned with such matters as tainted or otherwise poisoned foods, like the colored stick candy. So great was their thoroughly merited concern, Wiley and his cohorts created the Pure Food and Drug Act leading to the FDA. They needn't have bothered if all companies were as pure as Cracker Jack claimed to be.

In one ad that ran in 1916, the company stressed its product's purity *and* the benefits of eating it in volume, with a tag line that promised, "The more you eat, the more you want," and said, "You can eat Cracker Jack a plenty." This is the true beauty of old-time advertising. It's guilt-free, written as if weight gain never existed. As for purity:

> Here is the confection you can let your children eat to their heart's content. Eat it yourself. It can't harm you. It's made of the best materials, untouched by hands, in a spic-and-span factory, and packed so it comes to you good, fresh, and pure.[24]

As for the name, *Merriam-Webster* dictionary describes "crackerjack," first used around 1893, as meaning "a person or thing of marked excellence," as in, "a young prospect who's supposed to be a *crackerjack* on the baseball diamond."[25] In a less wholesome venue, "Cracker Jack" was a widely-publicized burlesque show with "40 chorus performers and 10 principals . . . [who] supply the riot of music and dances," according to one 1913 ad.[26]

The pivotal point of Cracker Jack's success was when the song "Take Me Out to the Ballgame" came along with the line "buy me some peanuts and Cracker Jack" taking center stage in the lyrics. It was simply a stroke of luck beyond anything a marketer could muster. Apparently Vaudeville lyricist, Jack Norworth jotted down the words after seeing a sign in the subway reading, "Baseball Today—Polo Grounds." The envelope where he jotted them resides at the National Baseball Hall of Fame.

Ironically, neither Norworth nor composer Albert von Tilzer had been to a ball game at that time. Lucky for them, and for Cracker Jack, almost no one who sings this "Second American Anthem" realizes the song is actually about a girl named Katie Casey who was so crazy about baseball she'd rather go to a game than on a date.[27] The song was first sung by Norworth's then wife, the Vaudeville singer Nora Bayes, at the *Ziegfeld Follies*.[28]

Cracker Jack also offered a trinket-sized prize inside, although practically every candymaker was doing so. Some gave the gifts outright while others, particularly penny candy stores, used them as a game that some, including New York City mayor Fiorello H. La Guardia, considered gambling. A *New York Times* article in 1937, reported that the mayor ordered the police to stamp out the penny candy "racket." Here is what it said:

> Mayor La Guardia has ordered the police to put an end to the penny candy "racket" it was announced yesterday. This "racket," it was explained, is the practice of selling penny candy or gum to children through the lure of prizes to lucky purchasers. The prizes range from pennies to pennants. . . . One method of candy gambling . . . consisted of the display of a number of pieces of candy, a few of which have a penny concealed inside their wrapping. Another gives prizes for pieces of candy with colored centers, white centers bringing no return. Lucky purchasers of colored gum balls also receive prizes, usually pennants. . . . "I have conferred with educational and social welfare authorities on this subject," said the Mayor, "and they are in agreement that this practice encourages and engenders gambling in children."[29]

The guilty would receive a warning, then would be arrested.

Rueckheim didn't force kids to win the prize; instead they gave the "prize" as a gift. The prizes were also wrapped and therefore hygienic, free of stickiness from the candy, and, as the label promised, they were suspense-mustering surprises. While other candymakers have dispensed with prize-giving, Cracker Jack soldiers on; the prize is now unique and nostalgic.

Fig. 14.3. An ad for Cracker Jack.

Another advertising advantage of F. W. Rueckheim & Browere the Cracker Jack mascots, Sailor Jack and his dog, Bingo, which were showcased in their ads and on their boxes. The sailor's image was modeled after the brothers' nephew Robert, who died of pneumonia when he was only eight. Sailor Jack and Bingo had just the right touch of trust-inspiring innocence. In one ad, a paternal sea captain stands behind them, with the caption:

Come, go on a trip to Crackerjack land
And see what the Cracker Jacks do—
How cleanly they work; how gladly they hand
The best of all candies to you![30]

Sailor Jack was also patriotic, especially during World War II when he usually appeared in a sailor suit. But the company went even further by advising consumers that if they ate Cracker Jack, they'd be supporting the war effort. The headline of one ad proclaimed:

Save Sugar, Wheat, and Fats, Cooperate with the Food Administration

The text of the ad told consumers to "Be sure to get the Genuine Cracker Jack. Look for the blue and red circles across the front of the package."[31]

Since then, Cracker Jack has had a long, patriotic, and profitable life.

CHAPTER 15

THE GREAT AMERICAN CANDY STORE

L ater that night, I dropped off my father, picked up a sleepy Moses, and Dan and I headed back to Rockport. Through the darkness at the Charlestown Bridge, I saw matron of the candy universe, Schrafft's Candy. The enormous, glass-and-gray building was built in 1928 and was the largest candy factory in the world, employing at least 1,600 people. Today, it's an office building, but in the dark it looks much like its former self.

And what was that self? William Schrafft started his business in 1861, making such items as gum drops and candy canes.[1] During the Civil War, he may have advertised for locals to send his candies, including the newly made jelly bean, to Union soldiers, although I couldn't find evidence of that.[2]

Schrafft's company was venerable when he owned it and more venerable, if not downright classy, after Frank G. Shattuck bought it in 1898. Originally from Upstate New York, Shattuck was a salesman for Schrafft's who executed his big ideas in the most tasteful of ways. The Schrafft's building made enrobed chocolates with the finest of fillings, sold in fashionable boxes with floral design.[3]

But Schrafft's was more. So much more. At the turn of the century it was unseemly for unescorted women to dine out alone. So, Schrafft's created an atmosphere with ice cream, fine candies, and food where women could dine alone or among themselves in an atmosphere of genteel civility. A few stores were in Boston, but most opened in New York City, where they were the first to hire women managers.

The food had no pretensions, but rather they *embodied* pretension. Men had their leather-encrusted men's clubs. Women had Schrafft's. There they could purchase such items as "Banana Stuffed with fresh Fruit Salad, a la Schrafft Sandwich Squares" and "Chopped Corn Beef Sandwiches with Tomato Juice Cocktail."[4] Another favorite was the chopped-egg sandwich cut into thirds with the crusts

Fig. 15.1. The Schrafft building.

removed. Ever connected to its candy past, the meal was polished off with an ice cream sundae or a box of chocolates from the signature candy counter.

Naturally, most Schrafft's had soda fountains, but they also had bars, where ladies gathered to sip Manhattans, martinis, grasshoppers, golden fizzes, pink ladies, and old fashioneds. Said great-grandson Frank M. Shattuck: "Everyone wore hats and handmade suits. And if you were a lady, it was safe to sit at the soda fountain and drink gin from a teacup."[5] For all its grandeur, Schrafft's sold its candy in retail stores all over the country, comfortably resting in nicely fitted boxes.

LET'S GO SHOPPING!

When I woke up the next morning, I looked out the motel window at the unfortunate view of a dumpster and parking lot, but I knew the sun was glistening off the sea, just a five minute walk away. I had two candy shops to visit. The day was going to be good. But first the fascinating story of Frederick Roeder.

A CONFECTIONER'S TALE

Frederick Roeder immigrated to the United States from Germany and, in the early 1850s, opened a confectionery that was typical of the pre-candy store times. Roeder's Confectionery is now a National Park Service museum in Harpers Ferry, West Virginia, separated from my shop by a narrow street called "Hog's Alley" because hogs were once driven down it to slaughter.

As you can guess, Roeder's confectionery was on the ground floor of the building and his family lived above. A back porch, where the family hung clothes to dry and likely slept to escape the summer heat, protruded from the upper story. Roeder's wife died the year the Civil War began,[6] leaving Roeder with seven children, two of them infants, which he and his oldest daughter cared for.[7]

Harpers Ferry was a thriving industrial town at that point, known for manufacturing munitions. Until the Civil War, it was part of Virginia where almost half of the population was African American, both free and enslaved.[8] It was also the site of John Brown's raid, which some believe triggered the Civil War. While the area had a clear Confederate presence, Roeder was a Unionist and abolitionist. The year the Civil War started, Harpers Ferry was one of its centers.

Fig. 15.2. Roeder's Confectionery.

On July 4, 1861 Harpers Ferry endured a dramatic day of fighting, ending in a Confederate victory. That evening, when things quieted down, Roeder left the bakery. Everyone seems to have a different idea of why—to explore the damage, have schnapps with friends, see the red, white, and blue flag flying. Regardless, while he was out, he was shot by a Union soldier. Roeder crawled back to the bakery and up to the back porch, where his daughter tended to him. A few hours later, he died. Frederick Roeder, the confectioner, was the first civilian casualty in a bloody period of Harper's Ferry history.[9]

PERSONAL PERSPECTIVE: DOROTHY VAN STEINBURG AND CHRIS HOUCK, FREDERICK ROEDER'S GREAT, GRAND-DAUGHTERS, CONFECTIONERY IN THE FAMILY

I met Frederick Roeder's great-granddaughter, Chris Houck, when she happened to come to my shop on a cold winter evening. We had a nice chat, and I got her contact information. Two years later, I called her for an interview. She brought her sister, Dorothy Van Steinburg. Since they finished each other's sentences, I thought it was fair to write one voice for both of them.[10]

We always went to Sunday dinner at our grandmother's house until I was four or five. Grandma was one of fifteen kids so there were lots of cousins and lots of baked goods. I think it runs in our blood. We had peach pie, apple pie, and one called "prune pig." That was dried prunes, wrapped in pastry, put in a muslin bag then tied, and put in boiling water. Oh, was that good. It was like a dumpling. We went to Harpers Ferry all the time. I loved going to Harpers Ferry because we could get ice cream and penny candy. They'd tell us, that's Frederick Roeder's confectionery. That's where he lived.

Frederick Roeder also owned a brewery down Hog's Alley and a small hotel by the tavern. He made yeast beer for the tavern, but his main business was the bakery. He provided provisions for Lewis and Clark. One day, after lots of fighting broke out, he was at the Hilltop House[11] getting a newspaper and meeting with friends. A drunk Union soldier on Maryland Heights shot him, probably because he thought everyone in Harpers Ferry was a Confederate.

His friends carried him to the bakery and put him on the back porch. His oldest daughter Louisa was with him when he died. Frederick Roeder is buried right straight up the road in the graveyard to the left. All the family is there,

there's a whole plot for the Roeders. You can see it if you want. The names are on the tombstones. They never stopped being for the Union.

FROM ROEDER TO ROCKPORT:
THE GREAT AMERICAN CHOCOLATE SHOP

American candy stores grew out of confectioneries like Roeder's, but were devoted to candy, chocolate, and often nuts. They seem to grow the fastest and healthiest at resorts, especially *seaside* resorts, where their delightful, albeit misguided selections of salt water taffy are still a hit. They're an enduring answer to fast-food candy making where their "factories" are smaller than a board room and have "conveyor belts" about three feet long.

One of the oldest candy stores in Rockport is "Tucks," which opened in 1929. The Tuck family still owns it today and even has an original taffy pull machine in the window. It's operated by a high school or college student in the summer, when tourists crowd around watching the pink, green, and white miracle of salt water taffy being made.

But, as I mentioned, this miracle is a bit off-kilter.

THE SECRET STORY OF SALT WATER TAFFY

The ingredients in salt water taffy will probably sound pretty standard by now: water, sugar, flavoring, a stabilizer such as corn starch, corn syrup,[12] and food coloring to give it that festive zing. Salt water taffy, and the widespread popularity of taffy in general, began in Atlantic City in the 1880s, where taffy makers John Ross Edmiston, Joseph Fralinger, and Enoch James were busily creating a taffy industry.

In those days the shops were built right by the sea,[13] which was a bad idea given the certainty of storms and floods. But no one seemed to notice. Then one dark night, a storm swept up from the sea, flooding the shops along the boardwalk. One belonged to John Ross Edmiston. As he was cleaning up the next morning, a little girl stopped by asking for taffy. Looking at the waterlogged mess, Edmiston shook his head and said the immortal words: "I only have 'salt water' taffy." And then he thought: *The name sounds right. So beach-like and fun. But salt water? In taffy? Not so right.* So Edmiston kept the name but left the salt water out of the recipe.

His neighbor Joseph Fralinger was the man who put salt water taffy on beachgoers' maps with his boundless marketing campaigns. He worked as a glass-blower, fish merchant, and bricklayer until he took over a taffy concession stand on the boardwalk in 1884. Soon he added favorites like molasses pulls, and his one store became six.

Fralinger loved taffy, but he didn't love his neighbor, Enoch James. James started out in the Midwest, then opened a taffy shop in Atlantic City where his two innovations made salt-water-taffy history. One was bite-size pieces that fit comfortably in the vacationers' mouths. No more half-eaten gobs of taffy. No more sticky pieces covered with sand. And what better place to put these morsels than in James's second invention, the festive taffy satchel, which can still be found in candy stores today.

Fralinger and James remained competitors well into the twentieth century when the Glasser's candy company, now in the fifth generation, bought them both[14]. They, like other candymakers, have the Supreme Court to thank for their "salt water taffy." Edmiston filed for a trademark on the name seeing how he invented it. In the early 1920s, the federal government agreed, but his competitors fought back. The US Supreme Court took their side, making the sea-saltless "salt water taffy" fair game for everyone.[15]

BRITTLE

The brittle is another candy store favorite, and well it should be. It has the perfect snap, a satisfying sweet and salty texture, and a lingering finish. The love of brittle isn't old, however—it's ancient.

The brittle originated thousands of years ago when inhabitants of China, the Middle East, Egypt, India, Greece, Rome, and elsewhere coated fruits, nuts, and seeds with honey as a tasty and healthful addition and as a preservative.[16] The combination was so popular, it's still around today, commonly referred to as the Greek pasteli.

The peanut brittle, the one in candy stores and even supermarkets, is the pasteli's much younger American cousin. Many peanut brittles contain corn syrup, while others, like the one Edith Elizabeth Lowe Higdon ate at her father's farm in South Carolina, are made with molasses. The creamiest brittle, and the first known in US history, also contains pure butter. In 1847, the recipe appeared in Sarah Rutledge's *The Carolina Housewife*, which is considered the quintessential pre–Civil War Southern cookbook. Here's what she advised in her "Excellent Receipt for Groundnut Candy" on page 219:

> To one quart of molasses add half a pint of brown sugar and a quarter of a pound of butter; boil it for half an hour over a slow fire; then put in a quart of groundnuts, parched and shelled; boil for a quarter of an hour, and then pour it into a shallow tin pan to harden.

George Washington Carver, a scientist, philanthropist, professor, and peanut proponent, also developed several recipes for peanut brittle. Although an accomplished man, Carver had a troubling early childhood. He was born into slavery and, at ten days old, was kidnapped with his mother and sister. Carver was found in a field and traded back to the original slaveholder in exchange for a racehorse. His mother and sister were never heard of again.[17]

One of Carver's recipes tastes like the sugar-coated peanuts you find in pushcarts in major cities:

Ingredients:

- 3 cups granulated sugar
- 1 cup roasted peanuts
- 1 scant cup boiling water
- 1/4 teaspoon soda

Melt all together over a slow fire; cook gently without stirring until a little hardens when dropped in cold water; add the nuts; turn the mixture in well-buttered pans and cut while hot. Stirring will cause the syrup to sugar.[18]

But how did the peanut brittle find its way to the United States in the first place? Most people believe it originated in the South, which makes sense since the peanut was growing there and not elsewhere, and the first peanut brittle recipe was also from the South. But how did the peanut get there? There are two possibilities. One makes the most sense. The other makes no sense at all, but I'll bet someone, somewhere, had the pleasure of believing it.

The first possibility is that the peanut reached the United States on slave ships from Africa. The enslaved people were the primary ones to grow and eat it. A Celtic version of brittle was brought to the United States in the 1800s[19] when scores of Irish were fleeing the potato famine. In 1847, the two were joined in Sarah Rutledge's cookbook. If so, then the peanut brittle has remarkable metaphorical, if not ironic, history. The peanut brittle, one of the nation's most popular candies, emerged from the catastrophic events in the lives of two peoples: African Americans, forced and held in slavery for generations, and the Irish, fleeing from starvation at home.

The second, less-likely story is about the contribution of Tony Beaver of West Virginia, a man who may explain why the state's motto is "Wild and Wonderful." Tony Beaver was a folk hero, along the lines of Paul Bunyan, whose stories were created by turn-of-the-century West Virginia lumbermen. Poet and author Margaret Prescott Montague, born in 1878 and the daughter of a Harvard graduate, compiled the lumbermen's stories, although some suspicious folk think she invented them.[20] Regardless, the stories, published in her 1928 book *Up Eel River*, are classic folk lore and have been enjoyed by legions of children for decades.

FOLK PERSPECTIVE: TONY BEAVER
AND THE PEANUT BRITTLE INCIDENT

When Tony Beaver was born, he was your average West Virginia baby: normal weight, normal size. But soon he went through a growth spurt that would not stop. He grew to be a large, strapping man with a fondness for the outdoors. In fact, he was so fond of the wilderness that he lived at a lumber camp he built near the mythical "Eel River." A congenial man, he made himself available to those in distress, their summons passed on to him by a seemingly tireless jaybird.[21]

To get a better idea of Tony Beaver's greatness, one cold winter, when the snow was so high the mountain folk couldn't gather firewood, Tony single-hand-edly crossed the snowbanks, cut off the tops of the trees, and dropped them down the townspeople's chimneys. When the spring crop failed, Tony, whose garden sprouted produce as oversized as he was, grew a potato that spread across four acres of ground and kept the entire town fed for weeks.[22]

So, you can imagine the magnitude of what occurred when peanut brittle was involved. Apparently, the Eel River breeched its banks, destroying every-thing, and threatened to flood the town. Quick-thinking Tony Beaver stopped the flood by pouring vast quantities of molasses into the river then adding, to ensure the safety of one and all, peanuts. The locals were saved and, in the process, a new candy was created. West Virginians, in their jubilation, started making the peanut brittle and have been making it ever since.[23]

SEX AND CHOCOLATE-COVERED CREAMS

Most candy stores weren't worried about bars and drops, they had something more sumptuous on their minds: variously called chocolate bonbons, chocolate creams, truffles, and enrobed chocolates. These voluptuous candies were a prized gift on Mother's Day and Valentine's Day, and if a date went well, a possible prelude to sex. And the best chocolates of all were French.

By French, the chocolates weren't necessarily *from* France, but were in the "French style," such as the very-French truffle, filled with ganache and surrounded by a deliciously dark shell. The French-style cream-filled candy was introduced in 1851 at the Great Exhibition in London.[24] It won an adoring audience in the United States, who have long been enamored by all things French.

So popular were these chocolates that some "chocolatiers" devoted themselves to their existence. Others, such as Schrafft's Candy Company, made them en masse then wholesaled them to smaller companies. Schrafft's also carried chocolates in their own retail shops, complete with French-sounding names, such as "D'Or Elegante," and distinct gold-hued packaging. Their ads said:

> From the French comes the motif for this distinguished package, but only Schrafft could have supplied such chocolates. Search among the most exclusive shops of London, Paris, Rome—you will find nothing to compare to them. The golden box of chocolates is now offered for the first time. It contains the daintiest of our French truffle, nuts, fruits, and cream centers.[25]

Mais oui!

Other chocolate makers matched Schrafft's in their advertising without using the word "French." Instead, they offered upscale sounding assortments with names like "Society Chocolates,"[26] "Lady Fairfax Chocolates,"[27] and "Paradise Chocolate."[28] Like most candies whose advertising hinges on style and class, this advertising subtly, but most definitely, alluded to sex. A Belle Mead chocolate advertisement describes their product with words that practically caress:

A box of Belle Mead chocolates is an open door to the magic realms of chocolatry where all's delicious. Made from the purest ingredients moulded into sweets of rare delight—into bonbons and raspberry creams, into peppermint and orange paste, mapled creams and caramels, and many other luscious morsels.[29]

The visuals that accompanied these ads were almost explicit: images of roses cast in chocolate that an ob-gyn would recognize immediately.

If enrobed chocolates were sexual, then there had to be people who were against them, and trust me, there were—but for reasons you might not expect. At the time, men gave women boxes of chocolates in courtship. The gesture was sexual yet subtle and didn't make most people nervous. If a woman bought herself chocolates . . . well, let's just say it was unseemly.

This concern was hardly hidden. For many in the nineteenth century, chocolate—especially chocolate consumed by women who read romance novels (seriously)—led to what was coined as "self-abuse." One of the most outspoken experts on the matter, although not from personal observation, I'm sure, was John Harvey Kellogg.[30] Kellogg, a physician who operated a get-healthy sanatorium in Battle Creek, Michigan, did not believe in sex; he believed in sex so little that he never engaged in it with his wife. But worse than sex with another was sex with yourself. "If illicit commerce of the sexes is a heinous sin," Kellogg wrote, "self-pollution is a crime doubly abominable."[31]

This was not a moral or religious belief that a quick Hail Mary or an act of contrition could resolve. It led to physical, emotional, and spiritual sickness. "Candies, spices, cinnamon, cloves, peppermint, and all essences powerfully excite the gentile organs," Kellogg said[32]. And this then led to uncontrollable desires, a more or less bonfire of lust. Personally, I'm not sure why that's a problem, but Kellogg had a solution. A cereal he called "Corn Flakes."

Whatever lust the chocolates may have inspired, you'd never guess it at the family-owned candy shop. The candies were displayed next to rows of marshmallow, caramels, and caramel biscuits, aka caramel-covered marshmallows. The shops were all about family values.

One example is Eiler's Candy in Dover, Ohio. I came across this candy store when my editor asked if I knew anything about a candy called "Orientals." His family got them from Eiler's Candy on the holidays when he was a kid, and he remembered the mouthwatering flavor.

My initial research indicated that (a) Eiler's is still around but (b) doesn't have a website with its history and (c) also doesn't have an online shop where I could explore its offerings. In other words, this old-fashioned candy store is still old fashioned. Looking through newspaper archives, I was able track down the Eiler story.

EILER CANDY: THE QUINTESSENTIAL AMERICAN CANDY STORE

What I found was a classic old-time chocolate store that Norman Eiler started in 1936, selling handmade jellies, chocolates, and brittles on 3rd Street in downtown Dover, Ohio.

It was a real community place, sponsoring toy drives and other events, and offering the occasional "Sidewalk Sale!" with fabulous discounts. Their advertisements started appearing regularly in the 1950s, all of them full of tempting and reasonably priced delights. No gold, no glitz. Eiler's candy was for everyone. One of their signature candies was the "Oriental."

PERSONAL PERSPECTIVES: JOHN GIBBS
AND THE DELICIOUS ORIENTAL

Today, John Gibbs, the nephew of Norman Eiler, owns the shop. Here is what he said:[33]

My uncle, Norman Eiler, bought the concession stand at the Bexley Movie Theater in 1936. In those days, they were full-serve concession stands with ice cream, sodas, milk shakes, and just a little bit of candy that was purchased from outside suppliers. In 1942, they moved the store around the corner, just one block, where it is today.

His dad, my grandfather, had worked in a steel mill and lost his job in the Depression. They didn't have money for gifts, so his mom gave homemade candy instead. Friends kept requesting it throughout the year . . . and Norman saw an opportunity to put his parents back to work. He added a line of candy that his mom and dad made in the basement of their home. Seventy-five to eighty percent of long-term candy operations began in the basement or the kitchen.

My grandmother got the recipe for Orientals from parts unknown. They weren't regular candies: the centers were softer and creamier than you would normally find, and if you waited a few weeks to eat them, the inside would turn to liquid. At Christmas time we'd make them a little bigger and wrap them in cellophane.

Grandpa made candy every year until he died. My Aunt Rosemary, his daughter, made the chocolate until she died in 1983, and my dad took over from 1983 to 1986, then my sister and I stepped in. We still own it today. We make the candy the same way, and we're true to our core candy. Not much has changed.

BRIDGE MIX!

You cannot, repeat, absolutely *cannot*, overlook this marvel of candy making and its place in polite society. And what is more polite than the game of bridge. From the 1920s to the 1950s, couples sat at designated "bridge tables" for hours, cards in their hands. But how to snack? How to enjoy some sweet refreshment? That would mean putting down the cards and stopping the game.

Enter the bridge mix, an assortment of chocolate-covered raisins, almonds, peanuts, and caramels served or stationed in candy bowls alongside bridge tables everywhere. A bridge player needed only to dip the fingers of one hand into the bowl to retrieve the delicious sustenance *without ever lowering their cards*. Other classics, such as licorice bridge mix or tastefully sugared mixes featuring the Jordon Almond were also present, depending on the players involved and, I bet, the décor of the house that was hosting the game.

BACK IN ROCKPORT: FROM HOTEL TO TUCK'S

Fig. 15.3. Bob Tuck making toffee at Tuck's Candy in Rockport, Massachusetts.

Dan, Moses, and I ate breakfast, then had a pleasant walk around Bear Skin Neck, where lobstermen were doing their rounds and Tuck's Candy was open. Today, the shop has a large glass window giving view to a candy counter and a display filled with pastel-hued taffy. Behind a wall in the rear, Dan Tuck, the third-generation owner, a few employees, and, on occasion, his father, make sweets by hand. The view from their workspace is of boats moored in the harbor and beyond that, the open sea.

Unfortunately, Dan Tuck was unavailable for the interview because, apparently, I had scheduled it for the previous day. But his father, who was dipping squares of toffee into rich, dark chocolate, was happy to talk. So, as he and an employee dipped the candy, I took out my laptop and prepared it for notes.

PERSONAL PERSPECTIVE: ROBERT TUCK, CANDYMAKER[34]

My grandfather and great-grandfather were dentists. My father, Walter, had a twin brother whose name was George. When they got out of high school, their father said he couldn't afford to send both of the boys to college. So he sent George to pharmacy school and he went there for about three years.

My father wanted to be a chef, and he started out in restaurants but he got a nasty infection from making baked stuffed lobster. He got really sick, and changed his mind. He decided to go into candy, instead. The only way to learn candy making is to apprentice. There are all kinds of schools for bakers and chefs but nothing for candy. You have to apprentice even today. No university of candy making.

He apprenticed in three different places . . . this was probably . . . well, he started the store in '29 so this was probably in 1923 or '24. One of the places where he apprenticed was Schrafft's in the "homemade" division. He specialized in everything, just learning the trade. Then his father helped set him up a candy store at 15 Main Street, which he owned. His father's dental office was on the top floor, and he took the place downstairs for the candy.

That's where he started. George was working out of town as a pharmacist for a couple years, then he moved back and brought the pharmacy with him. They put his pharmacy right in the candy store. The candy was on the right, the pharmacy was on the left, and there was a raised part in the middle where he made the candy.

I took over for my father when he was sixty-five. I made candy for well over fifty years. Probably sixty years of making candy. I started when I was fourteen; my summer job and my job after school was making candy, me and my sisters. I was growing up in World War II which had sugar rationing at the time. The national bank system tracked how much sugar my father used through the Rockport bank. The amount you could have was based on your sales from 1939.

It was a tough time. You had your regular customers. It was a commodity and it sold out pretty fast. Anything that came by ship was rationed. The ships were needed for the war effort, and they were randomly sunk by the Nazis. The more cargo ships the Nazis eliminated, the more they shut off the country's supplies. It was tough time, as I said, but we got through it.

What kind of candy did I like best? Not the kind my father made, I can tell you that. I went to Mrs. Savage's penny candy store. I bought root beer barrels, Squirrel Nut Zippers, the mint spearmint leaves. . . . They didn't have gum. At the time, gum was coming from Mesoamerica, and the government needed the gum rubber for tires. I remember going to one of many corner stores, standing in a line and waiting with a penny to get bubblegum. The kids were lined up all the way down the block. Bubblegum. That's what we always liked best.

After the interview, Bob took me to the back room near the taffy pull to show me the family's original recipes, and I really mean original: handwritten on time-worn pieces of paper, a few notes scrawled on the delicate pages. Dan still uses them today. His candies are delicious.

CHAPTER 16

THE PENNY CANDY EXPLOSION

After Tuck's we headed back to Boston, this time for an investigation that was any candy researcher's dream: the penny candy store. Those stores, sometimes no bigger than a closet, were a mecca of sizes, shapes, and smells; all affordable to the smaller fisted among us, whose spending money came from babysitting, delivering newspapers, and co-opting coins from grown-ups. The candies, artfully tucked into baskets and jars, were known as "penny candies" because a penny could get a kid anywhere from a sucker to a dozen little treats. Understanding candy in the industrial age means understanding, nay embracing, that bright and cheery sugar urchin of the confectionery world.

SUGAR BITS FOR LITTLE KIDS

Throughout the early days of candy history, confections were considered among the finer things of life, exclusively for the well-to-do. Then came penny candy. It was affordable, especially for children, and, even more shocking, children of the working class.

The early selections, as listed in the *Ohio Journal of Education* in 1857,[1] were cream candy, popcorn, peppermint, molasses, rose, clove, butterscotch, sugar plums, lemon drops, lemon candy, peppermint drops, French kisses, cinnamon, ice-cream, wintergreen, sour drops, horehound, lavender, gum drops, vanilla, rock, birch, cats-eyes, and kisses. They offered a variety of flavors from a literal world of places—the vanilla from Mesoamerica, the clove from Asia, and the wintergreen from right here, all available to kids whose world was closed off from such things in any other venue.

These candies were made available compliments of the early Industrial Revolution; that's when the price of sugar dropped, thanks in part to Norbert

Rillieux's sugar evaporator. Now, for the first time, candymakers could make and sell inexpensive and innovative concoctions geared to kids. The kids loved it. The confectionery peddlers loved it. But home economists, temperance enthusiasts, and other folk, were horrified. And their horror was deepened by antipathy for the working class.

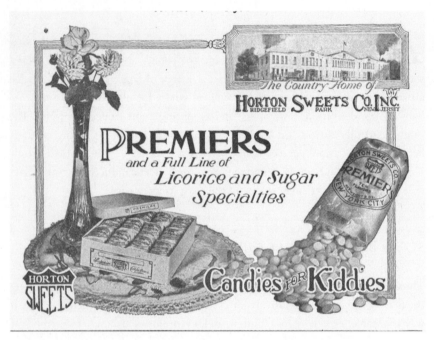

Fig. 16.1. A candy advertisement geared toward children.

This perspective was voiced with stunning clarity in such places as an article in an 1824 edition of *The Friend*. According to the author, candy could lead working class children into "intemperance, gluttony, and debauchery."[2] What exactly did they mean by this? The intemperance, gluttony, and debauchery was not free-wheeling. Sweets inflicted their wrath in a variety of ways, often depending on the specific candy.

One candy that remains villainous today is the candy cigarette. But modern candy moralists have it easy compared to turn-of-the-century reformers who had to worry about candy cigarettes with the red tips *and* "whisky" gum drops made with fruit flavoring. Activists, such as Reverend James E. Smith declared, "These candies may look harmless, but they are leading the minds of our boys toward temptation, they are enticing our children to become drunks and cigarette fiends."[3] Children were also indulging in a related hazard, the candy cigar. Apparently the Reverend was far from alone in his crusade. He praised one cohort, Miss Lucy Page Gaston, aka "the cigarette smasher."

Candy could also lead to alcohol abuse although the road to this particular vice was more convoluted. An issue of *Ladies Home Journal* of 1906 explained, "The first craving from ill feeding [of candy] calls for sugar; later for salt; then tea, coffee; then tobacco; then such fermented beverages as wine and beer; and lastly alcohol."[4] So, by that reasoning, candy is a gateway to . . . salt.

It wasn't just eating the candy that was the problem—it was the *act* of buying the candy. The power of the purchase could lead children to feelings of independence and self-assuredness. And that could get them to believe they were adults and cause them to start acting like adults, which inevitably led to drinking, smoking, and, yes, even gambling. The working-class children were most vulnerable since they lacked discipline and the principled background of their wealthier counterparts.

Even candy-defenders fell into the mire of classism. For example, one late nineteenth-century article encourages parents to let their children eat candy . . . but only if it's expensive and, in effect, out of reach of the working class. "Never pay less than 40 cents a pound" the piece advises, "for that is the only way you can get the purest candy available."[5]

Another article appearing in 1904 advised parents, "Children should be allowed to eat sweets, but the proper kind of sweets. Cheap, nasty confections should never be given to them. . . . Beware of cheap nasty candies; they are poisonous. But give the children candy in the form of pure chocolate, honey . . . A lump of sugar or a good stick of candy now and then will not hurt them. . . . Their systems crave them. They impart warmth and energy. They nourish and build up the tissues."[6]

By the 1870s, the penny candy had grown in popularity, appearing in such places as tobacco stores, newsstands, movie theaters, and five-and-dime stores.[7] And with its popularity came accusations that candy not only led kids to moral corruption and a lifetime of alcohol abuse, but also that it could kill them.

During this time, the nation had a mounting concern over the quality of what they ate. Under the auspices of Harvey Wiley, purity became the rallying call of the public. In 1906, an act garnishing the word appeared, the Pure Food Act, and with it the Bureau of Chemistry and its powerful personae later known as the FDA.

Candy, with its cheap, working-class associations, was at the center of attention, accompanied by alcohol, marijuana, and other foods and substances. Newspapers were ablaze with shocking reports. One headline in the *Pittsburgh Daily Post* announced "Merchants Store 100 Tons of Tainted Candy" and revealed that an attorney for the Pennsylvania Pure Food Department declared that the candy contained a poisonous drug that could jeopardize children's health. The dishonorable merchants were delaying trials until after the holiday season, so they could sell the tainted sweets in the meantime. Note: one hundred *tons*. The judge determined that the trial must be delayed "until after the Court House improvement work is completed."[8]

The *Salt Lake Tribune* reported at least two fatal incidents over the course of a year. The first, in 1909, were the deaths of a one-year-old and a three-year-old, who allegedly died from tainted candy. The coroner had yet to examine the children. The other incident, in 1910, was definitely the result of tainted chocolate. The victim, twelve-year-old Ivan Leroy Starmer, had bought the chocolate at a local grocer. It turns out the grocer had kept poisons by the candy counter. Some had leaked out and in cleaning up the mess, the grocer got poison on his hands, which he then transferred to the candy.[9]

Of course, the reports varied sharply. Just when the pure-food crowd were blaming candy on, well, everything, other reports dismissed their concerns. For example, after an investigation, Pennsylvania chemist Charles H. LaWall announced on the Pure Food bulletin that the candy in their area was pure. It wasn't always pure, LaWall stressed, but things had changed.[10]

Meanwhile, candy companies were busily convincing a skeptical public of their candy's food value. Editorials weighed in on candy's behalf, such as one by food writer and columnist Frederic J. Haskin. In an in-depth editorial, he asserted that candy is safe, a real boon for the economy, and good *food*.

But the apex of Haskin's piece, something candymakers must have set on a shrine, was his assertion that children actually *won't* overeat candy when a supply is "kept before them at all times." It's only when the supply is *limited* that they go overboard. Haskin's next assertion is even more remarkable: candy does *not* lead to cigarette smoking. In fact, it discourages it. "Few cigaret [sic] smokers eat candy," he said.[11]

Haskin did make another point—one that became the candy industry's saving grace. Candy was being used in war rations, and this, beyond all else, gave candy haters some perspective. Candy was what our boys on the front loved and needed. And it still is today.

THE BIRTH AND VERY LONG LIFE (BUT NOT LONG ENOUGH, IN MY OPINION) OF THE PENNY CANDY STORE

I dropped Dan and Moses off at a park and headed for Irving's Toy and Card Store. The shop, about the size of a living room, was tightly tucked in front of a brick apartment building with a grammar school close by. The small space was stuffed with candy bars, penny candy, cards, and small toys.

Fig. 16.2. Penny candy.

When I was young, visiting my grandmother near Sewall Avenue, I would go to Irving's with my cousin. Now, fifty years later, it hadn't changed. It really hadn't changed. I must have looked nostalgic as I locked my car because a man in his early fifties greeted me and told me his father's story. As a boy, his father lived on the outskirts of town. His family was poor, and they didn't go out—not to movies, not to restaurants—except on Saturday when his father went to Irving's. For years and years, he'd go to Irving's. He only had a few coins, but for a boy with so little, that was a lot. "It was the best part of his week," the man told me. Then he said good-bye and walked away.

Fig. 16.3. Irving's Toy Store.

At Irving's, a second man about ten years older was telling a cluster of visiting family members how he went to Irving's when he first arrived in this country. The family didn't look impressed, but I knew exactly what he meant. For years, he went there every day.

That's how it goes with penny candy stores.

The family wandered off, and he and I went into the candy store. I swear, Ethel Weiss, the owner, was sitting in the same seat as always. She didn't remember my cousin or my mother, who bought bubblegum there as a kid, or me. She didn't remember the man either. No matter, he took my picture sitting beside Ethel and I took his. There was a framed plaque on the wall congratulating Ethel on her hundredth birthday. She motioned to it.

PERSONAL PERSPECTIVE: ETHEL WEISS AT ONE HUNDRED

When I was a cub journalist, my editor asked me to write a "page brightener" about an old candy store, which, as it happened, was Irving's. I did. That was thirty years ago. I last bought penny candy there almost fifty years ago. When I interviewed Ethel again, she was over one hundred years old. Not a lot had changed.[12]

My father came over from England in 1914. He came here to work in the ship-yards in Virginia during World War I, and that's where I was born. Then he went to Portland, and I grew up there. I married someone from Boston. He came to play baseball against a team from Portland. The team was really from Chelsea, but they had kids from all over. All the players were Jewish: it was a Jewish league. We met at a restaurant after the game. Later on, we got married.

Irving, that was my husband, was working for a sausage house, and he lost his job because he sided with the workers instead of the concern over a strike. He heard a candy store was for sale. It seemed like a good idea, so we bought it. It was a success; everybody loved us. And that's where we are now. . . .

When the kids came in, I showed them how to make choices and how to prioritize. I showed them how to manage their money. I had them count the coins when they paid and count the change afterwards. They learned about manners and how to be polite. So many kids have come through here. . . . I can't say how many. I don't remember most of their names.

The earliest candies are mostly still in style. They were penny candy and nickel candy. Screamers and bubblegum, things like that. There isn't as much variety, though. There just isn't as many kinds of candy around. We used to carry marshmallows, but I don't sell them anymore and people don't ask. There's still peppermints and red licorice. I had the Candy Buttons, but kids don't ask for that now, either.

It's been seventy-six years that I've been here. If someone asks for something and we don't have it, I order it. That's all. There's really not much to say.

THE GREAT AMERICAN SEVENTEENTH-CENTURY SWEET

Of all the penny candy favorites that people today remember, the Fireball is at the top. The secret to the popularity of this spicy orb lies in its ancestry, going back to the seventeenth century "sugar plum."

Fig. 16.4. Sugar plums.

To make these sugar plums, a skilled craftsman apprenticed for years, absorbing the nuances of a trade that makes Julia Child look like a scullery maid in comparison. First, he coated seeds or nuts with gum arabic, then put them in a "balancing pan" suspended over a large, low fire, and rolled them in sugar syrup. To keep the coating even and the sugar from crystallizing, he kept the seeds and nuts in constant motion, stirring them with one hand and moving the pan with the other. He controlled the temperature of the heat by controlling the intensity of the fire.

Once the candy was coated, the confectioner set it aside where it dried for a day or two, then began the process again, stirring and moving, adding layer upon layer over a period of weeks.[13] In the last stage, with the sugar coating as smooth as glass, he often added a flourish of color, using mulberry juice or cochineal for red, indigo stone for blue, spinach for green, and saffron for yellow.[14]

These sugar-coated bits were no Gobstoppers, but eaten with great decorum, after medieval meals in fourteenth-century Paris. In the early 1700s, they were given as gifts, particularly sugar-coated almonds, with their symbol of joyous beginnings.[15]

The term "sugar plum" appeared in Thomas Decker's *Lanthorne and Candlelight*[16] in 1608 but had nothing to do with plums, prunes, or any sort of poached fruit. Instead "plum" referred to the word "good." "Sugar plum" equals "good sugar." Given the cost and time involved in producing them, the sugar plum was also associated with money. If someone was giving a bribe, they were said to be stuffing that person's mouth with sugar plums. "Plum" was also eighteenth-century slang for a large amount of money.[17]

FROM SUGAR PLUM TO FIRE BALL

So, how did the esteemed "sugar-plum" become a kid's penny candy? It's like asking how the Greek god Hercules became a Disney character. It took a long time, but it happened. Changes during the Industrial Revolution enabled confectioners to replace the balancing pan with a rotating drum and create sugar plums quickly and with relative ease. This may have been a moot point for early twentieth-century Americans were it not for Salvatore Ferrara, an Italian immigrant who arrived in the United States in 1900.

He started his American experience working on the Santa Fe Railroad until he moved to Chicago and opened a candy and pastry shop. One of his specialties was the quintessential Italian wedding candy, the Confetti almond, aka Jordan Almond. The candy was a hit and soon Ferrara was selling his sweets throughout the Midwest.[18]

In 1921, Farrara and his brothers-in-law, Salvatore Buffardi and Anello Pagano, expanded the business, and the Ferrara candy empire, makers of such iconic panned treats as Boston Baked Beans and Lemon Heads, was born. Their most time honored candy was the jawbreaker, a typical panned candy with a sugar crystal at its center instead of a nut or seed.[19] In 1839, the word "jawbreaker" meant a "hard-to-pronounce word" and later was slang for a dentist.[20] By the early 1900s, the Jaw-breaker had melted its way into the American fabric. In 1910, the *Monroe City Democrat* published this little page brightener:

A teacher in giving a lecture to her junior hygiene class had cautioned them against eating anything hard, such as nuts, hard candy, etc. A small boy held up his hand.

"What is it Sammy?" she inquired.

"Say, did you ever see any of these here candy jaw-breakers," he asked.

"Y-es, I believe so," she hesitated wonderingly.

"Well, Willie here," indicating another boy in the class, "stood right in front of Gregorie's store and et five of them right down."

"Ate," corrected the teacher.

"Aw, was it eight? I was thinkin' it was only five."[21]

THEN CAME THE HOT STUFF

Salvatore Ferrara's company was a hit, but no one knew it. It sold its candy in the nameless universe of wholesale and bulk until 1932 when the company introduced its first branded item: little, bright-red sensations called "Red Hots."

What followed had a great deal to do with Salvatore's son, Nello. His beginnings weren't what you'd expect of a candymaker: he started off as an attorney, then enlisted in the army during World War II where he ended up in the Army's Counter Intelligence Corps. After the war, he served in the International Military Tribunal for the Far East under the command of General MacArthur. Once he returned, Nello opened his own law practice but only for a short time.

By 1947, Nello quit the legal world and entered the universe of confections. His first step was to do away with the chocolates and other candies the company was making in order to focus exclusively on panned candies. He renamed the company Ferrara Pan Candy Company, developed a recognizable brand, and, in 1954, added a new candy to the lineup. The name of this candy was the Atomic Fireball.[22]

SUGAR PLUMS TODAY: WHAT THE FAIRY NEVER KNEW

Today panning is a huge industry, encompassing Ferrara's Boston Baked Beans, M&M's, jelly beans, and Skittles. Companies produce the sweets in a "pan" that looks like a small cement mixer. To do this today, the candymaker lets the candy dry then returns it to the pan, adding yet another layer of sugar, and so on. Like the old-time sugar plum, both the Jawbreaker and Fireball take about two weeks to make and has one hundred layers.[23]

WAX LIPS AND CRAZY DRAKE

The story of wax lips goes back to Crazy Drake, the man who figured out how to get petroleum out of the ground and thus invented the petroleum industry. His discovery also launched Daniel Peter's quest for milk chocolate. Petroleum was also responsible for another candy innovation closer to home in Buffalo, New York.

Drake's discovery ultimately led to paraffin wax, a by-product of petroleum production. A host of non-candy items were created from this substance, such as Robert Chesebrough's new balm, "petroleum jelly," aka Vaseline. Chesebrough believed in the health value of his product so much that he ate a spoonful of the stuff every day. Apparently, it worked; he died when he was ninety-six. Thomas Edison used paraffin in wax cylinders for his photographs in 1901, and, in 1903, Binney & Smith Company used the wax to create a product that combined the word "craie," French for "chalk," with "oleaginous," an adjective for "oily," to make "Crayola."

In the midst of all this arose one of the lesser known but much loved (in some circles) by-products of the petroleum industry: wax lips. Chewing gum mavericks, John Bacon Curtis and Thomas Adams had used paraffin wax as a chewing gum, but their efforts could not match the imagination of John W. Glenn.

This inspired Buffalo, New York, confectioner came to the United States from England in 1888 when he was fifteen and became the mastermind behind the "penny chewing gum novelties." For his chewable treats, Glenn used fully refined, food-grade wax straight from the Emlenton Refining Company, aka Quaker State Oil.[24] Among his many products were wax lips, wax horse teeth (seriously), and even a gum top that really did spin.[25]

Another favorite was Nik-L-Nip, little wax bottles with colored sugar water inside. Rumors circulated about the name, but most agreed that the "Nik-L" stood for "nickel," the cost of the tasteless industrial wonders. Some say "Nip" refers to the process of "nipping" off the top. Others believe that "Nip" refers to a nip of whisky, which is likely seeing that the temperance movement was in full swing, with people complaining about candy cigarettes and whisky gum drops. Glenn gave them yet another thing to complain about.

The chewing paraffin reached a peak in 1923 when Glenn boasted one

Fig. 16.5. Wax lips.

hundred employees. Since then, the wax lips have bounced around. One stop was a company owned by Franklin Gurley, who also made candles in shapes that ranged from Santas to pilgrims. The lips later moved from New York to Illinois, then to Selma, Alabama, as shops were downsized or closed.[26]

Today, they are made in Canada by Concord Confections, which is owned by Tootsie Roll Industries.

JELLY BEANS: ONE GOOFY GUY

Most people don't consider jelly beans a penny candy since they belong in a category unto themselves. Too small to be counted, they're set aside to be poured and weighed, even in candy stores today. Still, the jelly bean is a twentieth-century favorite with roots that go back to a surprising place: the Turkish delight.

In the mid-1800s, some unknown person added a sugar shell to the Turkish delight, coming up with a new candy called the "jelly bean." William Schrafft supposedly sent the new candy to the Union soldiers and advertised for others to do so, as well.[27] What's certain is the jelly bean was a mainstream candy by the late 1800s, selling for nine to twelve cents a pound according to one ad in the *Brooklyn Daily Eagle* on October 2, 1898.[28]

But why "jelly bean"? Obviously it resembled a bean. But culturally, the name referred to a gaudy, goofy fellow. F. Scott Fitzgerald wrote a story titled "The Jelly Bean" in 1922, in which he wrote: "'Jelly-bean' is the name throughout the undissolved Confederacy for one who spends his life conjugating the verb to idle in the first person singular—I am idling, I have idled, I will idle." And Phil Harris wrote a song "Jelly Bean (He's a Curb-Side Cutie)" in 1940. In other words, this "jelly bean" man was useless.

The jelly bean won its most enduring acclaim around 1930 as an Easter candy. The reasons are not entirely clear—perhaps because Easter, like other springtime rituals, is about rebirth, and the bean is an excellent symbol.

Then came Jelly Belly. The jelly bean was revolutionized by candy distributor and entrepreneur David Klein, who came up with the concept to infuse the entire bean with flavor. Later, as he was watching the TV show *Sanford and Son*, he thought the characters were talking about someone named "Jelly Belly." They were really talking about "Lead Belly."[29]

Klein outsourced production to the Herman Goelitz Candy Company who developed his concept into a candy. Later, in a move that ended in a lengthy legal battle, the Goelitz family pushed Klein out, paying him a relatively small settlement and shutting him out of his Jelly Belly legacy for good. An award-winning movie about the event, called *Candy Man: The David Klein Story*, came out several years ago and is now available on Amazon.

Regardless, the jelly bean entered a new and illustrious phase of life, making appearances everywhere from movie-theater concession stands to corner-store displays. They showed up at a presidential inauguration in1981 and were the first candy to go on a space mission in 1983. In fact, people ate enough jelly beans in 2014 to circle the earth five times.[30]

PERSONAL PERSPECTIVE: DAVID KLEIN,
INVENTOR OF THE JELLY BELLY

In the summer of 1952, when I was six years old, I started working at the liquor store my grandparents owned with my Aunt Ida. It was called "Lazy Bee Liquor" on the corners of Kester and Burbank Boulevard in Van Nuys, California. The clientele was actively involved in the movie business: acting, producing, and writing. A lot of movie stars were living around it . . . Lucille Ball, Desi Arnaz, Tony Dow from *Leave it to Beaver*. Annette Funicello's father owned the Union 76 gas station right next door.

My grandparents were immigrants from Russia. They were hardworking people who lived in a duplex about half a block away so they could walk to work . . . my grandfather never got his license. I lived a few blocks away, and walked to the store every morning and my aunt walked me home later in the day.

As part of my duties, I went with my Aunt Ida to a candy wholesaler called Smart and Final to select candy for the store. My aunt was about four feet eight and loaded with energy. My dad called her "Little Caesar" because she was always telling people what to do. Most people used to call her "Shorty." She never married and only went on one date. And the man tried to borrow money from her. On the first date. Can you believe that?

So, here's what I remember: At the warehouse we looked through the candy. Let's say you wanted to taste a sample like a Look bar, remember those? They retailed for a nickel. You could open the box, put a nickel in and taste a bar. If you liked it, you got the whole box. If not, you left the nickel there to let whoever did get the box start with a sale. And that's what you did. It wouldn't be like that today.

We brought the candy back to the store, and I would fill up the display case. As I filled it, I would look at the wrapper to see where they came from. . . . I became an expert in candy. . . . in Junior High if anyone wanted to know where their candy came from, I could tell them. I knew about liquor, too. I knew what a fifth of whisky meant. Hardly anyone else did. Hardly anyone knows today.

When I was eighteen, five years after the liquor store closed, I went into a popcorn and caramel-corn business called "Big Dave's" with my uncle Earl, Ida's brother, who we called "Itchy." We made no money. It just wasn't profitable. Later, I went into the candy and nut business. At first, I just focused on walnuts . . . and brought in millions after only three months.

One and a half years later, I came up with the idea for Jelly Belly. Instead of just having the flavor in the shell, my idea was to infuse the entire bean with new and unusual flavors. I thought up the name "Jelly Belly" when I was watching

Sanford and Sons—you remember that show, right? They were talking about Lead Belly. I didn't know who Lead Belly was. . . . If I knew he was in jail for murder, I may not have used the name.

I approached the Herman Goelitz Candy Company and asked them to be my contract manufacturer. And that's what they were. At first the jelly bean was a flop. Then I got the Associated Press to write an article about the beans and they really took off! The Goelitz Company bought me out four years later, including the trademark for the name. I can't use the name, and I couldn't compete with jelly beans for twenty years.

The twenty years is over now, and I've developed a new line of jelly beans [David's Signature "Beyond Gourmet" Jelly Beans]. They're different: they're delicious and all-natural. And my company, "Can You Imagine That!" won the Most Innovative Product Award for Farts Candy, which I developed with Leaf Brands. I'm also working on a project that raises money through candy sales to send kids with cancer to summer camp. I'm proud of that the most.[31]

LIFE SAVERS

The Life Saver was invented by Clarence Crane in 1912. Crane worked for his father in his maple sugar business until 1903, when he opened one of his own. As these things seem to happen in candy history, he soon became the largest maple sugar producer in the world and extremely wealthy. He was also married, but his wife, Grace Edna Hart, suffered from mental illness. Their marriage was volatile and combative and eventually they separated and then divorced.[32]

But one good thing came out of their union: their son, Hart Crane, one of the most influential poets of his time. Unfortunately, Hart had his own troubles, severe alcoholism among them. He died after falling off a ship at only thirty-three years of age, but whether he jumped, was pushed, or fell isn't clear.[33]

Crane's confectionery life was relatively easier than his personal one. He knew that most candymakers' profits nosedived in the summer when it was too hot to make chocolate. So, in 1912, Crane had an idea: Why not make hard candy that can be produced year round? The candy had to be delicious *and* interesting. He started making the usual flat candies, using a pharmacist's pill cutter. Then, to jazz it up, Crane put a hole in the middle. He called it a "Life Saver" because it looked like a life preserver.

Originally, Crane marketed the Life Saver as a breath freshener, focusing on the novelty of the "O" shape. For example, the first flavor was peppermint, which he called "Pep-O-Mint," with a complementary tagline, "For that Stormy Breath." The image was of a sailor tossing a life preserver to a young woman.[34] But weather proved to be a problem for Crane after all. He packaged the candy in cardboard tubes and the pieces stuck together in heat and humidity. In 1913 the Noble brothers, Robert and Edward, stepped in to help.

Here the story gets even more interesting. Edward was a marketer who first approached Crane with a marketing concept for the Life Saver. Instead of hiring him, Crane sold him the entire Life Saver business for $2,900, stickiness and all. That's where Robert came in. He had been an engineer at Westinghouse and developed foil and wax-paper wrappers that kept the candy fresh and unstuck year round.[35] However, Robert's packaging idea only mattered if people bought the product.

Back to Edward. Prohibition was around the corner, and alcohol was increasingly controversial. Still, people enjoyed a good drink and nothing was going to stop them. But how could they hide the tell-tale smell of alcohol on their breath from spouses and other judgment-prone people? For Edward, this situation reeked of opportunity, and he began selling the Life Saver as a breath mint in saloons.[36] He positioned his candy next to the cash register, each roll costing a nickel. Then he arranged for the cashier to give a nickel back to customers in change from their meal . . . conveniently the right amount to buy the Life Savers.[37]

Sales soared! The profits increased seven times the first year and tripled the second. Within ten years, the Noble brothers' sales reached $11.5 million.[38] As the profits grew, so did the variety of candy. Early on, the company made WintOgreen, CinnOmon, PepOmint, ClOve, LicOriche, and

Fig. 16.6. An ad for Life Savers.

ChocOlate Life Savers, adding a MaltOmilk flavor in 1921 and CrystOmint in 1925. In 1935, they introduced the now iconic Five-Flavor Roll.

Eventually, Edward Noble bought out the Beechnut Gum Company.[39] As for Clarence Crane—he started his own chocolate company and died a wealthy man. His son died a year after he did—Crane Senior was spared the grief of his son's death at sea and the irony of his candy being named the "Life Saver."

PERSONAL PERSPECTIVE: CAMILLA DHANAK, LIFE SAVERS IN THE HOLLER

I met Camilla Dhanak, a television producer from Michigan who lives in Los Angeles, when she was filming a show near my shop. It turned out her grandmother was from West Virginia and had a fascinating candy-related story.[40]

Whenever I see Smith Brothers Cough Drops or Wint-O-Green Life Savers, I always think of my grandmother and her mother, Halle Evelyn, who they called Miss Evey and who lived in the "Holler" of West Virginia. She married when she was fifteen or sixteen to a drunk. Even in her wedding picture you can see that she's holding him up—he was so drunk he couldn't stand straight. In the 1920s, he left Miss Evey with five kids and no money. Nothing. So, she started making food to sell to coal miners as they went into the mines. She was unbelievably poor, her kids didn't have shoes or anything like that, but at least they could eat.

She did okay but the miners said they wanted something stouter. Somehow she learned to make moonshine and started selling bootleg whiskey at the mines. This was Prohibition, don't forget, and she got busted five times. The authorities threw out the liquor but they never touched the still. I think they knew that was how she fed her children. She kept the still somewhere in the back, away from the house, and would just start it up again when they left.

Eventually she moved to Michigan, which is where I was born, and opened a successful chicken and dumplings restaurant. I still remember my great-grandmother from when I was little. She and my grandmother, who told me the story, always carried Smith Brothers and Wint-O-Green Life Savers so I think of her, and my grandmother, whenever I eat them. It's funny, when I feel lonely for family, I still get wintergreen Life Savers. I even text my cousin to tell her. One time, she texted me a picture of a roll. Not the fruit flavor, the Wint-O-Green. I still love them.

CHAPTER 17

THE HISTORY OF AN AMERICAN-MADE PASSION

The irony of the drug store, with its mission to protect health and its history of selling sweets, is obvious. Even I see the darker side: my father got diabetes in his early forties and my nana in her sixties. My father practically calculates every morsel that reaches his mouth: calories, quantities, amount of sugar. My nana didn't pay attention to her diabetes; she ignored it. And when she died a quick, sudden death at ninety-three, her bowls were chockfull of candy and her fridge was stocked with marshmallow- and chocolate-filled brownies. For her, no matter what the complication, candy would always win.

For years, drug stores stuck to their candy roots. Even into the 1960s, they still had soda fountains and shelves stacked with Good & Plenty, Broadway Licorice, Licorice Twists, Jawbreakers, and Swedish Fish. As a kid, I went to Davey's Drug Store, where a disgruntled clerk bagged candy from behind a counter for children who spilled in after school. The Pleasant Street pharmacy actually had a soda fountain plus a section devoted to candy. Cotter's Spa was first and foremost a candy store and soda fountain, and also happened to sell aspirins and such embarrassing items as sanitary napkins.

But one candy retained its medicine connection and to a small degree, still does today: chewing gum.

THE PHOTOGRAPHER AND THE PRESIDENT

It's odd that gum, historically one of the most medicinal candies, was largely made by inventors, candymakers, and businessmen who never contemplated a career in medicine. How gum became an American pastime has something of a marvel beginning, like the cacao, with the Aztecs. While the Native Americans of Maine were chewing spruce tree resin, the Aztecs were chewing resin from the sapodilla tree. Unlike the Native Americans, they had rules of decorum regarding their chewing gum habits.

According to sixteenth-century Spanish missionary Bernardino de Sahagún, "All the women who are unmarried chew chicle in public. One's wife also chews chicle, but not in public. . . . with it they dispel the bad odor of their mouths, or the bad smell of their teeth. Thus they chew chicle in order not to be detested." He added that women who openly chew were considered harlots, a precursor to the modern movie hooker snapping her gum on a damp, darkened street.[1]

The resin from the sapodilla eventually bumped out the spruce gum. How it arrived in the United States is an odd tale involving the deposed president of Mexico, General Antonio López de Santa Anna. He was the man who led the charge against the United States in the legendary Battle of the Alamo. He's also the man who killed Davy Crocket.

So how did Santa Anna wiggle his way into American candy history? Santa

Anna was an excellent politician. He was charismatic, ambitious, and handsome. He cared more about fame and adoration than fortune and was so adept at flip-flopping on issues that he set a standard today's leaders can only aspire to reach. With his excellent skills in waffling, Santa Anna won US favor, lost and regained the Mexican presidency, and was adored and detested by Mexicans. In the mid-1800s, battle-worn and deprived of one leg, Santa Anna went into exile. Yet Santa Anna, being Santa Anna, was determined to regain power and return to his former glory.[2]

Fig. 17.1. General Antonio López de Santa Anna. *Image from Wikipedia, user Scewing.*

So, if you were a deposed leader anxious to muster support and regroup, where would you go? Why, the resort town of Staten Island, NY, of course. It was there, in 1856, that he met Thomas Adams, whose name appears on Chiclet boxes and other old-time confections.

Here's what happened: When the two men met, Adams was a part-time inventor and full-time glass merchant. He later soloed as a photographer for the Union Army and served in the Army of the Potomac during the war.[3] How Santa Anna wound up living in his town is anyone's guess; he may have been swindled into making the trip to the United States and ended up in Staten Island. Or, he may have been rescued by US officials from a death sentence in Mexico and shuttled north. Most likely, Santa Anna arrived through official channels, thinking he might prove useful again. Once here, he was introduced to Adams.

At that time, the Industrial Revolution was gaining steam and rubber was the gold of the day. It was perfect for making tires, kitchen gadgets, machinery, and children's toys, and ultimately money. For Santa Anna, rubber was the key to amassing enough wealth to return to Mexico and regain power. It was his last chance.

This was no pipedream. Santa Anna brought the ingredients for a rubber empire—resin from the sapodilla tree—from his native land. In 1857, Santa Anna asked Adams to join in his scheme, using his supply of resin and a promise to get more as collateral.[4] Adams, the inventor, was intrigued. He and his two sons experimented with the chicle, using a vulcanizing process that Charles Goodyear had invented in 1839. Rubber for tires? Didn't work. Rubber for dolls? That didn't work, either. After repeated efforts and a personal investment of $30,000, Adams was ready to give up.

Then, an idea hit him. Adam's grandson tells the story in a 1944 speech at a banquet for managers at the American Chicle Company:

After about a year's work of blending chicle with rubber, the experiments were regarded as a failure; consequently Mr. Thomas Adams intended to throw the remaining lot into the East River. But it happened that before this was done, Thomas Adams went into a drugstore at the corner. While he was there, a little girl came into the shop and asked for a chewing gum for one penny. It was known to Mr. Thomas Adams that chicle, which he had tried unsuccessfully to vulcanize as a rubber substitute, had been used as a chewing gum by the natives of Mexico for many years. So the idea struck him that perhaps they could use the chicle he wanted to throw away for the production of chewing gum and so salvage the lot in the storage. After the child had left the store, Mr. Thomas Adams asked the druggist what kind of chewing gum the little girl had bought. He was told that it was made of paraffin wax and called White Mountain. When he asked the man if he would be willing to try an entirely different kind of gum, the druggist agreed. When Mr. Thomas Adams arrived home that night, he spoke to his son, Tom Jr., my father, about his idea. Junior was very much impressed, and suggested that they make up a few boxes of chicle chewing gum and give it a name and a label. He offered to take it out on one of his trips (he was a salesman in wholesale tailors' trimmings and traveled as far west as the Mississippi). They decided on the name of Adams New York No. 1. It was made of pure chicle gum without any flavor. It was made in little penny sticks and wrapped in various colored tissue papers. The retail value of the box, I believe, was one dollar. On the cover of the box was a picture of City Hall, New York, in color.[5]

Adams's groundbreaking gum eventually made him a fortune. As for Santa Anna, after the first few attempts to make rubber failed, he gave up. As Adams's chicle empire started to build, stick by stick, Santa Anna returned to Mexico where he died, sick, senile, and unaware of the fortune his chicle had won.[6]

ABOUT THAT EMPIRE . . .

Adams and his sons, Horatio and Thomas Jr., started making chewing gum just as Curtis had a few decades before, by boiling the resin and rolling it by hand at home—a slow and inefficient task. Soon, they opened the Adams and Sons Company in Jersey City, New Jersey, where they streamlined production in a more efficient manner, suitable to the times. But whoever heard of chewing gum? The spruce resin had been around, but we know what became of that. So, Adams developed a tagline for his new gum distinguishing it from the resins and paraffin wax: "Adams's New York Gum No. 1—Snapping and Stretching."[7]

Then Adams concocted a marketing plan based on the premium. Adams arranged for candy stores to give away a piece of his gum every time they purchased candy. Customers would enjoy the chew and buy the gum. The gum sold, but it didn't sell fast enough. So, Adams added sugar and sales skyrocketed. Next, he added licorice flavor, creating the first flavored gum called Black Jack Gum, which he also marketed as a remedy for colds. The Adams company still carries these flavors in limited batches every three years or so. Their arrival sends candy store owners (myself included) into a buying frenzy, although big-budget Cracker

Barrel is usually first in line. Adams later invented Tutti Frutti Gum the first fruit-flavored gum, followed by a sour orange flavor.[8]

For Adams, attempting to build an empire had its limitations. The Industrial Revolution was in its adolescence, and the machinery he needed wasn't available, largely because it wasn't invented yet. Years before, Curtis had encountered the same problem, so he invented the machinery himself; Adams did the same. Among his new machines was a gum dispenser for drugstores, actually more of a gum-*making* machine that kneaded the gum and pressed it into strips that the shopkeeper could break and sell for a penny. In 1888, Adams commissioned a vending machine that would carry 100% fully made chewing gum in New York City subway stations. They were a hit.[9] These efforts, and a good deal of advertising, paid off, and, in the late 1880s, Adams's company employed over three hundred people who produced five tons of gum daily.

HOW RICH WAS THOMAS ADAMS, REALLY?

When Thomas Adams Senior died in 1905, he and his family were extremely rich. How rich? Perhaps nothing describes their fortunes so well as this bizarre little story that took place in New York City.

It was 1888, and a twenty-five-year-old architect named C. P. H. Gilbert designed a two-family mansion for Thomas Adams Junior and John Dunbar Adams. The illustrious mansion was across the street from the equally illustrious mansion belonging to Charles Feltman, a German Jewish immigrant who invented the hot dog. Feltman's success was so great, he went from pushing a pie wagon on the sands of Coney Island to building Feltman's Ocean Pavilion with a ballroom, carousel, outdoor movie theater, pavilion, roller coaster, hotel, Tyrolean village, and the world's largest restaurant serving five million customers a year.[10]

The Adams family had a cadre of servants, gorgeous landscaping, and one thing that Feltman definitely did not: Gilbert had installed the first elevator in New York City in their house. Soon after moving in, the family headed out to spend their summer at the beach. Unfortunately, the Adams family didn't realize before they left that four servants had gotten stuck in the elevator, where they starved to death. They were found six months later when the family returned home.[11] As for Gilbert—his career flourished.

OTHER KIDS ON THE BLOCK

Adams wasn't alone. Two important gum makers are long forgotten. One is Louisville native and pharmacist John Colgan who, in 1880, invented a way to make chewing gum taste better by adding powdered sugar.[12] The other is the illustrious William J. White, maker of the Yucatan gum. In 1892, White was the largest chewing gum manufacturer in the United States, with three hundred employees who churned out three to four tons of gum a day. He was also a snappy dresser and high roller who owned a mansion, a racetrack, and a yacht, and was frequently seen locking arms with high-style women, including the wives of other men.[13]

While his lifestyle was alarming, especially to his wife (they divorced in 1906), White's chutzpah may have helped him in the end. In 1869, although he had little education or political experience, White became mayor of West Cleveland, and, in 1893, he became a congressman.[14] Famous for passing out samples of his chewing gum to fellow members of Congress, he used his position to pull off other, more impressive advertising stints. While visiting England, for example, he managed to get an introduction to King Edward VII. He handed the unsuspecting royal a piece of Yucatan gum and later reaped huge marketing value by claiming the king endorsed it.

Later, White founded and became president of the American Chicle Company.[15] His more conservative business fellows first kicked him out of the conglomerate then tried to push him out of the Mexican chicle market altogether. White exacted his revenge. For now, though, a look at other gums.

BEEMAN'S: FROM PIG'S GUTS TO CANDY SHOP

The popular Beeman's gum was invented in the late 1800s by Dr. Edward E. Beeman, an Ohio-based physician and researcher who discovered that pepsin, derived from the stomach of hogs, could aid digestion. He began selling pepsin powder, but sales were not what he'd hoped. So, Nellie Horton, his bookkeeper (or local shopkeeper, depending on who you ask), suggested that he make a delicious-tasting pepsin chewing gum to increase sales.[16] Some say she was chewing White's Yucatan gum at the time.

Beeman made the gum. It tasted good and was individually wrapped, but sales were lackluster. And why? Beeman was a doctor, not a marketer, and called his company the unappealing "Beeman's Chemical Company." Worse, he put the unfortunate picture of a pig on the wrapper until Nellie Horton convinced him otherwise.[17] By 1892, Dr. Beeman's bearded and, I might add handsome, face was on wrappers, billboards, ads, and newspaper pages. With his good looks and tasty concept, Beeman eventually became the owner of a million-dollar enterprise.

In 1899, Beeman's was absorbed into White's newly formed American Chicle Company. They eventually added pepsin to "Adam's Pepsin Gum," whose many attributes included relieving nervous tension. The company hired numerous big names to proclaim the merits of his product—pilots, actors, and athletes, among them. As for the charming Nellie Horton—she was richly rewarded as Beeman had given her stock as a thanks for her help.[18]

THE QUICK CLEAN STORY OF DENTYNE

This familiar gum was invented by pharmacist Franklin V. Canning in New York in 1899. The name stood for "Dental Hygiene" and Canning was the first—since the Aztecs, anyway—to position gum as a breath freshener. His special ingredient was *cassia*, also known as cinnamon. Canning's tagline was: "To prevent decay, To sweeten the breath, To keep teeth white."[19]

HOW THE CHEWING GUM SAVED BABY FOOD
AND QUITE POSSIBLY HAM

Bartlett Arkell was born into a prominent family in 1862. His father was a publisher and state senator, and Arkell carried on the tradition as an editor for eleven years. He left to cofound the Imperial Packing Co., which produced packaging for hams, bacon, and lard. His friend and mentor was none other than bacon baron Arthur Armour.

Soon Arkell became president of the Imperial Packing Co., and, under his direction, the company excelled. Regardless, a friend said the name "Imperial" was ill-suited for an American ham since it spoke of kings, queens, and knighthood. So, Arkell changed the name to Beech-Nut, conjuring images of the noble American tree and the smoky flavor of his hams. Over the years, Arkell pioneered the use of glass and vacuum-packed containers and branched the company into

Fig. 17.2. Bartlett Arkell with Beech-Nut workers, Canajoharie, NY, ca. 1925.
*Image used with permission from the collection of the Arkell Museum at
Canajoharie, Beech-Nut Archive [1996.1.1087].*

everything from peanut butter to soup. Around 1910, Arkell's brother-in-law,
whose own brother helped start the American Chicle Company, suggested that
Beech-Nut enter the chewing gum arena. So, they did.[20]

As a person, Arkell was a devoted patron of the arts; an active supporter of the
Canajoharie, New York, community where he lived; and a great employer, giving
his turn-of-the-century employees health benefits, pensions, and bonuses. And,
like all chewing gum magnets, Arkell was also a stealthy marketer. Among his
stunts, he hired a traveling circus to showcase his candy and gum and created the
personas of the convincingly attractive "Beech-Nut Girls."[21]

But the pièce de résistance was when he contracted Amelia Earhart to fly a
plane brandishing the Beech-Nut name from New Jersey to Oakland, California,
and back. With funding made possible from the publicity from this flight, and
additional support from Beech-Nut, Earhart was able to fly from New York to
Europe in 1932, from Hawaii to California in 1935, and also embark on the
around-the-world flight in 1937 that was her end.[22]

Fig. 17.3. Amelia Earhart with a Beech-Nut plane. *Image courtesy of the International Women's Air & Space Museum, Cleveland, Ohio.*

Eventually, Beech-Nut became one of the three biggest gum companies in the nation, along with the American Chicle Company and Wrigley's Gum. During the Depression, when Beech-Nut's food profits faltered, the chewing gum kept them afloat, accounting for $11 million of the $18 million in profits that year. In 1931, Beech-Nut introduced strained baby food, which they are most known for today.[23]

WINTERGREEN, DOUGHBOYS, AND THE
GREAT AMERICAN SUCCESS STORY

David Clark's story is as much about the American dream as any imaginable. Born in 1864, he started his life in Cork, Ireland, right around the time of the deadly potato famine. After only one year of school, he dropped out to help the family get by. Yet, even as youngster, he had ambition. He and his family immigrated to the United States, where, at age twelve, Clark worked by day and sent himself to business school by night.

In 1886, after selling goods from a pushcart and working for other merchants, he founded the D. L. Clark Company in Allegheny, Pennsylvania, which is now Pittsburgh's North Side. He eventually moved into an empty cracker factory, where he manufactured a variety of candies—by 1920 there were 150 on the list including the famous (and delicious) Clark Bar, which was made for the rations of World War I soldiers.

Clark's business was so successful he opened a second factory across the street, where he manufactured the Teaberry chewing gum.[24] The teaberry is actually the

Fig. 17.4. Assorted chewing gum.

berry from the wintergreen plant, which has a pleasant, minty flavor and grows throughout New England.[25] For reasons unknown, Clark's tagline was "It's On the Level" and a carpenters level, complete with a grainy look, was in the background. Gradually, the carpenter's level changed until it became a simple red band. By 1931, the candy bar business became too demanding (and successful) so Clark sold the Clark Brothers Chewing Gum Company, which then became the Clark Gum Company.[26]

THE AMERICAN CHICLE COMPANY: A GIANT ARISES

Two changes occurred for the Adams and Sons Company in 1899. First, Thomas Adams retired. Second, the company merged into the American Chicle Company, aka "the Chicle Trust." Founded by the ever-flamboyant William White, with Thomas Adams Jr. as the chairman, the nine-million-dollar venture brought together six top gum companies, including J. P. Primley (Chicago), the Kiss-Me Gum Company (Louisville), and S. T. Britten & Co. (Toronto) and later absorbed such favorites as Dentyne, Maine-based Sen-Sen, and Chiclets.[27]

There was only one problem: the board disliked their leader. He was too ostentatious and focused too many resources on promoting his own gum. After voting White out of the company in 1905, they conspired to push him out of the gum business for good. Their plan was to corner the market of raw chicle from the coast of Mexico, drive up the prices, and force White out. Unlucky for them, White learned of their plans and sent buyers to secretly purchase chicle from the middle of Mexico at twenty-five cents a pound. The price of chicle skyrocketed to $1.25 a pound, and, without White there to buy it, American Chicle lost hundreds of thousands of dollars.[28]

The American Chicle Company was bought by Warner-Lambert, a pharmaceutical company, in 1962, which was later acquired by Pfizer in 2000. Pfizer sold their candy brands to Cadbury in 2003, Cadbury was bought by Kraft in 2010, and Kraft merged with Heinz in 2014. The brand is called Cadbury Adams.[29] For now.

WHEN SNAPPING AND STRETCHING
MEETS BLOWING AND POPPING

The Fleer brothers have a unique place in gum history. Their story starts when Philadelphia native Frank Fleer, born in 1860, joined and later took over his father-in-law's flavor extracts company in the 1800s.[30] Fleer was in good company; his father-in-law was a Quaker, one of the oldest, most influential groups in candy history. Within five years, Fleer began making chewing gum, some of which he sold in vending machines in the lobbies of buildings just when Adams was installing his machines in New York subway stations.

One of the Fleer company's most impressive accomplishments was created by Frank's brother, Henry. He added a candy coating to pieces of chicle[31] and named the resulting gum "Chiclets." It was a hit—a big hit—and American Chicle could hardly resist. They bought the gum and put Adam's logo on the package.

As part of the deal, the Fleer gum company could make chewing gum, but they could not make it with chicle. Three years before, Frank had experimented with doing something the big three in gum making—Wrigley, the American Chicle Company, and Beech-Nut—had not attempted: make a gum that could blow bubbles. Frank succeeded, using natural rubber latex, and launched the first bubblegum ever, called Blibber-Blubber. Shortly after, the Blibber-Blubber bubble popped. The texture was grainy and broke apart, and the bubbles were hard to blow. Worse, the gum adhered to skin with the ferocity of superglue. In short, the Blibber-Blubber bubble popped and Fleer was left with little to do.

But in 1913, Frank Fleer rose again, this time with the Frank H. Fleer Corporation in Philadelphia. The company made candy and trading cards featuring such celebri-

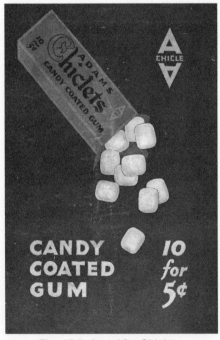

Fig. 17.5. An ad for Chiclets.

ties as Babe Ruth, Gloria Swanson, and Mary Pickford. All the while, the pursuit of bubblegum continued, even after Fleer retired and his son-in-law, Gilbert Mustin, took over the business, but they still didn't have much luck.

During the late 1920s, the company's accountant, twenty-three-year-old Walter Diemer, would sneak into the lab after hours and play around with the bubblegum recipe. He wasn't a cook, chemist, or scientist and didn't aspire to any of these things. What drove him was probably curiosity mixed with a sense of adventure. Numerous batches failed until finally, he got it right. Well, almost right. The gum didn't stick, and he could blow bubbles, but not if he let the gum sit overnight. In 1928, after more fiddling, Diemer figured out a solution. He also added pink dye to the mix, the only coloring he could find in the lab, which is why bubblegum is pink to this day.[32]

Fig. 17.6. Walter Diemer. *Image courtesy of Tootsie Roll Industries.*

Diemer presented his creation to the company, and Mustin dubbed it the deliberately misspelled Dubble Bubble. When they were ready to market the gum, Diemer himself went into shops to teach shopkeepers how to blow bubbles so that they could teach their customers to blow bubbles, and their customers could then teach their kids to blow bubbles, and their kids could teach their kids . . . and an American tradition began.

Dubble Bubble has lived a long and fruitful life ever since, even appearing in the rations of GIs during World War II. It rose above competition from Topps, whose Bazooka gum took off in the 1950s, and from the Bowman Company of Brooklyn New York, an early maker of trading cards, who produced a brand called Baloney. Today, Marvel Entertainment Group produces fifteen million pieces of gum a day.[33]

Frank Fleer died in 1921 and never lived to see his bubblegum succeed. Still, his obituary said he was fit and healthy until the end.[34] Walter Diemer never trademarked his gum recipe, never invented any other new confections, and never left the company. Instead, he became a senior executive and had a career that his wife said, after his death in 1998, was happy.[35]

THE BAKING POWDER SALESMAN

Every parent with a kid who misbehaves, runs away, lacks direction, and is a terrible student, take heart. William Wrigley, who died a millionaire in 1931, started his youth as what could only be described as a truant. If he were alive today, he probably would have been sent to reform school but fortunately for him, the nineteenth century was more forgiving, or indifferent, depending on your view.

Born in 1861, Wrigley was the oldest of nine children whose father was a soap manufacturer. At age eleven, Wrigley ran away from his home in Philadelphia to New York City, where he sold newspapers during the day and slept by the *Tribune* presses at night. He held other equally unsavory jobs until he returned home at age fourteen. Back at school, he was not a calmer, more focused student, as you might imagine. He was expelled numerous times, until his father pulled him out altogether and set him to work stirring soap with a paddle in his factory. Apparently, the difficult job and ten-hour work schedule suited Wrigley, and within a year he was promoted to salesman.

For the next ten years, Wrigley remained in sales, where he learned the greatest lesson of his life and one that ultimately put Wrigley gum on the map: the strategic art of persuasion. In his first job, he learned how to interact convincingly with customers while navigating a horse-drawn wagon weighted with soap throughout the Northeast. When he later moved to Chicago to set up a Western agency for his father, he needed to find a more complex strategy. The problem was that the retail price of the soap was too low for merchants to make a profit, and a higher price would be off-putting to customers.[36] But Wrigley had a plan—one used by John Curtis, the Fleer brothers, and Thomas Adams: premiums.

Wrigley being Wrigley put a twist on the concept. He convinced his father to double the retail price of the soap, then gave vendors premiums—in this case sixty-five thousand umbrellas. Sales went wild. Soon, Wrigley decided to go it alone, and in 1891, opened the William Wrigley Jr. Company where he continued to sell soap. This time, he encouraged customers to buy his soap with premiums of baking powder. The customers liked the baking powder more than the soap, so he sold baking powder, instead. And the premium for the baking powder?

Fig. 17.7. William Wrigley Jr. Image from Wikipedia, user Dogears.

Sticks of spruce resin gum. The spruce gum was more popular than the baking powder, and Wrigley's career in the gum business began.

Initially, Wrigley hired Zeno Manufacturing, the company that produced gum using the paraffin wax John Curtis sold years before. Wrigley convinced them to use chicle instead. The result was the short-lived Vassar and Lotta Gum. In 1893, Wrigley introduced two additional selections: Juicy Fruit and Wrigley's Spearmint. True to their names, the gums really did contain fruit juice and spearmint and were successful enough for Wrigley to cut Vassar and Lotta from production. Wrigley bought out Zeno Manufacturing in 1911.

In 1899, William Wrigley got an invitation from William J. White to join a trust that he and five other companies were forming. The trust, of course, was the American Chicle Company. But Wrigley, who lived life his way, refused the invitation and unwittingly became engaged in an intense competition in an overflowing gum market. In an attempt to stay afloat, and win the shelf space of his retail customers, Wrigley upped the premiums to coffee grinders, cash registers, scales, lamps, and other appliances. When this tried-and-true marketing strategy failed, Wrigley had to find a plan B. And he did. It was called advertising. He moved the company to New York and invested in two large advertising campaigns. Unfortunately they both failed, and Wrigley went broke.

Like American icons Mark Twain and Groucho Marx, William Wrigley has plenty of sayings attributed to him. One of them is: "Whatever the condition of a business, never stop advertising." Another is "Tell 'em quick and tell 'em often." In spite of his initial advertising debacle, Wrigley remained faithful to plan B. He moved back to Chicago, saved up money, borrowed money, and initiated a major campaign during the economic crisis of 1907. By steering the bad economy in his favor, Wrigley purchased $1.5 million of advertising space for a mere $250,000.

That campaign was a wild success. What followed was a career as much about PR and marketing as gum. Wrigley implemented the first national direct-marketing campaign, sending free samples of Wrigley gum to every address listed in US phone books. His reasoning: people with telephones could afford to buy gum. And they did. Next time, he sent samples to seven million households. He built the Wrigley Building on the north side of the Chicago River, which launched

Fig. 17.8. An ad for Wrigley's gum.

Chicago's "Magnificent Mile" and became a centerpiece for newspaper articles and tourist catalogues.[37]

Throughout that time, Wrigley's personality was his own marketing machine, and he achieved the greatest exposure for free. Articles about him regularly appeared in leading newspapers and magazines; he made the cover of Time Magazine in 1929, and his image was posted on the ten-cent stamp in Belize. It didn't hurt that Wrigley was the primary shareholder of the Chicago Cubs and, through purchasing top players, helped the team win the 1929 pennant, or that he bought Catalina Island, which he developed into a major tourist attraction.[38]

Ultimately, Wrigley's identity as a marketer/fortune maker eclipsed any other aspect of his life—it's his enduring legacy and the role that defined him best. While articles about gum makers of the early 1900s, such as Adams, Canning, and Beeman, focused on gum and the making of gum, articles about Wrigley's focused on making money.

Newspapers, magazines, and other venues even spotlighted Wrigley's success with advertising to encourage would-be advertisers to sign up. The *Daily Register* devoted an entire campaign to Wrigley in 1921 in a series of ads whose headline read: "Wrigley's Rules for Results." One of his rules is more like an adage but is still quintessential Wrigley: "Advertising is like running a furnace—you've got to keep shoveling the coal. Once you stop stocking, the fire goes out."[39] Doubtless, the *Daily Register* increased its profits from advertisers.

Wrigley was also the man you went to for business guidance. In one 1916 article in Washington, DC's *Evening Star*, the author states: "The man behind the Spearmint gum, which is one of the best examples of big fortunes created from the little nickel-chasing products, is William Wrigley Jr."[40] He goes on to use Wrigley as an example for all small-business owners striving for success.

During a slump in the economy in 1922, the *Richmond Daily Register* turned to Wrigley in a piece titled, "Wrigley on Prosperity." In it, the chewing gum baron acknowledged that the downturn of 1921 was bad for some people, but was the best year in all of his thirty years of gum manufacturing. And why? The best cure for hard times is to stop talking about hard times and get to work. And how did Wrigley get to work? "We are spending $11,000 a day just to push Wrigley's Chewing Gum," he said.[41]

By 1935, Wrigley's company produced 60 percent of all chewing gum in the United States, while Beech-Nut produced 20 percent and the American Chicle Company, 15 percent. When he died in 1931 at seventy years of age, William

Wrigley, the wild kid and terrible student, was one of the most influential and affluent men in the United States.

William Wrigley's legacy and fortune lives on. When William Wrigley III died in 1999, his estate was worth over $3 billion. William Jr.'s great-grandson, William Wrigley IV, is consistently ranked among the top fifty on the Forbes 400 list of richest Americans. The company, which is now owned by Mars, is the largest gum manufacturer in the world.[42]

WHERE DID ALL THE RESIN GUM GO?

In the mid-1900s, chewing gum changed. Tree resin, which was central to the human chewing experience for at least nine thousand years, was replaced by synthetic rubbers. The reasons, while complex, can be boiled down to trees and money. But before we discuss that monumental shift, let's take a quick behind-the-scenes look at the making of chicle.

CHICLE MAKING: A QUICK INTERLUDE

The production of chicle occurred chiefly in Mexico but also took place in Guatemala and Belize. The workers were called "chicleros," and their lives were like the pickers who harvested spruce resin for John Curtis, only more grueling and intense. Turn-of-the-century newspapers were speckled with articles about these intriguing foreigners, typically depicting them as hardworking men born into a life of servitude. One article explains:

> When our American chewing gum season is at its height, while the people are on summer vacation, the daring chiclero looks toward the jungle. . . . About a hundred cutters compose the chicle expedition. Added to this number are cooks, camp attendants, mules and a hold full of provisions. Then the boat sails away for the cutting, not to return until February.[43]

Another article tells readers that the chicleros "go into the deep forest under experienced leaders, armed with heavy knives of special make with pails and ladles for the sap, and each one is provided with a strong rope, more than eighty feet long to be used in climbing the lofty sapota [sic]tree from which the gum is procured"[44]

The chicleros were divided into groups of "ten or a dozen" then climbed the trees and shimmied back down, cutting a crisscross pattern in the bark as they went. They collected the sap that dripped from the wounds in canvas bags adhered to the tree trunks. Once a week, they boiled the sap in large pots over a fire, stirring constantly, then poured the lava-like substance into molds where it hardened into bricks.

The native Mayas were the most careful and prudent of the chicleros; the itinerant ones were slower and more likely to make mistakes. All knew how to navigate the jungle: how to hunt, find fresh water, and identify caves. They were also default archeologists, who discovered ancient ruins in their search for chicle and later shared their findings as guides for professional archeologists. Most important, though, they knew how to extract sapodilla resin without harming the tree.

The lives of the chicleros depicted by the newspapers only touched on reality. Their camps were violent and dangerous, and many of the chicleros were outcasts, loners running from the law or fleeing from disastrous lives. Others were more settled; some brought their families to accompany them through long months in the jungle. Many encampments had a woman cook who doubled as a whore.

Outside of work, the chicleros had to clean the tools they got from the company, cook the food they bought from the company, wash the clothes they bought from the company, and chop wood to light fires beneath pots they bought from the company. The chicleros weren't "provided with rope" and other supplies as the articles indicated, but had to purchase these items on credit that the company later withdrew from their wages.

Given their expenses, and the chicleros' habit of blowing their pay on drink, many lived in a constant state of debt. Should accidents, bites, dysentery, or disease afflict them, they had no medical care or time off. Eye infections, malaria, cuts, and poisonous lacerations were common. Still, the chicleros were experts at their jobs; it was one of few ways to make a living, and the jungle, even with all its dangers, was their home. They harvested the resin for generations.[45]

AS FOR THE RESIN . . .

So, why did the companies the chicleros ultimately worked for forsake them? From early on, gum makers were concerned about the availability of chicle. An article in the *Wenatchee Daily World* of 1909 leads with: "Dire woe is in store for the American gum chewer." It goes on to quote Franklin Canning, maker of Dentyne and board member of the American Chicle Company, as saying that the trees were over-tapped and were "being destroyed at a rapid rate."[46]

The trees held out, but not indefinitely. The demand for chicle escalated during World War II, in part to satisfy the demands of soldiers abroad, and the forests were quickly being depleted. To protect these resources, Mexico and Guatemala imposed new regulations and added taxes that increased the price of chicle, ultimately making it harder for companies to obtain. Synthetic rubber was increasingly cheaper and more readily available. Besides, no one seemed to notice a difference.

By the 1940s, the days of chicle had essentially ended.[47]

MAKE THAT *ALMOST* ENDED

Today, some small companies, such as Tree-Hugger, Glee Gum, and Mexico's Consorcio Chiclero, are producing chicle-based gum again. They still rely on chicleros to harvest the chicle, but they now pay honest wages and insure that the working conditions are safe.

CHAPTER 18

STILL WRAPPED IN
BAG AND BASKET

One of the beauties of the penny candy store was how you collected your stash. Some candies were unwrapped, and you picked these up with a small scoop, a set of tongs, or, at the beachside shops when no one was looking, your bare hands. Others were individually wrapped. These candies were what got penny candy out of the apothecary and grocers and into mainstream shops. Wrapped and ready, these candies were labeled, sanitary, and above all, self-contained. What better way to end our penny candy search than with a few favorite wrapped selections.

TOOTSIE ROLL: AN ENIGMA WRAPPED IN A MYSTERY
WRAPPED IN CHOCOLATE

The history of the Tootsie Roll began with an Austrian immigrant named Leo Hirshfield. The rumor—actually a published and respected rumor—was that Hirshfield started making his candy in a little shop in Brooklyn, New York. He named his penny candy the "Tootsie Roll" because it was a roll of toffee-like chocolate and his daughter Claire was nicknamed "Tootsie." Later, a larger company, Stern & Staalberg, bought Hirshfield out. Somewhere along the way, Hirshfield hand-wrapped his candy so it was clean, hygienic, and could travel from one store to another without needing to be poured and weighed.[1] Hirshfield, the immigrant candymaker, was the American dream and success story all rolled into one.

That's the story I love, and I'll stick to it.

But the truth is more like this: Leo Hirshfield really was an Austrian immigrant, but he was an inventor at the confectionery company Stern & Staalberg with numerous patents to his name. He worked his way up the company ladder, eventually becoming a vice president. He did invent the Tootsie Roll and likely named it for his daughter, although "Tootsie" had been a term of endearment since the early 1900s[2] as well as a loving name for a young one's foot. As for Hirshfield, after some wrangling with Stern & Staalberg, he either lost or left his job. He attempted to start another, but that, too, failed. The wealthy but defeated inventor went on to shoot himself in a New York hotel.[3]

See why I like the first story better?

Other Tootsie Roll insights: The Tootsie Roll was a heat-safe chocolate that held up well all year round. Among the many candies appearing in the rations of World War II soldiers, it was so durable and dependable, soldiers used "Tootsie Roll" as another name for bullets.[4] Stern & Staalberg later became known as the Sweets Company of America, then Tootsie Roll Industries, which it remains today.

STICKY CANDIES WRAPPED IN WAX PAPER HELD IN A BAG

Caramels are an American invention[5] that emerged from the European caramelized sugar of the seventeenth century.[6] They are the essence of the praline, which

Fig. 18.1. An ad for Tootsie Rolls.

the French brought to Louisiana in the 1760s.[7] The caramel came into its own in the late 1800s, around the time when Hershey started the Lancaster Caramel Company. The *Encyclopedia of Food and Beverages*, published in 1901, gives this definition of caramel: "Sugar and corn syrup cooked to a proper consistence in open stirring kettles, run out in thin sheets on marble slab tables and cut into squares when cooled."[8] That recipe is not an industry standard: Hershey, compliments of his Denver caramel-making employer, knew to substitute milk for paraffin wax.

Either way, caramel played a welcome part in candy where, with nuts, a chocolate coating, or simply solo, it is one of America's favorite candies today.

MILK DUDS BECAUSE IT IS ONE

Milk Duds were invented by the F. Hoffman Company of Chicago in the 1920s and later made by Holloway. This was at a time when marketing was becoming ever more sophisticated, and marketers knew that a product's name meant everything. No more putting the candymaker's name on the label—it worked for Hershey, the Smith Brothers, and Oliver Chase, but times were changing. The name needed zing!

But how do you give zing to a candy you intended to be a perfectly round chocolate-covered caramel ball that sagged and dented? It wasn't a ball. It was a dud. And that's when someone in the company came up with a great idea. *Let's call it "Milk Chocolate Duds!" Too long? OK, then just "Milk Duds!"* It's too bad that person's identity has been lost in the annals of history. It was the first and only time, as far as I know, that a candy was named for its liability.[9]

Another caramel favorite with a spicy name was the Sugar Daddy, invented by Robert Welch, a chocolate salesman for the James Welch Co. The Sugar Daddy was named for the *other* sugar daddy, an older gentleman who obliges a younger woman—his wife, his mistress, or whoever she may be—with all the comforts his fortune can supply. Apparently, *that* sugar daddy originated with one Alma Spreckels. It's the pet name she gave her considerably older husband, heir to the Spreckels's sugar fortune in 1908. Originally, the candy was called the "Papa Sucker."[10] We're all glad they changed it. Can you imagine calling it "Papa Sucker" today? It's almost too embarrassing to talk about.

TOFFEES OR TAFFY OR TURKISH TAFFY?

The Mary Jane was one of the earliest toffees, and its beginnings in Paul Revere's former home is beyond the greatness any toffee can reasonably expect. Still, a rush of other toffees followed, such as the Bit-O-Honey, first made in Chicago in 1924, using honey instead of the standard corn syrup and sugar. It's not clear if the name was influenced by Clarence Crane's increasingly popular Life Saver family with the pronounced "O."

Another old timer is the sassy Squirrel Nut Zipper, which has one of the most perplexing names in candy history. The Squirrel Nut Company, then called the Austin T. Merrill Company, started in 1890 in Boston, Massachusetts. The business soon moved to Cambridge, Massachusetts, where the new owner Mr. Perley G. Gerrish sold his freshly roasted nuts throughout the Boston area by horse and carriage.

The company produced candy as well as nuts and came out with the Squirrel Nut Zipper in 1926. The name "Squirrel Nut," is for the company, obviously. The "Zipper" was an illegal Prohibition-era cocktail.[11] Remember how the temperance crowd claimed candy would lead to alcoholism in kids? Well, the candy companies had their say, putting a humorous twist on the old adage, "If you can't beat them, join them."

Eventually the Squirrel Nut Company's nuts went to south to Antarctica with Admiral Richard Byrd, alongside its stateside neighbor's NECCO Wafer. Also like the wafer, the nuts were also sent out during World War II. A soldier stationed in the Philippines wrote home: "I received a Christmas box with a pack of your peanuts in it. They were the only nuts that arrived without worms."[12]

Today, the company, now called Squirrel Brand and Southern Style Nuts, is based in McKinney, Texas. The Zipper is still in Massachusetts, where it's now made by none other than NECCO.

HEATH TOFFEE LAXATIVE?

In the penny candy store, the toffee found itself in places in-between its naked self and fully dressed in candy bar chocolate. One example is the Heath Toffee Bar, a candy quite different in nature from the other misbehaving Prohibition-era candies we've discussed. The Heath Toffee Bar was started by a school teacher, L. S. Heath, in Illinois. Heath was actually looking for a line of work for his two oldest sons when he found a small confectionery for sale.

In 1914, the shop opened selling ice cream, fountain drinks, and sweets. One thing lead to another, and soon candy salesmen were hanging around Heath's store, talking, as they do, about candy. One of them was raving about another candymaker's toffee recipe. The Heath brothers were intrigued. I bet you know what happened next. They called it Heath Toffee.

In 1931, L. S. Heath quit his job teaching school after twenty years and joined the candy business, as did his two sons. It was the younger generation who thought up a great marketing idea: Why not sell our candies through dairymen who went from house to house with their milk, ice, and cheese? Just add Heath Toffee to the list, and customers will add it to their purchases along with other products. And, of course, they did.[13]

But the Heath Toffee Bar was different from other bars, which initially caused confusion. First, the bar was one ounce, while others were four; this convinced consumers they were buying a penny candy and not a five-cent bar. Second, the design had a large "H" at either end, with the "eat" in small caps in the middle: HeatH. Shoppers thought the name of the company was H&H with the "eat" telling them what to do with it. A third problem was that the packaging, name aside, made it look like the laxative Ex-Lax. Salesmen weren't sure what they were supposed to sell.

The Heath Toffee Bar took off anyway and is made by Hershey today.

THE BOSTON CHEW

Don't be deceived by the title. We really are talking about the Charleston Chew, which is not exactly a taffy and not exactly a toffee, and to be perfectly honest, I'm not exactly sure what it is. But I can tell you this: the Charleston Chew, that dense marshmallow-taffy-toffee substance covered with chocolate is more like the Squirrel Nut Zipper, in spirit anyway, than the Heath Toffee Bar.

It was first made in 1925 and spent most of it life in Boston, which is one Zipper connection, although most people think its name refers to Charleston, South Carolina. I imagine it has a pretty good following there. The other connection is that the Charleston Chew is tied to Prohibition, named for the *dance*, the Charleston, which showed up in movies with flappers dancing merrily in-between sips of the Zipper (quite possibly) and other speakeasy drinks.

While we're discussing theater and dancing, the Fox Cross company that invented the Charleston Chew began when Donley Cross, a Shakespearean actor in San Francisco, fell from the stage, injuring his back and ending his career. The logical next step for Cross was to start a candy company with his friend, Charlie Fox.[14] I know, it doesn't make much sense, but that's candy.

TAFFY DUD

The Turkish Taffy was another flop that rose in stature to become a pop-culture favorite and, after a brief hiatus, remains so today. I remember eating it as a kid and feeling the sticky sweetness warm my mouth.

Bonomo Turkish Taffy was not made by a Turkish candymaker but by Austrian immigrant Herman Herer in 1912. At the time, he was trying to create a marshmallow candy for M. Schwarz & Sons of Newark and added too many egg whites. The candy was a dud. But it got Herer thinking. He experimented with the recipe, then sold his business to M. Schwarz & Sons who hired Herer back. Herer kept experimenting and finally succeeded in making the only flat taffy in the world. Its name was Turkish Taffy.

In nearby Coney Island, the Bonomo family was looking for something new to do. Albert, who really was Turkish and had immigrated to the United States in 1892, started his career selling candy from a pushcart in Coney Island. He then owned an ice cream company, where he sold ice cream from a horse-drawn covered wagon. Eventually he opened a candy and ice cream factory on the first floor of his house, living on the second floor and housing about thirty workers on the third floor.

In 1919, Bonomo's two sons, Vic, who had just returned from World War I, and Joe, a bodybuilder and football player, joined the business. In 1936, Bonomo bought M. Schwarz & Sons and with it the Turkish Taffy, making the taffy truly Turkish. Eventually the brothers took over and ran the company until Joe left to pursue a career in Hollywood as an actor, stuntman, strongman, and health writer. Vic then ran the company on his own.[15]

The Turkish Taffy remained a mainstay of American confections, thanks in part, to its signature tag line "Crack it up," and instructions on the packaging: "Crack It Up!—Hold Bar in Palm of Hand—Strike against Flat Surface—Let It Melt in Your Mouth." Tootsie Roll eventually bought the candy and ran it into the ground. But only temporarily. The Turkish Taffy is back, now owned by a company called Bonomo. There is no relation between the company and the Bonomo family, but the taffy still tastes good.

SOFT STUFF AND PIXY STIX SWITCH
AND BANANA-FLAVORED PEANUTS

Another centerpiece of the candy store was the wild flavors, colors, and textures that promised kids a culinary (of sorts) experience. The endurance of these sprightly selections has much to do with their flexibility, sometimes shifting purpose as well as packaging and taste. One example is Pixy Stix, the paper straws filled with sugar so powdery and light it practically vanishes when eaten.

Originally a drink flavoring, much like Kool-Aid, the sugar powder was made in the 1930s and called "Frutola." But when inventor J. Fish Smith found that kids preferred eating it, he turned it into an eating candy, which he sold with a spoon. In the 1950s, Sunline Inc. made it the fun-lover's candy it is today. Outside of its straw-like wrapper, it would just be another tasty but highly processed sugar. But who cares?[16]

Fig. 18.2. Circus peanuts.

Another candy that is perplexing in flavor, texture, and history are the much loved (and loathed) Circus Peanut. This curious candy originated in the 1800s. It was quite possibly for sale at travelling circuses but was also found in candy stores, general stores, and other places where penny candy was sold. The texture is soft as a sponge, spongy as a marshmallow, and flavored like a banana. The circus peanut was never what you'd call prestigious and various versions entered the candy arena for decades. One in particular is a surprise.[17]

AS FOR THAT SURPRISE

In 1963, General Mills used the circus peanut as a prototype for the charms in Lucky Charms. Today, knockoff Charms are cropping up at candy stores every-where, minus the flakes. As you may remember, I sampled a few on my way back from Wilbur's. Very satisfying in a lighthearted way.

CHICKEN BONES TO CHICK-O-STICK

Is Chick-O-Stick another Life Saver rip off with the "O" at its center? If so, that's about all the two sweets have in common aside from their presence in candy stores. The orange- and coconut-speckled Chick-O-Stick began its life in Canada, known as Chicken Bones. It was invented by Frank Sparhawk, an employee of brothers James and Gilbert W. Ganong, who opened their shop in 1873. The candy was a cinnamon-flavored candy shell filled with bittersweet chocolate, that looked like chicken bones. The Ganong's company is still operating today and is still family owned.[18]

So successful were Chicken Bones that they spread south, all the way to Texas, where another family-owned business, Atkinson Candy Company, apparently found them. The Atkinson Candy Company began in 1932 after Basil Atkinson was laid off from his job at a foundry. He borrowed a truck, dug up some cash, and loaded his wife and sons into the cab for the two-day drive to Houston. There he loaded up on candy and tobacco. He began selling these items to small shops, eventually setting up a wholesale distribution center.

Eventually, Basil realized he could make candy just as well, make that *better*, than the other guys. With help from his wife, he got to work. In the late 1930s, he came up with a candy that looked like Southern-fried chicken bones (and the

Chicken Bones candy that already existed). Basil decided he should name them "Chicken Bones," but Ganong decided he shouldn't. Atkinson renamed his candy Chick-O-Stick, with the Life Saver-esque "O" in the middle. It was a southern favorite for years and is nationally known today.

PERSONAL PERSPECTIVE: WILMA GREEN, CHICK-O-STICK IN CHICAGO

Wilma Green is an artist whose life could be her own portrait. She is an activist, a community organizer, a mother, a teacher, and a friend. This is her candy story.[19]

When I was a kid, my mother would send my twin brother, William, and me to Star Foods Grocery with empty RC Cola bottles and some money. We'd exchange the bottles for more RC for her and two Chick-O-Stick; one for her and one for my brother and me to share. They had to be Chick-O-Stick. She loved Chick-O-Stick. I don't know if it was her background coming from the South, but she did.

That was in the '60s in Chicago. We lived in the largest public housing development in the world—the Robert Taylor housing project. People had migrated from the South during the Depression and built these communities over the years. It was a black metropolis. We did everything there—went to school, saw the doctor. Everyone who went to the Star Foods Grocery knew the owners and everyone got credit. Some people say it was segregation, but I don't know. I always felt good. . . . I always knew everyone was watching out for me there.

My mom was raising ten kids on her own since my father had died. My brother and I were the youngest. The three oldest were in Arkansas picking cotton with my grandparents. All of us went there in the summer to help out, but my brother and I were too young to pick. It was because of that work my grandparents were able to buy their own house.

During WWII, when my mom was a teenager, she had the opportunity to work at a plant that made parts for bombs like Rosie the Riveter. She paid someone else to pick the cotton; the owners didn't mind because they didn't know the people who worked there—just the number of hands. They weren't really people to them. Eventually she worked at an electronics company that was right next to a candy company. She would go there and get the second-rate candy, you know like broken pieces of chocolate, which she'd also give to us. My brother and I would sell it to other kids and get the good stuff for ourselves, like Now and Laters.

But, as I said, once a week, my brother and I would take the RC bottles and get more RC for my mother and Chick-O-Stick for all of us. I think the candy originated in the south—it was probably a piece of her memory. It's amazing how candies bring up memories.

It's nice to revisit those memories. I really love that.

AND, AT LAST, THE LOLLIPOP

No one knows when people started enjoying lollipops, although Charles Dickens wrote about hard candy on a stick in the 1800s. In the United States, around the time of the Civil War, people started sticking pencils into hard candies to eat them. At home, people basically dropped a mound of hard candy onto parchment or wax paper, stuck in a stick, let it dry, and then enjoyed the treat. But commercially not a lot was going on.[20]

Then, in 1895, Chicken Bones owners Gilbert and James Ganong began inserting sharp wooden sticks into their hard candy, creating one of the first commercial lollipops in the northern hemisphere. They called it an "all day sucker."[21] That changed in 1908 when the Bradley Smith Company starting manufacturing the "Lolly Pop," which was named after George Smith's favorite racehorse. Their inspiration was a chocolate-caramel taffy on a stick, made by Reynolds Taffy of West Haven, Connecticut, that resembled the Sugar Daddy.

George Smith attempted to get ownership of the name "Lolly Pop," but the US Patent Office turned him down, as the term was listed in an English dictionary of the early 1800s, spelled "lollipop." There it was described as "a hard sweetmeat sometimes on a stick." Eventually, Smith got the rights to "Lolly Pop" with that specific spelling, but it was negligible. People began using both names interchangeably and have ever since.[22]

By the 1920s, numerous lollipops seemed to appear in penny candy stores and other places. There was the Dum Dum, made in 1924 by the by the Akron Candy Company, which evidently knew the marketing potential of a name; the company's salesman named the lollipop "Dum Dum," thinking kids could easily remember it and ask their parents to buy some. Obviously, he was right. The Tootsie Pop, essentially a panned Tootsie Roll, came around 1931, and, in the 1940s, after parents expressed concern that kids would choke on the stick, the Saf-T-Pop, with a round holder, was released.[23]

CHAPTER 19

CANDY BOWLS AND
ICE CREAM TRUCKS

After Irving's, I made a quick stop at my parents' house to interview both of them before heading home. Dan, Moses and I stayed a short time, but I got what I went for . . . although it was not what I wanted.

SUMMARY OF AN INTERVIEW WITH MY FATHER, A CANDY LOVER

My father seemed distracted and quiet, not depressed exactly, but distant. Things weren't good. When I asked what candy my nana enjoyed, he said he didn't remember her eating any. She liked pies and cakes, but he didn't remember candy. He didn't even remember the candy bowls in her house. There were soap dishes and ashtrays that she had made in arts-and-crafts class, but candy dishes? No. When I asked what candy he liked, my father thought for a moment then said that he never cared for candy. He liked cakes and pies, too.

ABOUT THOSE CANDY BOWLS

Candy bowls were different from penny candy stores, chocolate stores, drugs stores, and five-and-dimes. They were in a class all their own. They represented affluence and abundance. They were *classy*. Their stature was all about the Depression-era generation who remembered when sugar was expensive or rare. As for the sparkling gems that filled the hollowed interior—Jordan Almonds, fruit slices, candy ribbon, art candy, Hershey kisses, bridge mix—they were available without ceremony or fee, especially enchanting to the younger generations who were lucky enough to enjoy them. Above all, the bowls (and their contents) were about love.

Fig. 19.1. A classic candy dish.

Today, kids have no memory of the candy bowl, but some grandmother, aunt, great–aunt, or *someone* should restart the trend. It will give the kids something spectacular to remember in adulthood.

INTERVIEW WITH A CANDY HATER

I interviewed my mother at her kitchen table. What she said is this:[1]

Nana always loved candy and always was fat. I tried keep you kids away from candy because it has no nutritional value, is bad for your teeth, and adds weight. So why eat it? It has no value. I tried to keep you kids away from eating candy and from sugared cereal.

Nana tried to get you to eat candy, I don't know if you really liked it, but she did it just to spite me. She would take you behind the house when I wasn't looking and give you candy. It made me so angry. She visited homes for the elderly and volunteered even though she was elderly herself. And what did she bring them? She brought them candy. I thought that was pretty bad. They don't have a good diet in those places. Bring them fruit or something.

I know Grandma [her mother] ate candy, but that was different. They were sour balls and Life Savers. I don't consider Life Savers or sour balls or any of those candies Grandma ate candy. They were in a different class. They're for bad breath or a dry mouth. If you want a little something at a movie you would have Life Savers. They weren't really candy, like chocolate. They were in a different class altogether.

We also liked that sugar, the rock sugar on a stick, which old people stirred their tea with. They used to have a sugar cube, and the elderly people would put it between their teeth and sip their tea. That would flavor the tea. It wasn't as though you were eating candy.

Didn't I like any candies? Well, occasionally there was a candy bar called Little Nick or something like that. I liked that. And I liked bubblegum, too. I used to go to Irving's and get bubblegum. That's just as bad. We liked to chew it. We'd blow bubbles. My dentist told me it was ruining my teeth.

Candy—that was an addiction. You just took it because you had to. Like Nana. It was all over her house. I was always a health food person, I guess.

QUICK ANALYSIS OF THE INTERVIEW

Opinions like my mother's—that candy is addictive, valueless, and so on—have bubbled up throughout our nation's history. Oddly, my mother is the one who introduced me to S'mores at a family outing. While not exactly a candy, the S'more, which first appeared in 1927, was the Girl Scouts' version of the new and very popular candy bar, with its marshmallow and chocolate center.[2]

WHAT HAPPENED NEXT

A few weeks after the visit to my parents' house, I called to speak with my father. My mother said he was in the hospital for reasons relating to dementia. When I spoke to my father, I asked if I could send him anything from the shop. He seemed to perk up. He thought a moment and said "fudge."

I felt immensely relieved about that. I can't say why, but I did.

At the time of this writing, his spirits are up.

PERSONAL PERSPECTIVE: HOWARD NACHAMIE, FORMER GOOD HUMOR MAN WITH AN INDIRECT BONOMO CONNECTION

Sweets were available in plenty other out-of-shop places besides the candy bowl. The most beloved was the ice cream truck. Not only was the ice cream good, but these trucks also carried such extras as candy cigarettes and Life Savers. When I called Howie for an interview, I hadn't talked to him since our dinner in New York.[3]

In the '20s, my maternal grandmother owned the Yale Hotel on Coney Island. It was a peak destination back in the day. They had fireworks and the Mermaid Parade where my mom was a beauty-pageant queen. The men would show off their physics and exercise on the beach.

I remember being there a long time after she died; it was on a dirt road with a goat in the yard. One of the boarders at my grandmother's hotel was Albert Bonomo. He would experiment with candy, chocolate, nuts, and frozen chocolate-covered bananas in the kitchen. He'd sell those bananas on the beach.

My father was a pharmacist. He had a couple of pharmacies; one was on Staten Island. I used to go with him on the ferry and hang out at the store. He had a vast array of candy. I would get Sky Bars, Zagnuts, so many candy bars. He also had a lunch counter, with a woman who made burgers and fries, and a fountain. My father would make me malted milk. I can hear the old, green machine purring now.

When I got older, I'd shoot pool or hang out with the girls, and on the way home, I'd get an egg cream and a straight pretzel. Most of the candy stores were owned by Jewish immigrants with [Holocaust] tattoos on their arms. They had newsstands next to subway stops.

In Brooklyn, where I was growing up, an ice cream man would come by selling Bungalow bars. Good Humor was a rival. Once the two were on the same street and had a yelling match. When I was in college, I started working for Good Humor. I drove in an open Good Humor truck. You'd load up the night before with whatever you wanted, chocolate éclair with toasted almonds, ices, Dixie Cups they called Good Humor Cups that had movie stars on the lids. We had bells that we would ring-ding-ding-ding, and I would yell "Ice Cream!" The kids would wave like they would for a taxi. Their parents would come out, too.

THE ICE CREAM MAN!

While the colonists ate ice cream early on, mobile ice cream didn't appear for a few hundred years with down-on-their-luck immigrants searching for ways to make money. The result was the pushcart, weighted with ice and frozen treats.[4]

But the real ice-cream-truck breakthrough came in 1920 with Harry Burt, a candymaker from Youngstown, Ohio. Harry was experimenting by coating a slab of vanilla ice cream with chocolate. His daughter Ruth reached for the treat and . . . what a mess! Harry, being entrepreneurial, seized the moment and inserted a lollipop stick in the middle so she could eat it, neat and clean. He called the result "Good Humor Ice Cream Suckers." "Humor" referred to the old-world belief that the humors were responsible for health. For three years, Harry waited for word of his patent application, but none was forthcoming. So he headed for Washington, DC, with a five-gallon pail full of ice cream bars that he handed out to patent officers. The patent was approved.[5]

Soon, Harry started selling his ice cream on a spotlessly white truck,[6] reassuring to a public concerned with the purity of their food. The truck's bells were from the family bobsled. Harry added more trucks, whose drivers bowed to women and saluted men. One truck led to another, and soon the Good Humor Man, with his white uniform and white truck, became an American icon, a confectionery white knight appearing in comics and children's books and on radio shows.[7]

But Good Humor did encounter some bad-humored men. In 1929, when Good Humor opened a plant in Chicago, the mob demanded $5,000 in protection money, the equivalent of $70,000 today. In true Good Humor spirit, Harry refused, and the mob destroyed part of his fleet.[8]

But the Good Humor Man prevailed and is still around today. Good Humor-Breyers is one of the largest branded ice cream producers in the nation.[9]

PERSONAL PERSPECTIVE:
THE AUTHOR'S ICE CREAM MAN MEMORIES

I was never happy growing up on Valley Hill Drive. It was a characterless street with 1950s ranch houses. I was sick a good deal of the time, and I was a terrible student, often bullied at school. One memory stands out now, fifty years later, of a summer evening when I was in my room, already in my pajamas. My father suddenly appeared in the doorway. "I just heard the ice cream man . . . you want something?"

I shouted my order, a Creamsicle, and hurried after him down the carpeted stairs. By the time he reached the street, the ice cream truck was several houses up, with no one there to stop it. So my father ran, waving his arms and calling out- I don't remember ever seeing him run before. I stood on the front steps, watching as he ran and shouted, and then it happened: the truck stopped and after a brief, delicious moment, my father came back, victorious, Creamsicle in hand.

AFTERWORD

It's been three months since I finished this book; since then, much has happened. Dabney Chapman, who I interviewed about his mother's toffee and his father's family's rock candy, died. Bob Tuck's wife of fifty-four years also passed away. My husband, Dan, left to spend a year in a war-torn part of Afghanistan, something neither of us quite expected. As for my father: he's now in an assisted living facility. My mother rarely visits him.

Shortly after I completed the text, my editor, Steven Mitchell, suggested I write some kind of conclusion about where candy is today. He was right—I did need a conclusion. After considering the message for several weeks, here's what I have to say: Today's candy is cheaper than it was before, largely mass-produced, and void of cultural meaning. The flavors are largely concocted in a lab, as are the textures and colors. Marketers play a bigger part in candy making than ever before, and visionary candymakers—like John Curtis and Mary Spencer—are hard to find.

But it's important to remember that plenty of candies are still made in small stores, and all sweets, from the mega-sized gummies to the super-sour hard candies, share a remarkable, uniquely American history. Besides, so many of those who have passed, those who survive, and those who go on to do brave things, have held candy at some central place, a truly dear and love-filled place, in their lives. Love it, hate it, or consider it deliciously sweet as sin, candy occupies that place in most of us today.

ACKNOWLEDGMENTS

I have so many wonderful people to thank for helping me write this book. Most important, is my husband, Dan, who has been supportive on every front. He tended to my candy business so I could stay home writing, and he cooked and cleaned, brought coffee to my desk, and was always ready with love and laughs. You were right . . . I am still a writer. And you helped me have the chance.

Then there's my agent, Grace Freedson, who convinced me that after writing nine books, a tenth was in order. It's been years for us, and I owe you many thanks.

I'm also so appreciative of my neighbor and friend Karen McMullen, who checked in, gave help whenever I needed it, and came up with ideas and glasses of wine—as always, a mensch! And Michael Spencer, who has taught me much about plants, history, and legacy, and further helped with insights and books.

Television director Tucia Lyman was amazingly supportive of this book, even while coping with my acting. She and her crew were wonderful. The show must go on and it did. Big thanks to the folks at Four Seasons Books for finding impossible-to-find books for my research on a truly impossible timetable. And to the wonderful David Klein—thanks for your story, your ongoing interest, and above all, for inventing the Jelly Belly!

And speaking of stories, big thanks to those who shared their stories with me for this book: David Rawls, Dabney Chapman, Wilma Green, Timothy Keady, Paul Palmer, John Gunther, Shelli Dronsfield, Bob Burkinshaw, John Gibbs, sisters Dorothy Van Steinburg and Chris Houck, Bob Tuck, Ethel Weiss, Howard Nachamie, and Edith Elizabeth Lowe Higdon and her granddaughter, Michelle Robinson, who arranged the interview. Many thanks also to Lois Nachamie for her wonderful encouragement, and to Leni Sorenson, whose insights were so helpful. Also, thanks to my brother, Mark Benjamin; my father, Richard; and my mother, who agreed to an interview.

Finally, thanks to Steven L. Mitchell, my editor, and the folks at Prometheus for giving me the opportunity to write this book. Last, and hardly least, Jan Hafer, Donna McAleese, and the others in my sign language group; we did it! We came up with a title, finger spelling and all.

NOTES

CHAPTER 2: SWEET AT THE START

1. Daphne Derven, "Native American," in *The Oxford Companion to Sugar and Sweets*, ed. Darra Goldstein (New York: Oxford University Press, 2015), p. 469.

2. "Century Plant, Maguey, Flowering Aloe, Spiked Aloe, American Aloe," Texas A&M University, http://aggie-horticulture.tamu.edu/ornamentals/nativeshrubs/agaveamer.htm (accessed August 21, 2015).

3. Derven, Oxford Companion to Sugar and Sweets, pp. 469–70.

4. "Bahidaj: Saguaro Cactus Fruit," TOCA: Tohono O'odham Community Action, http://www.tocaonline.org/bahidaj.html (accessed August 18, 2015).

5. Jim Griffith, "Big Jim: More on Saguaro Fruit Harvesting," *Arizona Daily Star*, June 11, 2013, http://tucson.com/news/blogs/big-jim/big-jim-more-on-saguaro-fruit -harvesting/article_4fca769e-ca63-11e2-92e2-001a4bcf887a.html (accessed August 18, 2015).

6. Peter Hull, *Glucose Syrups: Technology and Application* (Hoboken, NJ: Wiley-Blackwell, 2010), p. 2.

7. Ibid., pp. 3–4.

8. Andrew F. Smith, *Sugar: A Global History* (Chicago: University of Chicago Press, 2015), p. 188.

9. Deborah Jean Warner, *Sweet Stuff: An American History of Sweeteners from Sugar to Sucralose* (Washington, DC: Smithsonian Institution Scholarly Press, 2011), p. 119.

10. Melody Krauss, "Maple Sugaring: Native American Lore and History," Master Gardeners, http://www.emmitsburg.net/gardens/articles/adams/2010/maple_sugaring.htm (accessed August 18, 2015).

11. James Smith and William McCullough Darlington, An Account of the Remarkable Occurrences in the Life and Times of Colonel John Smith (Now a Citizen of Bourbon County, Kentucky) During His Captivity with the Indians in the Years 1755, '56, '57, '58 and '59 (Cincinnati, OH: Robert Clarke, 1907), p. 69.

12. Autumn Arthur, "Maple Syrup Madness," Emmitsburg News-Journal, February 8, 2015, http://www.emmitsburg.net/archive_list/articles/ce/fairfield/2015/maple_suger.htm (accessed August 18, 2015).

13. Mary Holz-Clause, "Maple Sugar Profile," Agricultural Marketing Research Center, March 2014, http://www.agmrc.org/commodities__products/specialty_crops/maple-sugar-profile/ (accessed August 18, 2015).

14. Jason Stover, employee at Native American Natural Foods, in a discussion with the author, August 24, 2015.

CHAPTER 3: SUGAR FROM FRUIT AND FRUIT FROM FRUIT

1. "Massachusetts," Ocean Spray, http://www.oceanspray.coop/Our-Cooperative/Locations/Grower-Regions-and-Stations/Cranberries/Massachusetts.aspx (accessed August 20, 2015).

2. "Cranberry History," Ocean Spray, http://www.oceanspray.com/Who-We-Are/Heritage/Cranberry-History.aspx (accessed August 20, 2015).

3. "History of Cranberries," Cape Cod Cranberry Growers Association, http://www.cranberries.org/cranberries/history.html (accessed August 20, 2015).

4. "Our Commitment to Your Health," Ocean Spray, http://www.cranberryhealth.com/The-Cranberry/ (accessed August 20, 2015).

5. Julia Sexton, "Thanksgiving, the Civil War, and Cranberry Sauce," *Westchester*, November 2010, http://www.westchestermagazine.com/Westchester-Magazine/November-2010/Thanksgiving-The-Civil-War-And-Cranberry-Sauce/ (accessed August 20, 2015).

6. "Cranberry History."

7. U. P. Hedrick, ed., *Sturtevant's Notes on Edible Plants* (Albany, NY: J. B. Lyon, 1919), p. 402.

8. "Welcome to Historic Whitesbog Village," Whitesbog Village, http://www.whitesbog.org/ (accessed August 21, 2015).

9. Ginny Knackmuhs, "The Blueberry: Born & Bred in New Jersey," *Garden State Legacy* 5 (September 2009): 6, http://gardenstatelegacy.com/files/The_Blueberry_Born_Bred_in_NJ_Knackmuhs_GSL5.pdf (accessed August 21, 2015).

10. United States Department of Agriculture, "Systems for Marketing Farm Products and the Demand for Such Products at Trade Centers," George K. Holmes, Report no. 98 (Washington, DC: US Government Printing Office, 1913), p. 233.

11. "Elizabeth C. White," Whitesbog Village, http://www.whitesbog.org/whitesbog-history/elizabeth-c-white/ (accessed August 21, 2015).

12. Ad in the *Evening World*, October 9, 1922 (New York, N.Y.), p. 11.

13. "Ten Ways to Eat More Cranberries," American Cranberry Exchange, MSU Libraries, http://archive.lib.msu.edu/DMC/sliker/msuspcsbs_eatm_americacr1/msuspcsbs_eatm_americacr1.pdf (accessed August 20, 2015).

14. "1 - 2 of 2 Search Results for cranberry products," Jelly Belly, http://www.jellybelly.com/search?query=cranberry (accessed August 21, 2015).

15. Image of Ice Chips product by Vitamin Life, http://www.vitaminlife.com/common/images/products/large/72167-20130723.jpg (accessed August 21, 2015).

16. "Real Cranberries Dipped in Silky Smooth Dove Dark Chocolate Stand Up Pouch," Dove Chocolate, http://www.dovechocolate.com/Product/detail?p_id=57 (accessed August 20, 2015).

17. "Fruit & Nut Clusters," Kind, http://www.kindsnacks.com/store/types/healthy-grains-clusters/fruit-nut-clusters.html (accessed August 24, 2015).

18. "History of Blueberries," US Highbush Blueberry Council, http://www.blueberrycouncil.org/about-blueberries/history-of-blueberries/ (accessed August 20, 2015).

19. Kenneth F. Kiple and Kriemhild Coneè Ornelas, eds., *The Cambridge World History of Food*, vol. 2 (Cambridge: Cambridge University Press, 2000), p. 1734.

20. "The Origin of Blueberries," Food History, June 3, 2011, http://www.world-foodhistory.com/2011/06/origin-of-blueberries.html (accessed August 21, 2015).

21. Author interview with Joel, June 2, 2015.

22. Author interview with Mark Benjamin, June 7, 2015.

23. Frederick V. Colville, *Experiments in Blueberry Culture* (Washington, DC: US Government Printing Office, 1910), p. 11.

24. Ibid., p. 24.

25. Ibid., p. 14.

26. Arlene Voski Avakian and Barbara Haber, eds., *From Betty Crocker to Feminist Food Studies: Critical Perspectives on Women and Food* (Amherst: University of Massachusetts Press, 2005), pp. 32–33.

27. "Blueberry Season," Kitchen Clinic, *Ames Daily Tribune*, June 28, 1938, p. 6.

28. "Elizabeth C. White."

29. Ibid.

30. "Blueberry Cultivation," Whitesbog Village, http://www.whitesbog.org/whitesbog-history/blueberry-cultivation/ (accessed August 21, 2015).

31. Knackmuhs, "Blueberry," p. 3.

32. "Elizabeth C. White."

33. Knackmuhs, "Blueberry," p. 4.

34. Ibid., p. 5.

35. Anthony J. Cichoke, *Secrets of Native American Herbal Remedies* (New York: Penguin, 2001), p. 74.

36. Peter J. Hatch, "Strawberries: Arcadian Dainties with a True Paradisiacal Flavor," *Twinleaf Journal Online* (1997), https://www.monticello.org/site/house-and-gardens/strawberries-arcadian-dainties-true-paradisiacal-flavor (accessed August 21, 2015).

37. George M. Darrow, *The Strawberry: History, Breeding and Physiology* (New York: Holt, Rinehart and Winston, 1966), p. 23.

38. Ibid., p. 22.

39. Ibid., p. 28.

40. Ibid., p. 35.

41. Ibid.

42. Hatch, "Strawberries."

43. Darrow, *Strawberry*, pp. 27–28.

44. S. W. Fletcher, *The Strawberry in North America* (New York: Macmillan, 1917), pp. 16–17.

45. Ibid.

46. B. June Hutchinson, "A Taste for Horticulture," *Arnoldia 40*, no. 1 (January 1980): 31–35.

47. Ibid.

48. Fletcher, Strawberry in North America, pp. 23–25.

49. Ibid.

50. Ibid.

CHAPTER 4: ROOTS, BARK, AND BEANS

1. Dave Fuller, "Remembering Spruce Gum," *Northern Woodlands*, Autumn 2011, p. 16, http://northernwoodlands.org/knots_and_bolts/remembering-spruce-gum (accessed August 20, 2015).

2. Leela Ramaswamy, "Yum, It's Chewing Gum!," *Deccan Herald*, October 21, 2011, http://www.deccanherald.com/content/199431/yum-its-chewing-gum.html (accessed August 20, 2015).

3. Scott Conroy, "Ancient Chewing Gum Found in Finland," CBS News, August 21, 2007, http://www.cbsnews.com/news/ancient-chewing-gum-found-in-finland/ (accessed August 20, 2015).

4. Dioscorides, *De Materia Medica: Being an Herbal with Many other Medicinal Materials*, trans. Tess Anne Osbaldeston (Johannesburg: Ibidis, 2000), p. 4.

5. "Mastic Candy," Anemos, http://www.e-anemos.gr/contents/en-us/d7_Mastic _candy_mastiha_karameles_mastixa_bon_bon.html (accessed October 29, 2015).

6. Farhad U. Huwez et al., "Mastic Gum Kills *Helicobacter Pylori*," *New England Journal of Medicine* 339, no. 26 *(December 24, 1998): 1946;* "Student Dig Unearths Ancient Gum," BBC News, August 20, 2007, http://news.bbc.co.uk/2/hi/uk/6954562. stm (accessed August 20, 2015); José Roberto de Magalhães Bastos et al., "Utilization of Xylitol as a Preventive Substance in Dentistry," *Brazilian Journal of Oral Sciences* 4, no. 15 (October–December 2005): 891–93.

7. Charles Bancroft Gillespie, *Portland Past and Present* (Portland, ME: Evening Express, 1899), p. 218.

8. George Thomas Little, ed., *Genealogical and Family History of the State of Maine* (New York: D. Lewis Historical, 1909), http://dunhamwilcox.net/me/me_bio_abbott.htm (accessed August 24, 2015).

9. Laura Rice, "Let's Eat: Adirondack Spruce Gum," Adirondack Almanack, May 25, 2010, http://www.adirondackalmanack.com/2010/05/lets-eat-adirondack-spruce-gum.html (accessed August 20, 2015).

10. Fuller, "Remembering Spruce Gum," p. 16.

11. Little, Genealogical and Family History.

12. Ibid.

13. Ibid.

14. "Life Savers: 'A Hole Lot of Fun,'" Wrigley, http://www.wrigley.com/global/brands/life-savers.aspx (accessed August 20, 2015).

15. "Plant Guide: Sassafras *Sassafras albidum* (Nutt.) Nees," United States Department of Agriculture Natural Resources Conservation Service, http://plants.usda.gov/plantguide/pdf/cs_saal5.pdf (accessed August 20, 2015).

16. Jason Wilson, "A Liqueur Named Root," *Washington Post*, June 1, 2011, http://www.washingtonpost.com/lifestyle/food/a-liqueur-named-root/2011/05/25/AGwDsaFH_story.html (accessed August 20, 2015).

17. "Root Beer," Food Timeline, http://www.foodtimeline.org/foodbeverages.html#rootbeer (accessed August 20, 2015).

18. David Schmidt, "Hires and the Root of Root Beer," Lower Merion Historical Society, http://www.lowermerionhistory.org/texts/schmidtd/hires.html (accessed August 20, 2015).

19. Charles E. Hires, "Seeing Opportunities," *American Druggist and Pharmaceutical Record* 61 (October 1913): 27–28; "Sarsaparilla," rootbeerbarrels.com, www.rootbeerbarrels.com/sarsaparilla.html (accessed August 24, 2015).

20. Ad in *New York Times*, June 21, 1888, p. 6.

21. Ibid.

22. Merry Citarella, "The History of Root Beer," Jaquo, http://jaquo.com/the-history-of-root-beer/ (accessed August 15, 2015).

23. Ad in New York Times.

24. "Choose Cold Soda Specialties Now," *American Druggist and Pharmaceutical Record* 63 (January–December 1915): 164.

25. Ibid.

26. "Charles E. Hires" Cook's Info, http://www.cooksinfo.com/charles-hires (accessed August 20, 2015).

27. Ad in *Alton Evening Telegraph*, February 18, 1932, p. 10.

28. "History," A&W, http://www.rootbeer.com/history/ (accessed August 20, 2015).

29. Nate Barksdale, "Fries with That? A Brief History of Drive-Thru Dining," May 16, 2014, http://www.history.com/news/hungry-history/fries-with-that-a-brief-history -of-drive-thru-dining (accessed August 20, 2015).

30. "History."

31. E. Sortomme, "The History of Root Beer," gourmetrootbeer.com, http://www .gourmetrootbeer.com/history.html (accessed August 20, 2015).

32. "History."

33. "The History of Dad's Root Beer," Dad's Old Fashioned Root Beer, http://www .dadsrootbeer.com/dads/dads.nsf/vwcontent/History (accessed August 20, 2015).

34. Ad in *Decatur Daily Review*, May 20, 1953, p. 5.

35. Ad in *Lincoln Evening Journal*, May 10, 1954, p. 3.

36. "The History of Dad's Root Beer."

37. "Baked Navy Bean," State Symbols USA, http://www.statesymbolsusa.org/ symbol-official-item/massachusetts/state-food-agriculture-symbol/baked-navy-bean (accessed August 15, 2015).

38. "All About Candy," National Confectioners Association, http://www.candyusa .com/allaboutcandy (accessed August 20, 2015).

CHAPTER 5: ALL THE FOOD IN THE WORLD

1. Claire Shaver Haughton, *Green Immigrants: The Plants That Transformed America* (New York: Harcourt, Brace, Jovanovich, 1978), pp. 253–55.

2. Ibid.

3. Kenneth F. Kiple and Kriemhild Coneè Ornelas, *Cambridge World History of Food*, vol. 2 (Cambridge: Cambridge University Press, 2001), p. 1830.

4. Eliza Leslie, *Directions for Cookery in Its Various Branches*, 10th ed. (Philadelphia: E. L. Carey and A. Hart, 1840), pp. 244–48.

5. *Martha Washington's Booke of Cookery and Booke of Sweetmeats*, transcribed by Karen Hess (New York: Columbia University Press, 1981), p. 284.

6. Haughton, *Green Immigrants*, pp. 241–44.

7. John F. Mariani, *The Encyclopedia of American Food & Drink* (New York: Lebhar-Friedman, 1999), pp. 223–24.

8. "Beeman, Edwin E.," Encyclopedia of Cleveland History, July 10, 1997, http:// ech.case.edu/cgi/article.pl?id=BEE (accessed: August 21, 2015).

9. Haughton, *Green Immigrants*, pp. 341–46.

10. Alan Davidson, *The Oxford Companion to Food* (New York: Oxford University Press, 1999), p. 673.

11. Jane Levi, "Nougat," in *The Oxford Companion to Sugar and Sweets*, ed. Darra Goldstein (New York: Oxford University Press, 2015), p. 486.

12. Andrea Rocco, "Candied Flowers," in *The Oxford Companion to Sugar and Sweets*, ed. Darra Goldstein (New York: Oxford University Press, 2015), p. 100.

13. *Martha Washington's Booke of Cookery and Booke of Sweetmeats*, transcribed by Karen Hess (New York: Columbia University Press, 1981), p. 434.

14. Rufus Estes, *Rufus Estes' Good Things to Eat: The First Cookbook by an African-American Chef* (Chicago: printed by author, 1911; reprinted, Mineola, NY: Dover, 2004), p. 111.

15. "Spices, Exotic Flavors & Medicines: Vanilla," UCLA Historic and Special Collections, Louise M. Darling Biomedical Library, https://unitproj.library.ucla.edu/biomed/spice/index.cfm?displayID=27 (accessed August 24, 2015).

16. Georges M. Halpern, *The Healing Trail: Essential Oils of Madagascar* (North Bergen, NJ: Basic Health Publications, 2004), p. 118.

17. "History," Nielsen Massey Fine Vanillas & Flavors, http://www.nielsenmassey.com/culinary/history-of-vanilla.php (accessed August 24, 2015).

18. Robert Krulwich, "The Little Boy Who Should've Vanished but Didn't," *National Geographic*, June 15, 2015, http://phenomena.nationalgeographic.com/2015/06/16/the-little-boy-who-shouldve-vanished-but-didnt/ (accessed August 24, 2015).

19. Ibid., pp. 116–18.

20. "FAQs," International Bee Research Association, http://www.ibra.org.uk/categories/faq#FAQ_15 (accessed August 24, 2015).

21. Anita Chu, *Field Guide to Candy: How to Identify and Make Virtually Every Candy Imaginable* (Philadelphia: Quirk Books, 2014), p. 48.

22. "Nougat," Honey Traveler, http://www.honeytraveler.com/honey-gastronomy/nougat (accessed August 24, 2015).

23. Tom Turpin, "Honey Bee Not Native to North America," On Six Legs, Perdue University news column, November 11, 1999, https://www.agriculture.purdue.edu/agcomm/newscolumns/archives/OSL/1999/November/111199OSL.html (accessed August 24, 2015).

24. Eliza Leslie, The Lady's Receipt-Book: A Useful Companion for Large or Small Families 1847 (Philadelphia: Carey and Hart, 1847), p. 300.

25. "The Food Timeline," Food Timeline, http://foodtimeline.org (accessed August 24, 215).

26. "Abolitionists and Free Produce," Mid-Hudson Antislavery History Project, http://pages.vassar.edu/mhantislaveryhistoryproject/abolitionists-and-free-produce/ (accessed August 20, 2015).

27. Benjamin Quarles, *Black Abolitionists* (New York: Da Capo Press, 1969), pp. 74–75.

28. "Peanuts," Poplar Grove Plantation, http://www.poplargrove.org/discover/gullah-geechee-2/peanuts/ (accessed August 24, 2015).

29. Haughton, *Green Immigrants*, p. 260.

30. Mark McWilliams, *The Story behind the Dish: Classic American Foods* (Santa Barbara, CA: ABC-CLIO, 2012), p. 164.

31. "History of Peanuts & Peanut Butter," National Peanut Board, http://nationalpeanutboard.org/the-facts/history-of-peanuts-peanut-butter/ (accessed August 24, 2015).

32. "Peanuts."

33. "History of Peanuts & Peanut Butter."

34. McWilliams, *Story behind the Dish*, pp. 164–65.

35. "History of Peanuts & Peanut Butter."

36. "About Almonds," Just Almonds, http://www.justalmonds.com/About_Almonds_s/21.htm (accessed August 20, 2015).

37. Andrew Dalby, *Food in the Ancient World from A-Z* (London: Routledge, 2003), p. 6.

38. Tamra Andrews, Nectar and Ambrosia: An Encyclopedia of Food in World Mythology (Santa Barbara, CA: ABC-CLIO, 2000), pp. 5–6.

39. Levi, "Nougat."

40. Katie Liesner, "Marshmallow," in *The Oxford Companion to Sugar and Sweets*, ed. Darra Goldstein (New York: Oxford University Press, 2015), pp. 430–31.

41. Kristine Krapp, How Products Are Made: An Illustrated Guide to Product Manufacturing, vol. 3 (Detroit: Gale, 1997), pp. 276–77.

42. Eleanor Parkinson, The Complete Confectioner, *Pastry-Cook, and Baker: Plain and Practical Directions for Making Confectionery and Pastry* (Philadelphia: J. B. Lippincott, 1864), p. 162.

43. Susan Campbell, "Diversity of Plants," in *Encyclopedia of Food and Culture*, ed. Solomon H. Katz, Scribner Library of Daily Life, vol. 2 (New York: Scribner, 2003), pp. 104–105.

44. "The History of Gelatin, Gelatine, and JELL-O," What's Cooking America?, http://whatscookingamerica.net/History/Jell-0-history.htm (accessed August 24, 2015).

45. "History," Knox Gelatine, http://www.knoxgelatine.com/history.htm (accessed August 24, 2015).

46. "First Annual Cookbook," *Monroe News Star*, November 20, 1935, p. 24.

47. "Marshmallow Roasts," *Wichita Daily Eagle*, October 13, 1892, p. 6.

48. Ibid.

49. Steve Annear, "What the Fluff? The History of Your Favorite Sandwich Confection," *Boston Magazine*, http://www.bostonmagazine.com/arts-entertainment/blog/2013/09/26/where-was-fluff-invented-festival-somerville-2013/ (accessed August 21, 2015).

50. Katie Holdefehr, "The Peeps Chick Is Turning 60," *Good Housekeeping*, http://

www.goodhousekeeping.com/institute/a13881/history-marshmallow-candy-peeps/ (accessed August 24, 2015).

51. Associated Press, "The History of Peeps," Fox News, http://www.foxnews.com/ leisure/2013/03/08/history-peeps/ (accessed August 24, 2015).

52. Mishelle Knuteson, "Licorice," Dr. Christopher's Herbal Legacy, http://www .herballegacy.com/Knuteson_History.html (accessed August 24, 2015).

53. *The Randolph Regulator*, July 26, 1876, p. 3 and 4.

54. "The Cultivation of Licorice," *Raleigh Christian Advocate*, September 12, 1888, p. 8.

55. "The History of Bassett's Liquorice Allsorts & Bertie Bassett," Recipe Reminiscing, February 17, 2015, https://recipereminiscing.wordpress.com/2015/02/17/ the-history-of-bassetts-liquorice-allsorts-bertie-bassett/ (accessed August 24, 2015).

56. Frank Dougherty, "Lester Rosskam, 68; 'Mr. Good & Plenty,'" *philly.com*, October 28, 1992, http://articles.philly.com/1992-10-28/news/25998972_1_national -confectioners-association-candy-family-business (accessed August 24, 2015).

57. Mallory Russell, "Former Ogilvy Creative Director Russ Alben Dies," *Advertising Age*, August 28, 2012, http://adage.com/article/people-players/ogilvy-creative -director-russ-alben-dies/236893/ (accessed August 24, 2015).

58. Joe Heim, "What's Your Candy Personality Profile?," *Amarillo Globe-News*, October 28, 2007, http://www.amarillo.com/stories/102807/fea_8777088.shtml (accessed August 24, 2015).

59. Andrew F. Smith, Food and Drink in American History: A "Full Course" Encyclopedia (Santa Barbara: ABC-CLIO, 2013), p. 528.

60. "Company History," American Licorice Company, http://www.americanlicorice .com/about/companyhistory/ (accessed August 24, 2015).

CHAPTER 6: THEN COMETH THE SUGARCANE

1. Deborah Jean Warner, *Sweet Stuff: An American History of Sweeteners from Sugar to Sucralose* (Washington, DC: Smithsonian Institution Scholarly Press, 2011), p. 5.

2. Andrew Coleman, "Sugarcane Plantations of Louisiana," Media Nola, A Project of Tulane University, http://medianola.org/discover/place/987/Sugarcane-Plantations-of -Louisiana (accessed August 21, 2015).

3. Andrew Smith, *Sugar: A Global History* (London: Reaktion Books, 2015), pp. 19–20.

4. "The World of Shakespeare's Humors," NIH US National Library of Medicine, September, 19 2013, http://www.nlm.nih.gov/exhibition/shakespeare/fourhumors.html (accessed August 21, 2015).

5. Ibid.

6. Ed Crews, "Rattle-Skull, Stonewall, Bogus, Blackstrap, Bombo, Mimbo, Whistle Belly, Syllabub, Sling, Toddy, and Flip: Drinking in Colonial America," *Colonial Williamsburg Journal* (Holiday 2007), http://www.history.org/foundation/journal/Holiday07/drink.cfm (accessed November 2, 2015).

7. Warner, *Sweet Stuff*, p. 25.

8. John Adams and Charles Francis Adams, The Works of John Adams, *Second President of the United States; With a Life of the Author, Notes and Illustrations* (New York: Little Brown & Company, 1856), p 35.

9. Smith, *Sugar*, p. 30.

10. Ibid., p. 31.

11. Warner, *Sweet Stuff*, p. 33.

12. "Prisoners Refuse to Go on Rock Pile on Bread and 'Yup,'" *Topeka Daily Capital*, October 13, 1908, p. 3.

13. "Witnesses Describing Striking Conditions in Lawrence," *Washington Times*, March 7, 1912, p. 1.

14. Federal Writers' Project, "Slave Narratives, A Folk History of Slavery in the United States with Interviews with Former Slaves," (Washington, DC: Library of Congress, Work Projects Administration, 1941), pp. 133 and 136.

15. Janet Clarkson, The Food History Almanac: *Over 1,300 Years of World Culinary History, Culture, and Social Influence* (Lanham, MD: Rowman & Littlefield, 2013), p. 1247.

16. Billie Spencer, "An Old-Fashion Taffy Pull," *Boys' Life*, July 1964, p. 63.

17. Laura Mason, "Toffee," in *The Oxford Companion to Sugar and Sweets*, ed. Darra Goldstein (New York: Oxford University Press, 2015), p. 738.

18. "Sugar History," *Fort Wayne News*, January 3, 1917, p. 14.

19. "Domino Sugar Corporation History," Funding Universe, http://www.funding universe.com/company-histories/domino-sugar-corporation-history/ (accessed August 21, 2015).

20. Ibid.

21. Ibid.

22. "Frederick C. Havemeyer," *New York Times*, July 29, 1891, p. 5; "Death of Frederick C. Havemeyer," *Chicago Tribune*, July 29, 1891, p. 3.

23. "America's Most Successful Men of Affairs, Henry Hall," *New York Tribune*, 1895, pp. 301–302.

24. "Domino Sugar Corporation History."

25. Ibid.

26. Coleman, "Sugarcane Plantations of Louisiana."

27. Smith, *Sugar*, p 22.

28. Ibid., p 32.

29. Elizabeth Abbott, *Sugar: A Bittersweet History* (New York: Overlook, 2009), p. 281.

30. Coleman, "Sugarcane Plantations of Louisiana."

31. "The News," *Fort Wayne Daily Gazette*, March 25, 1868, p. 1.

32. "Of General Interest," *Hornellsville Weekly Tribune*, October 10, 1890, p. 6.

33. W. F. Therkildson, "Do You Know?," *Panama City News Herald*, October 7, 1943, p. 4.

34. Ad for the Weilepp-Cox Agency, *Decatur Herald*, March 20, 1910, p. 42.

35. Warner, *Sweet Stuff*, p. 70.

36. "Company History," US Sugar Corporation, http://www.ussugar.com/company/history.html (accessed August 23, 2015).

37. Javier A. Galván, "Sugar and Slavery: The Bittersweet Chapter in the 19th Century Cuba, 1817–1886," *Revista de Humanidades: Tecnológico de Monterrey* 16 (2004), pp. 214–17.

38. "Cuban Sugar Duty Free," *Hawaiian Star*, April 12, 1901, p. 2.

39. Smith, *Sugar*, p. 42.

40. Galván, "Sugar and Slavery," pp. 214–17.

41. Edward Greaney, "Hawaii's Big Six: A Cyclical Saga," in *The Encyclopedia of Hawaii, a 1976 Bicentennial Project* (Honolulu: The University of Hawaii Press, 1976).

42. Charles Brewer, *Reminiscences*, 1884, p. 5.

43. Ibid., pp. 10–11.

44. "Ladd & Company: Koloa Plantation—Hawaii's First Sugar Plantation," Ladd Family: Koloa Plantation, http://www.laddfamily.com/Files/Koloa%20Plantation/Hawaii.htm (accessed August 23, 2015).

45. Greaney, "Hawaii's Big Six."

46. "Big Five," HawaiiHistory.org, http://hawaiihistory.org/index.cfm?fuseaction=ig.page&PageID=29 (accessed August 23, 2015).

47. Frank Cho, "C. Brewer to End Era," *Honolulu Advertiser*, August 1, 2001.

CHAPTER 7: A BAD CASE OF SUGAR BLUES

1. "Ladd & Company: Koloa Plantation—Hawaii's First Sugar Plantation," Ladd Family: Koloa Plantation, http://www.laddfamily.com/Files/Koloa%20Plantation/Hawaii.htm (accessed August 23, 2015).

2. "Hawaii: Life on a Plantation Society," Library of Congress, http://www.loc.gov/teachers/classroommaterials/presentationsandactivities/presentations/immigration/japanese2.html (accessed August 23, 2015).

3. Ibid.

4. "Homesick Jamaicans Land in US Jail," *Council Bluffs Nonpareil*, October 10, 1943, p. 1.

5. Andrew Smith, *Sugar: A Global History* (London: Reaktion Books, 2015), p. 34.

6. Elizabeth Abbott, *Sugar: A Bittersweet History* (New York: Overlook, 2009), p. 281.

7. Ad in *Times-Picayune*, "Succession Sale. Extended Plantation," January 18, 1860, p. 9.

8. Author phone interview with Leni Sorenson, August 2, 2015.

9. Ibid.

10. The Kitchen Sisters, "Hercules and Hemings: Presidents' Slave Chefs," Kitchen Stories, NPR, http://www.npr.org/2008/02/19/18950467/hercules-and-hemings-presidents-slave-chefs (accessed August 21, 2015).

11. "Arlington House, the Robert E. Lee Memorial," National Park Service, www.nps.gov/arho/learn/historyculture/george-custis.htm (accessed August 21, 2015).

12. George Washington Parke Custis, *Recollections and Private Memoirs of the Life and Character of Washington*, ed. Benson J. Lossing (New York: Derby & Jackson, 1860), pp. 422–24.

13. "Hercules," George Washington's Mount Vernon, http://www.mountvernon.org/research-collections/digital-encyclopedia/article/hercules/ (accessed August 21, 2015).

14. Ibid.

15. Craig LaBan, "A Birthday Shock from Washington's Chef," *Philadelphia Inquirer*, February 22, 2010, http://articles.philly.com/2010-02-22/news/24957476_1_oney-judge-hercules-slave (accessed August 21, 2015).

16. Ibid.

17. Fritz Hirschfeld, *George Washington and Slavery: A Documentary Portrayal* (Columbia: University of Missouri Press, 1997), p. 71.

18. Custis. Recollections and Private Memoirs, pp. 422–24.

19. Rufus Estes, *Rufus Estes' Good Things to Eat: The First Cookbook by an African-American Chef* (Chicago: printed by author, 1911; reprinted, Mineola, NY: Dover, 2004), preface.

20. "Bowser, Mary Elizabeth (1839–?) Union Spy during the Civil War," Hutchins Center for African and African American Research, Harvard University, http://hutchinscenter.fas.harvard.edu/bowser-mary-elizabeth-1839-union-spy-during-civil-war (accessed August 21, 2015).

21. Angela M. Zombek, "Libby Prison," Encyclopedia Virginia, May 14, 2009, http://www.encyclopediavirginia.org/Libby_Prison (accessed August 21, 2015).

22. "Bowser, Mary Elizabeth."

23. Lois Leveen, "A Black Spy in the Confederate White House," *New York Times*,

June 21, 2012, http://opinionator.blogs.nytimes.com/2012/06/21/a-black-spy-in-the -confederate-white-house/?_r=2 (accessed August 20, 2015).

24. Leveen, "A Black Spy."

25. James M. Brodie, "Created Equal: The Lives and Ideas of Black American Innovators," African American Registry, http://www.aaregistry.org/historic_events/view/ sugar-evaporator-patented (accessed August 21, 2015).

26. Gaius Chamberlain, "Norbert Rillieux, The Black Inventor Online Museum," Black Inventor Online Museum, November 26, 2012, http://blackinventor.com/norbert -rillieux/ (accessed August 21, 2015).

27. "Norbert Rillieux and a Revolution in Sugar Processing," American Chemical Society, http://www.acs.org/content/acs/en/education/whatischemistry/landmarks/ norbertrillieux.html (accessed August 21, 2015).

28. Ibid.

29. Deborah Jean Warner, *Sweet Stuff: An American History of Sweeteners from Sugar to Sucralose* (Washington, DC: Smithsonian Institution Scholarly Press, 2011), p. 7.

30. *Martha Washington's Booke of Cookery and Booke of Sweetmeats*, transcribed by Karen Hess (New York: Columbia University Press, 1981), p. 284.

31. Estes, *Rufus Estes' Good Things to Eat*, p. 104.

32. "Messenger of Joy," *Mattoon Gazette*, October 20, 1893, p. 5.

33. Ibid.

34. Maggi M. Morehouse and Zoe Trodd, eds., *Civil War America: A Social and Cultural History with Primary Sources* (New York: Routledge, 2013), p. 145.

35. "Dryden & Palmer Rock Candy," Bogdon's, http://rbcweb.shopfactory.com/ contents/en-us/d30_Dryden___Palmer.html (accessed August 21, 201).

36. "A Yankee in the Smith Family," *Democratic Pioneer*, March 15, 1859, p. 1.

37. "Paying the Fiddler," *Berkshire County Eagle*, August 14, 1862, p. 1.

38. "The Conflict between Freedom and Slavery," *Liberator*, March 8, 1861, p. 1.

39. "Sugar Candy," *Independence Daily Reporter*, March 20, 1886, p. 2.

40. Author interview with Edith Elizabeth Lowe Higdon, August 14, 2015.

CHAPTER 8: AN ARSENAL OF SUGAR

1. "People and Events, Benjamin Rush, 1745–1813," PBS, Africans in America, part 3, http://www.pbs.org/wgbh/aia/part3/3p458.html (accessed August 24, 2015).

2. Donald J. D'Elia, "Dr. Benjamin Rush and the Negro," *Journal of the History of Ideas* 30, no. 3 (July–September 1969), p. 413.

3. Brycchan Carey, "Anthony Benezet (1713–1784)," brycchancarey.com, http:// www.brycchancarey.com/abolition/benezet.htm (accessed August 24, 2015).

4. "People and Events, Benjamin Rush."

5. "An Address to the Inhabitants of the British Settlements in America, upon Slave-Keeping," New York Historical Society, http://www.nyhistory.org/exhibit/address -inhabitants-british-settlements-america-upon-slave-keeping (accessed August 24, 2015).

6. "Sugar Maple," Monticello, http://www.monticello.org/site/house-and-gardens/ sugar-maple (accessed August 24, 2015).

7. Ibid.

8. William Drown, Compendium of Agriculture or the Farmers Guide in the Most Essential Parts of Husbandry and Gardening (Providence, RI: Field & Maxcy, 1824), p. 255.

9. Benjamin Rush, "Letter of Thomas Jefferson Regarding the Maple Tree," in Essays, Literary, Moral, and Philosophical, 2nd ed. (Philadelphia: Thomas and William Bradford, 1806).

10. "Sugar Maple."

11. "From Thomas Jefferson to Benjamin Vaughan, June 27, 1790," National Archives, http://founders.archives.gov/documents/Jefferson/01-16-02-0342 (accessed August 24, 2015).

12. "Sugar Maple."

13. Herbert C. Covey and Dwight Eisnach, What the Slaves: Recollections of African American Foods and Foodways from the Slave Narratives (Santa Barbara, CA: ABC-CLIO, 2009), p. 190.

14. Helen Nearing and Scott Nearing, The Maple Sugar Book: Together with Remarks on Pioneering as a Way of Living, 50th anniversary ed. (White River Junction, VT: Chelsea Green, 2000), p. 266.

15. Nevin Martell, "Birch for Breakfast? Meet Maple Syrup's Long-Lost Cousins," NPR, October 28, 2013, http://www.npr.org/sections/thesalt/2013/09/28/226856804/ meet-maple-syrup-s-long-lost-cousins (accessed August 24, 2015).

16. Deborah Jean Warner, Sweet Stuff: An American History of Sweeteners from Sugar to Sucralose (Washington, DC: Smithsonian Institution Scholarly Publishing, 2011), p. 165.

17. International Confectioner, January 1917, p. 41.

18. Warner, Sweet Stuff, p. 166.

19. "Ingredients," Aunt Jemima, http://www.auntjemima.com/aj_products/syrups/ orginal.cfm (accessed August 20, 2015).

20. Author phone interview with Paul Palmer, July 15, 2015.

21. "Sorghum June Grain of the Month," Whole Grains Council, http:// wholegrainscouncil.org/whole-grains-101/sorghum-june-grain-of-the-month (accessed August 24, 2015).

22. A. Hugh Bryan, "Sorghum Syrup Manufacture," US Department of Agriculture, Farmers' Bulletin 477 (February 9, 1912), University of North Texas Digital

Library, http://digital.library.unt.edu/ark:/67531/metadc85696/m1/6/ (accessed August 24, 2015).

23. "Migrations in History," Smithsonian Education, http://www.smithsonianeducation.org/migrations/zoofood/sor.html (accessed August 24, 2015).

24. "Continuity and Change: Geographical Societies: The Mid- to Late-1800s," *AAG Newsletter* 31, no. 10, reprinted by St. Michael's College, http://academics.smcvt.edu/geography/history2.html (accessed August 24, 2015); "Paris, France 1851," University of Wisconsin American Geographical Society Library Digital Map Collection, http://collections.lib.uwm.edu/cdm/ref/collection/agdm/id/928 (accessed August 24, 2015).

25. "The Sorgho Sucre: A Rival of the Sugar-Cane," *Hunt's Merchants' Magazine and Commercial Review* 33, 1855.

26. Harry Nelson Vinall et al., "Identification, History, and Distribution of Common Sorghum Varieties," in *Standardized Plant Names* (US Dept. of Agriculture, 1936), p. 66.

27. "James Henry Hammond," National Park Service, http://www.nps.gov/resources/person.htm?id=160 (accessed August 24, 2015).

28. Annie Besant, "Colonel Henry Steel Olcott," *Theosophist* 27 (March 1907), https://www.theosophical.org/files/resources/articles/ColonelHenryOlcott.pdf (accessed November 2, 2015).

29. Ibid.

30. Henry Steel Olcott, *Sorgho and Imphee, the Chinese and African Sugarcanes* (New York: A. O. Moore, 1857), p. 15.

31. Eric Sloane, *Once Upon a Time: The Way America Was* (New York: Dover, 2005), http://www.appalachianhistory.net/2014/10/sorghum-season-is-on.html (accessed June 4, 2015).

32. Deborah Jean Warner, *Sweet Stuff: An American History of Sweeteners from Sugar to Sucralose* (Washington, DC: Smithsonian Institution Scholarly Publishing, 2011), p. 146.

33. Ibid.

34. Eric Colleary, "Recipe: Abraham Lincoln and his Gingerbread Men (1847)," American Table, January 5, 2013, http://www.americantable.org/2013/01/recipe-abraham-lincoln-and-his-gingerbread-men-1847/ (accessed August 24, 2015).

35. Samuel Hawkins Marshall Byers, *What I Saw in Dixie* (Dansville, New York: Robins & Poore, 1868), p. 14.

36. Douglas Schar, "Featured Article: Sweet Sorghum," Doctor Schar, http://doctorschar.com/features/sweet-sorghum-sorghum-bicolor/#sorghum-history (accessed August 24, 2015).

37. "Grover Cleveland," Miller Center, University of Virginia, http://millercenter.org/president/cleveland (accessed August 24, 2015).

38. "Harvey W. Wiley," US Food and Drug Administration, http://www.fda.gov/AboutFDA/WhatWeDo/History/CentennialofFDA/HarveyW.Wiley (accessed August 24, 2015).

39. A. Hunter Dupree, Science in the Federal Government: A History of Politics and Activities to 1940 (Cambridge, MA: Belknap, 1957), p. 177.

40. "Anheuser-Busch Introduces First Nationally Available Sorghum Beer: Redbridge," Anheuser-Busch, http://anheuser-busch.com/index.php/anheuser-busch-introduces-first-nationally-available-sorghum-beer-redbridge-2/ (accessed August 20, 2015).

41. "Sorghum," CGIAR, http://www.cgiar.org/our-research/crop-factsheets/sorghum (accessed August 20, 2015).

42. Author interview with John Guenther, July 16, 2014.

43. "History of Sugar Beet Production and Use," University of Nebraska Crop Watch, 2014, https://cropwatch.unl.edu/sugarbeets/sugarbeet_history (accessed August 24, 2015).

44. Ibid.

45. Lewis S. Ware, The Sugar Beet: Including a History of the Beet Sugar Industry in Europe, Varieties of the Sugar Beet, Examination, Soils, Tillage, Seeds and Sowing, Yield and Cost of Cultivation, Harvesting, Transportation, Conservation, Feeding Qualities of the Beet and of the Pulp, Etc. (Philadelphia: H.C. Baird, 1880), p. 26; "History of Beet Sugar," The American Beet Sugar Association, https://www.americansugarbeet.org/who-we-are/sugarbeet-history.html (accessed August 24, 2015).

46. Warner, Sweet Stuff, p. 85.

47. "Ohio Beet," Sandusky Clarion, October 30, 1822, p. 4.

48. "Beet Sugar," Liberator, September 17, 1836, p. 1.

49. Warner, Sweet Stuff, p. 97.

50. "The Beet Sugar Industry," Goodwin's Weekly: A Thinking Paper for Thinking People, June 1, 1912, p. 43.

51. "Beet Sugar Making at Home," Ranche and Range, December 13, 1897, p. 13.

52. "American Crystal Sugar Company: An Inventory of Its Records at the Minnesota Historical Society," Minnesota Historical Society, http://www2.mnhs.org/library/findaids/00341.xml (accessed August 24, 2015).

53. Advertisement section, American Sugar Industry and Beet Sugar Gazette 13 (April 1911): pp. 19–35.

54. "Trust Wars on U.S. Producers, Control of Market Threatened by Beet Sugar Industry," Cut Bank Pioneer Press, May 23, 1913, p. 6.

55. "The Sugar Investigation," American Sugar Industry and Beet Sugar Gazette, p. 340.

56. Deborah Warner, "Sugar Beet," in The Oxford Companion to Sugar and Sweets, ed. Darra Goldstein (New York: Oxford University Press, 2015), p. 676.

57. "American Crystals Sugar Company," Encyclopedia.com, http://www
.encyclopedia.com/topic/American_Crystal_Sugar_Company.aspx (accessed August 24,
2015).

58. "Dark Brown Sugar," C&H, https://www.chsugar.com/sugar/detail/dark-brown
-sugar (accessed August 24, 2015).

CHAPTER 9: A GIFT FROM THE GODS

1. Esmé E. Deprez, "What Are the World's Most Popular Candies?," Bloom-
berg Business Week, June 24, 2009, http://www.businessweek.com/globalbiz/content/
jun2009/gb20090624_590587.htm (accessed August 25, 2015).

2. "The Global Online Media Landscape," Nielsen, April 2009, http://www.
nielsen.com/content/dam/corporate/us/en/newswire/uploads/2009/04/nielsen
-easterpassover-april-09.pdf (accessed November 2, 2015).

3. Intelligent Travel, "The 10 Best Chocolatiers in the World," *National
Geographic*, December 28, 2012, http://intelligenttravel.nationalgeographic
.com/2012/12/28/the-10-best-chocolatiers-in-the-world/ (accessed November 2, 2015).

4. "Theobroma Cacao," Encyclopedia of Life, http://eol.org/pages/484592/
overview (accessed August 25, 2015).

5. B. J. Hernández, "Insect Pollination of Cacao (*Theobroma cacao L.*) in Costa
Rica" (thesis, University of Wisconsin, 1965), pp. 162–67.

6. "Carl Linnaeus," University of California, Berkeley, http://www.ucmp.berkeley
.edu/history/linnaeus.html (accessed August 25, 2010).

7. "The Maya and the Ka'kau' (Cacao)," Authentic Maya, http://authenticmaya
.com/cacao.htm (accessed August 25, 2010).

8. Deborah Cadbury, *The Chocolate Wars* (New York: Public Affairs, 2010), pp.
26–27.

9. "Food of the Gods," Albert R. Mann Library, Cornell University, 2007, http://
exhibits.mannlib.cornell.edu/chocolate/theobromacacao.php (accessed August 25, 2010).

10. Mort Rosenblum, *Chocolate: A Bittersweet Saga of Dark and Light* (New York:
North Point, 2005), p. 10.

11. "Making Heritage Chocolate at the Historic Crossing," Pennsylvania Historical
& Museum Commission, http://www.portal.state.pa.us/portal/server.pt/community/
fall/21063/heritage_chocolate/135717 (accessed August 25, 2010).

12. Cadbury, *Chocolate Wars*, p. 26.

13. "The Maya and the Ka'kau' (Cacao)."

14. "Ekchuah," Encyclopedia Mythica, http://www.pantheon.org/articles/e/
ekchuah.html (accessed August 25, 2015).

15. "The Maya and the Ka'kau' (Cacao)."

16. "Discovering Chocolate: The Great Chocolate Discovery," Cadbury, https://www.cadbury.com.au/About-Chocolate/Discovering-Chocolate.aspx (accessed August 25, 2015).

17. Cadbury, *Chocolate Wars*, p. 27.

18. "Discovering Chocolate."

19. Keith Peterson, review of *Conquistador: Hernán Cortés, King Montezuma, and the Last Stand of the Aztecs*, by Buddy Levy, *Washington State Magazine*, http://wsm.wsu.edu/r/index.php?id=103#. VUgyuJNQChEIn1520 (accessed August 25, 2015).

20. Rosenblum, *Chocolate*, p. 58.

21. Ibid.

22. "Discovering Chocolate."

23. Tim Richardson, *Sweets: A History of Candy* (New York and London: Bloomsbury, 2002), p. 220.

24. "History of Chocolate," Nibble, September 2006, http://www.thenibble.com/reviews/main/chocolate/the-history-of-chocolate.asp (accessed August 25, 2015).

25. Wendy Woloson, *Refined Tastes: Sugar, Confectionery, and Consumers in Nineteenth-Century America* (Baltimore, MD: John Hopkins University Press, 2002), p. 113.

26. "History of Chocolate."

27. Woloson, *Refined Tastes*, p. 113.

28. "Types of Chocolate," Godiva, http://www.godiva.com/collections (accessed August 25, 2015).

29. R. R. Allen et al., "*Daily Consumption of a Dark Chocolate Containing Flavanols and Added Sterol Esters Affects Cardiovascular Risk Factors in a Normotensive Population with Elevated Cholesterol," Journal of Nutrition 138, no. 4* (April 2008), pp. 725–31.

30. "*Can Chocolate Lower Your Risk of Stroke?," American Academy of Neurology*, February 11, 2010, https://www.aan.com/PressRoom/Home/PressRelease/799 (accessed August 24, 2015).

31. Magdalena Cuenca-García et al., "*Association between Chocolate Consumption and Fatness in European Adolescents," Nutrition* (October 2013).

32. "Key Chocolate Ingredients Could Help Prevent Obesity, Diabetes," American Chemical Society, April 2, 2014, http://www.acs.org/content/acs/en/pressroom/presspacs/2014/acs-presspac-april-2-2014/key-chocolate-ingredients-could-help-prevent-obesity-diabetes.html (accessed August 25, 2015).

33. "Granola Bars," Cascadian Farm Organic, http://www.cascadianfarm.com/products/granola-bars (accessed August 245, 2015).

34. Rosenblum, *Chocolate*, p. 37.

35. "Spices as Aphrodisiacs," UCLA Louise M. Darling Biomedical Library, http://unitproj.library.ucla.edu/biomed/spice/index.cfm?spicefilename=Aphrodisiacs.txt&itemsuppress=yes&displayswitch=0 (accessed August 2, 2015).

CHAPTER 10: CHOCOLATE OVER WATER

1. Gerald Ward, "Silver Chocolate Pots of Colonial Boston," in *Chocolate: History, Culture, and Heritage*, ed. Louis Grivetti and Howard Yana Shapiro (Hoboken, NJ: Wiley, 2009), p. 143.

2. Carla Martin, "Brownies," US History Scene, April10, 2015, http://ushistory scene.com/article/brownies/ (accessed August 25, 2015).

3. Ward, "Silver Chocolate Pots of Colonial Boston ," p. 143.

4. Samuel Sewall, *The Diary of Samuel Sewall* (Boston, MA: Massachusetts Historical Society, 1878).

5. Wendy Woloson, *Refined Tastes: Sugar, Confectionery, and Consumers in Nineteenth-Century America* (Baltimore, MD: John Hopkins University Press, 2002), p. 114.

6. "Samuel Sewall," Celebrate Boston, http://www.celebrateboston.com/biography/samuel-sewall.htm (accessed August 25, 2015).

7. Nicholas Westbrook, Christopher D. Fox, and Anne McCarty, "Breakfasting on Chocolate: Chocolate in Military Life on the Northern Frontier, 1750–1780," in *Chocolate: History, Culture, and Heritage*, ed. Louis Grivetti and Howard Yana Shapiro (Hoboken, NJ: Wiley, 2009), p. 399.

8. James F Gay, "Chocolate Production and Uses in 17th and 18th Century North America," in *Chocolate: History, Culture, and Heritage*, ed. Louis Grivetti and Howard Yana Shapiro (Hoboken, NJ: Wiley, 2009), p. 289.

9. "Virtual Tour of Lower Mills, Dorchester, Massachusetts," Bostonian Society, p. 1, http://www.bostonhistory.org/sub/bakerschocolate/Lower%20Mills%20Then%20 and%20Now%20Tour.pdf (accessed August 27, 2015).

10. Peter F. Stevens, "James Baker and John Hannon: Pioneer Chocolatemeisters," *Dorchester Reporter Online*, February 16, 2012, http://www.dotnews.com/2012/james -baker-and-john-hannon-pioneer-chocolatemeisters (accessed August 27, 2015).

11. "Virtual Tour of Lower Mills, Dorchester, Massachusetts."

12. Stevens "James Baker and John Hannon."

13. Thomas Jefferson, "Thomas Jefferson Letter to John Adams, dated November 27, 1785," in *The Papers of Thomas Jefferson*, vol. 9, ed. J. P. Boyd (Princeton, NJ: Princeton University Press, 1954), p. 63.

14. "Unsweetened Chocolate," Bostonian Society, http://www.bostonhistory.org/sub/bakerschocolate/prod_unsweet.htm (accessed August 27, 2015).

15. Ibid.

16. Committee of the Dorchester Antiquarian and Historical Society, *History of the Town of Dorchester, Massachusetts* (Boston: Ebenezer Clapp Jr., 1859), p. 638.

17. "Unsweetened Chocolate."

18. Herbert S. Houston, *The World's Work: A History of Our Time* (New York: Doubleday, Page, 1903), pp. 3372 and 3373.

19. Walter Baker & Company, *Cocoa and Chocolate: A Short History of Their Production* (Dorchester, MA: W. Baker, 1904), p. 32.

20. Houston, *The World's Work*, p. 3374.

21. Neil Jeffares, "LIOTARD, Jean-Étienne Geneva 1702–1789," *Dictionary of Pastellists before 1800 Online Edition*, August 3, 2015, http://www.pastellists.com/Articles/LIOTARD.pdf?zoom_highlight=buste (accessed August 25, 2015).

22. Ad for Baker's Chocolate, *Richmond Dispatch*, February 26, 1899, p. 6.

23. Ad for Baker's Chocolate, *Commoner.* March, 17, 1905, p. 1.

24. Ad for Baker's Chocolate, *Overland Monthly*, January 1919, on Wikipedia, https://en.wikipedia.org/wiki/Baker's_Chocolate_%28brand%29 (accessed August 27, 2015).

25. Ad in *Salt Lake Herald.* November 14, 1903, p. 5.

26. Ad in *Salt Lake Herald*, March 1907, p. 2.

27. "Native American Tribes, State of Massachusetts" Geni Project, http://www.geni.com/projects/Native-American-Tribes-State-of-Massachusetts/9825 (accessed August 25, 2015).

28. Francois Auguste Peter Sr., "Daniel Peter—The Inventor of Milk Chocolate," What's Cooking America, http://whatscookingamerica.net/History/MilkChocolate.htm (accessed August 25, 2015).

29. "Edwin Drake, Oil Digging" Who Made America, PBS, http://www.pbs.org/wgbh/theymadeamerica/whomade/drake_lo.html (accessed August 25, 2015).

30. Peter, "Daniel Peter."

31. Lee Mccoy, "Cailler Chocolate," Chocolatiers, April 22, 2014, http://www.chocolatiers.co.uk/blogs/profiles/13841997-cailler-chocolaterie (accessed August 25, 2015).

32. Deborah Cadbury, *The Chocolate Wars* (New York: Public Affairs, 2010), p. 78.

33. Peter, "Daniel Peter."

34. Laurent Bijard, "Daniel Peter or How the Small Squares of Tenderness Were Invented," *Journal Francais d'Amerique* 8, no. 21 (October 24–November 6, 1986), http://whatscookingamerica.net/History/MilkChocolate.htm (accessed August 27, 2015).

35. Peter, "Daniel Peter."

36. Ad in *Evening Star*, Sept 25, 1910, p. 45.

37. Ad in *New York Tribune*, July 23, 1911, p. 37.

38. Ad in *Evening star.* August 8, 1920, p. 62.

39. Bijard, "Daniel Peter."

CHAPTER 11: THE MYSTERY OF THE MARVELOUS WILBUR BUDS

1. Trip to Wilbur Chocolate on May 15, 2015, author interview with Kathy Blankenbiller and Ann Charles.

2. "The History of Wilbur Chocolate," Wilbur Chocolate, http://www .wilburbuds.com/Wilbur-History.html (accessed August 20, 2015).

3. "Our History," Cargill, http://www.cargill.com/company/history/ (accessed November 30, 2015).

4. "Our Rich History," Peters Chocolate, http://www.peterschocolate.com/pages/ history.html (accessed August 20, 2015).

5. Deborah Cadbury, The Chocolate Wars: *The 150-Year Rivalry between the World's Greatest Chocolate Makers* (New York: Public Affairs, 2010), pp. 107–110.

6. "Milton Hershey, 1857–1945: He Built a Successful Business and a Sweet Town," Manythings.org, http://www.manythings.org/voa/people/Milton_Hershey.html (accessed August 25, 2015).

7. "Milton S. Hershey: The Young Apprentice," Hershey Company, https://www .thehersheycompany.com/about-hershey/our-story/milton.aspx (accessed November 30, 2015).

8. Tim Richardson, *Sweets: A History of Candy* (New York: Bloomsbury, 2002), pp. 265–66.

9. Cadbury, *Chocolate Wars*, pp. 112–14.

10. Author interview with Jan at the Hershey Story Museum, May 28, 2015.

11. Ibid., p. 145.

12. "Hershey, Catherine Sweeney; 1871–1915," Hershey Community Archives, http://www.hersheyarchives.org/essay/details.aspx?EssayId=11&Rurl=/resources/search -results.aspx?Type=BrowseEssay (accessed August 25, 2015).

13. Ibid.

14. "Telegraphic Notes," *New-York Tribune*, August 11, 1900, p. 1.

15. "A Big Price Was Paid, Lancaster Company Was Sold for a Million Dollars," *Lebanon Daily News*, August 11, 1900, p. 1.

16. "Hershey Chocolate Corporation," *Evening Public Ledger*, June 10, 1920, p. 21.

17. Rachel Janik, "How the Hershey's Kiss Conquered Valentine's Day," *Time Magazine*, February 14, 2015, http://time.com/3707086/hershey-kiss-history-valentines/ (accessed August 25, 2015).

18. "Hershey's History," Hershey Company, https://www.thehersheycompany.com/ about-hershey/our-story/hersheys-history.aspx (accessed August 25, 2015).

19. "Hershey Entertainment and Resorts Company," Hershey Archives, http:// www.hersheyarchives.org/essay/details.aspx?EssayId=20&Rurl=%2fresources%2fsearch -results.aspx%3fType%3dSearch%26Text%3dTown%2bof%2bHershey%26StartMonth %3d%26EndMonth%3d%26StartDay%3d%26EndDay%3d%26StartYear%3d%26End Year%3d (accessed August 25, 2015).

20. Cadbury, *Chocolate Wars*, pp. 132–34.

21. Annie Diggs, "Cosmopolitan New York, 1903," in *The Chocolate Wars*, Deborah Cadbury, p. 146.

22. Richardson, *Sweets*, p. 146.

23. "Building Book on at Hershey," *Harrisburg Telegraph*, August 11, 1911, p. 2.

24. "Hershey Industrial School Making Real Men of Boys within Its Doors," *Harrisburg Telegraph*, November 19, 1915, p. 22.

25. "Hershey, Catherine Sweeney."

26. "Cuba, Central Hershey, 1916–1946," Hershey Community Archives, http:// www.hersheyarchives.org/essay/details.aspx?EssayId=16&Rurl=/resources/search-results .aspx?Type=BrowseEssay (accessed November 29, 2015).

27. Ibid.

28. "Chocolate King Sails for Europe with Murrie," *Lebanon Daily News*, July 28, 1931, p. 9.

29. "Reese Candy Company," Hershey Community Archives, http://www .hersheyarchives.org/essay/details.aspx?EssayId=29 (accessed November 29, 2015).

30. Cadbury, *Chocolate Wars*, pp. 251–52.

31. Author interview with Shelli Dronsfield, May 12, 2015.

32. Linda Stradley, "The History of Ice Cream Cones," What's Cooking America, 2004, http://whatscookingamerica.net/History/IceCream/IceCreamCone.htm (accessed November 2, 2015).

33. Jim McClure, "York Peppermint Patties May Go to Hot Clime," York Town Square, April 30, 2007, http://www.yorkblog.com/yorktownsquare/2007/04/30/cool-york-peppermint-patties-g/ (accessed November 2, 2015).

34. "James O. Walsh," Cambridge Historical Society, The History of Candy Making in Cambridge, http://www.cambridgehistory.org/discover/candy/jwelch.html (accessed November 2, 2015).

35. Andrew F. Smith, *Encyclopedia of Junk Food and Fast Food* (Santa Barbara, CA: Greenwood, 2006), p. 145.

36. "Nabisco Names James O. Welch Chairman of the Board," Associated Press News Archives, January 12, 1987, http://www.apnewsarchive.com/1987/ Nabisco -Names-James-O-Welch-Jr-Chairman-Of-The-Board/id-3d7ffe0322b00ac4f6eef 7d3712646b4 (accessed November 2, 2015).

37. "James O. Walsh."

CHAPTER 12: CANDY BAR BLITZ

1. Melissa Ziobro, "Military" in *The Oxford Companion to Sugar and Sweets*, ed. Darra Goldstein (New York: Oxford University Press, 2015), p. 453.

2. "Brooklyn Leads Country in Candy Export," *Brooklyn Daily Eagle*, March 7, 1908, p. 17.

3. Robert Fitzgerald, *Rowntree and the Marketing Revolution, 1862–1969* (Cambridge University Press, 2007), p. 317.

4. Jennifer Justus, "Goo Goo Gets a Makeover," *Tennessean*, May 11, 2011, http://archive.tennessean.com/article/20110511/LIFE02/305110080/Goo-Goo-gets-makeover (accessed August 26, 2015).

5. "Much Candy for Soldiers," *Bend Bulletin*, August 12, 1918, p. 1.

6. "Hersey's Chocolate Plays Important Part of War Effort," Hershey Community Archives, http://www.hersheyarchives.org/essay/details.aspx?EssayId=26&Rurl=%2fresources%2fsearch-results.aspx%3fType%3dBrowseEssay (accessed August 26, 2015).

7. "Hershey's Tropical Chocolate Bar," The Price of Freedom: Americans at War, http://amhistory.si.edu/militaryhistory/collection/object.asp?ID=42 (accessed August 26, 2015).

8. "Six Army Field Rations Lead Soldiers in Any Circumstance," *Portsmouth Herald*, August 26, 1942, p. 2.

9. "Hersey's Chocolate Plays Important Part of War Effort."

10. "About Mars," Mars.com, http://www.mars.com/global/about.aspx (accessed August 26, 2015).

11. Joel Rath, "East Asia," in *The Oxford Companion to Sugar and Sweets*, ed. Darra Goldstein (New York: Oxford University Press, 2015), pp. 233–34.

12. Deborah Cadbury, The Chocolate Wars: *The 150-Year Rivalry between the World's Greatest Chocolate Makers* (New York: Public Affairs, 2010), p. 234.

13. "History of Mars, Inc.," Reference for Business, http://www.referenceforbusiness.com/history2/16/Mars-Inc.html (accessed August 26, 2015).

14. Joel Glenn Brenner, "Mars," in *The Oxford Companion to Sugar and Sweets*, ed. Darra Goldstein (New York: Oxford University Press, 2015), pp. 426–27.

15. Cadbury, *Chocolate Wars*, p. 234.

16. Brenner, "Mars," p. 427.

17. "History of Mars, Inc."

18. "History of Mars," English Tea Store, http://www.englishteastore.com/mars-history.html (accessed August 26, 2015).

19. Cadbury, *Chocolate Wars*, p. 241.

20. "The History of Kit Kat," Nestleprofessional.com, https://www.nestleprofessional.com/uk/en/SiteArticles/Pages/History_of_KitKat.aspx?UrlReferrer=https%3a%2f%2fwww.google.com%2f (accessed August 26, 2015).

21. "History of Mars, Inc."

22. Brenner, "Mars," pp. 415–16; "Hungry History," History Channel, http://www.history.com/news/hungry-history/the-wartime-origins-of-the-mm (accessed August 26, 2015); Roy Rosenzweig, "Why Did Soldiers Make M&M's a National Institution," Center for History and New Media, http://chnm.gmu.edu/sidelights/why-did-soldiers-make-mms-a-national-institution/ (accessed August 26, 2015).

23. "Smarties," Rowntree Society, http://www.rowntreesociety.org.uk/smarties/#sthash.74GJKoyW.dpuf (accessed August 26, 2015).

24. Cadbury, *Chocolate Wars*, pp. 249–50; Brenner, "Mars," pp. 415–16.

25. David Kaplan, "Mars Incorporated: A Pretty Sweet Place to Work," *Fortune*, January 17, 2013, http://fortune.com/2013/01/17/mars-incorporated-a-pretty-sweet-place-to-work/ (accessed August 26, 2015).

26. Ibid.

27. Ibid.

CHAPTER 13: CANDY FOR FUN AND FLAVOR

1. "1912 Bread and Roses Strike," Massachusetts AFL-CIO, http://www.massaflcio.org/1912-bread-and-roses-strike (accessed August 25, 2015).

2. Author interview with Bob Berkinshaw at Ye Olde Pepper factory, June 4, 2015.

3. Laura Mason, *Sugar-Plums and Sherbet: The Prehistory of Sweets* (Devon: Prospect Books, 2004), pp. 89–91.

4. Author interview with Bob Burkinshaw, June 1, 2015.

5. "The Latest Buzz: Eating Insects Can Help Tackle Food Insecurity, Says FAO," UN News Centre, http://www.un.org/apps/news/story.asp?NewsID=44886#.UyrYxaLl6So (accessed August 26, 2015).

6. Jean Condit, "Grasshoppers a la Mode: Strange Things Are Tickling Palates These Days, Coming Soon—Fried Bees, Chocolate-Covered Ants," *New York Times*, April 29, 1956, p. 264.

7. Victor J. Hillery, "Specialty Foods: Snails, Grasshoppers, Caviar, Ants Pop Up On More US Menus," *Wall Street Journal*, November 9, 1956, p. 1.

8. Massachusetts Charitable Mechanic Association, First Exhibition and Fair of the Massachusetts Charitable Mechanic Association, at Faneuil and Quincy Halls, in the City of Boston, September 18, 1837 (Boston: Dutton and Wentworth, 1837), https://archive.org/details/exhibitionfairof00mass (accessed August 26, 2015).

9. "Confectionery—How It Is made, and What It Is Made Of," *Scientific American*, December 2, 1868, p. 358.

10. Ibid.

11. Ibid.

12. Mason, Sugar-Plums and Sherbet, p. 82.

13. Elesha Coffman, "Raising Cane, The Origins of the Candy Cane," Christian History, August 8, 2008, http://www.christianitytoday.com/ch/news/2004/cane.html (accessed August 26, 2015).

14. "The History of Christmas Trees," Grindstone, Amherst Historical Society, November/December 2014, http://www.amhersthistoricalsociety.org/nov%20dec%20 2014.pdf (accessed August 26, 2015).

15. Coffman, "Raising Cane."

16. Will O. Rigby, Rigby's Reliable Candy Teacher, 19th ed. (Topeka, KS: Rigby, 1919), p. 213.

17. "Candy Butchers," Food Timeline, http://www.foodtimeline.org/foodcandy .html#candybutcher (accessed August 28, 2015).

18. George Conklin and Harvey Woods Root, The Ways of the Circus: Being the Memories and Adventures of George Conklin (New York: Harper and Brothers, 1921), p. 151.

19. Ad in Weekly Roundabout, August 14, 1880, p. 4.

20. P. Sapertos, "Not Loafers" The Day Book, March 1, 1915, p. 13.

21. Ad in Confectioners Journal 46 (1920), p. 54.

22. "Boston's North End History," Northendweb.com, http://www.northendweb .com/history.htm (accessed August 26, 2015).

23. Richard Peevers, "Mary Janes: A Candy History," Roadside Attraction, http:// roadside-attraction.com/mary-janes/ (accessed August 26, 2015).

24. "Richard Outcault," Ohio State University Libraries Exhibitions, http://library .osu.edu/projects/ohio-cartoonists/outcault.html (accessed August 26, 2015).

CHAPTER 14: JUST A SPOONFUL OF *WHAT*?

1. "About the Company," NECCO, http://www.necco.com/about.aspx (accessed August 26, 2015).

2. Tim Richardson, Sweets: A History of Candy (New York: Bloomsbury, 2002), p. 164.

3. Charles Dickens, The Mystery of Edwin Drood (New York: Hurd and Houghton, 1871), p. 31.

4. "About the Company."

5. Ad in Public Ledger, February 23, 1921, p. 3.

6. "Legend of the Smith Bros," Smith Brothers, http://www.thesmithbrothers .com/history-pages-28.php (accessed August 26, 2015).

7. "Maynards Cough Candy, Recommended by the Leading Physicians as a Tonic and Expectorant," Weekly Graphic, April 1, 1887, p. 2.

8. Ibid.

9. "Legend of the Smith Bros."

10. Tony Lucia, "The Luden Story," *Reading (PA) Eagle*, August 15, 2007, http://www2.readingeagle.com/article.aspx?id=54964 (accessed August 26, 2015).

11. "Health and Wellness Products," Smith Bros. Co, http://www.thesmithbrothers.com/health---wellness-products-pages3.php (accessed August 26, 2015).

12. "Confectionery—How It Is Made and What It Is Made Of," *Scientific American* (December 2, 1868), p. 358.

13. Wendy Woloson, *Refined Tastes, Sugar, Confectionery, and Consumers in Nineteenth-Century America* (Baltimore, MD: John Hopkins University Press, 2002), pp. 146–48.

14. Simira Kawash, *Candy: A Century of Panic and Pleasure* (London: Faber and Faber, 2013), p. 32.

15. "American Patents," *Journal of the Franklin Institute* 50, no. 6 (December 1850), p. 367.

16. Laura Mason, *Sugar-Plums and Sherbet: The Prehistory of Sweets* (Devon: Prospect Books, 2004), p. 146.

17. "Confectionery Trade in America," in *Americana*, ed. Frederick Converse Beach and George Edwin Rines (New York: Scientific American Compiling Department, 1912), https://books.google.com/books?id=MYFRAAAAYAAJ&printsec=frontcover &source=gbs_ge_summary_r&cad=0#v=snippet&q=Confectionery&f=false (accessed August 28, 2015).

18. Ibid.

19. "New England Confectionery Company (NECCO)," Local Legacies, Library of Congress, http://lcweb2.loc.gov/diglib/legacies/loc.afc.afc-legacies.200003102/default .html (accessed August 28, 2015).

20. "About the Company."

21. John (Jack) Podojil, Popcorn Favorites: Everything You Want to Know about Popcorn and More (Bloomington, IN: Trafford, 2013), pp. 28–29.

22. "Cracker Jack Co.," Encyclopedia of Chicago, http://www.encyclopedia.chicago history.org/pages/2630.html (accessed August 26, 215).

23. Podojil, *Popcorn Favorites*, p. 29.

24. Ad in *(New York) Evening World*, March 6, 1916, p. 9.

25. "Crackerjack," *Merriam-Webster*, http://www.merriam-webster.com/dictionary/ crackerjack (accessed August 26, 2015).

26. "Cracker Jacks," *Evening Star*, November 9, 1913, p. 21.

27. "Take Me Out to the Ball Game," Library of Congress, http://www.loc.gov/ item/ihas.200153239 (accessed August 26, 2015).

28. "History and Legends of Popcorn, Cracker Jacks and Popcorn Balls," What's

Cooking America, http://whatscookingamerica.net/History/PopcornHistory.htm (accessed August 26, 2015).

29. "Mayor Orders End of Penny Candy 'Racket'; Encourages Gambling in Children, He Says," *New York Times*, April 4, 1937, p. 1.

30. Ad in *Evening World*, March 6, 1916, p. 9.

31. Ad in *Washington Post*, January 27, 1918, p. 7.

CHAPTER 15: THE GREAT AMERICAN CANDY STORE

1. "When New England Candy Was King: 15 Sweet Facts," New England Historical Society, http://www.newenglandhistoricalsociety.com/new-england-candy-king-15-sweet-facts/ (accessed August 26, 2015).

2. Tim Newcomb, "Nine Things You Didn't Know about Your Easter Candy," *Time*, April 5, 2012, http://newsfeed.time.com/2012/04/06/nine-things-you-didnt-know-about-your-easter-candy/slide/a-wartime-snack/ (accessed August 26, 2015).

3. "When New England Candy Was King."

4. "Menus," New York Public Library, http://menus.nypl.org/menu_pages/56754/explore (accessed August 26, 2015).

5. Christopher Gray, "Midday Havens, Lost to a Faster-Paced City," *New York Times*, Real Estate, June 29, 2008, http://www.nytimes.com/2008/06/29/realestate/29scap.html (accessed August 26, 2015).

6. "Harpers Ferry," National Park Service, http://www.nps.gov/hafe/index.htm (accessed August 26, 2015).

7. Author interview with Roeder's great-grandchildren in Harpers Ferry.

8. Author interview with park anthropologist in Harpers Ferry.

9. "Harpers Ferry" Harper-Ferry-Bolivar, Historic Town Foundation, http://www.historicharpersferry.com/ (accessed August 26, 2015).

10. Author interview with Dorothy Van Steinburg and Chris Houck, August 7, 2015.

11. The Hill Top House was built after the Civil War. At that time, it may have been a hotel or store.

12. Beth Kracklauer, "Taffy," in *The Oxford Companion to Sugar and Sweets*, ed. Darra Goldstein (New York: Oxford University Press, 2015), pp. 727–28.

13. "History," Fralinger's, http://www.fralingers.com/history/ (accessed August 26, 2015).

14. Karen L. Schnitzspahn, *Jersey Shore Food History: Victorian Feasts to Boardwalk Treats* (Charleston, SC: History Press, 2012), p. 153.

15. "Who Were the Other Contenders & What Was the Outcome of the Legal

Battle?," Food Timeline, http://www.foodtimeline.org/foodcandy.html#saltwater (accessed on August 25, 2015).

16. Maguelonne Toussaint-Samat, *History of Food* (New York: Barnes & Noble Books, 1992), pp. 565–66.

17. "George Washington Carver," Biography, http://www.biography.com/people/ george-washington-carver-9240299#synopsis (accessed August 25, 2015).

18. "Fruit and Nut Resources: How to Grow the Peanut and 105 Ways of Preparing it for Human Consumption" Texas A&M AgriLife Extension, http://aggie -horticulture.tamu.edu/fruit-nut/carver-peanut/ (accessed November 2, 2015).

19. "Where Did Peanut Brittle Come From? It Depends on Whom You Ask," National Peanut Board, http://nationalpeanutboard.org/history/where-did-peanut -brittle-come-from-it-depends-on-whom-you-ask/ (accessed August 26, 2015).

20. Debra K. Sullivan, "Margaret Prescott Montague," *West Virginia Encyclopedia*, October 20, 2010, http://www.wvencyclopedia.org/articles/2026 (accessed August 26, 2015).

21. Noel W. Tenney, "Tony Beaver," *West Virginia Encyclopedia,* http://www .wvencyclopedia.org/print/Article/412 (accessed August 26, 2015).

22. Sullivan, "Margaret Prescott Montague."

23. Ibid.

24. John F. Mariani, *Encyclopedia of American Food and Drink* (New York: Lebhar-Friedman, 1999), pp. 54–55.

25. Ad in *New-York Tribune*, December 13, 1922, p. 6.

26. Ad in Goodwin's Weekly: A Thinking Paper for Thinking People, December 11, 1909, p. 10.

27. Ad in *Washington Times*, October 13, 1915, p. 3.

28. Ad in *(New York) Evening World*, December 30, 1921, p. 11.

29. Ad in *New York Tribune*, October 31, 1920, p. 11.

30. Wendy Woloson, *Refined Tastes, Sugar, Confectionery, and Consumers in Nineteenth-Century America* (Baltimore, MD: John Hopkins University Press, 2002), p. 139.

31. Matt Soniak, "Corn Flakes Were Invented as Part of an Anti-Masturbation Crusade," *Mental Floss*, December 28, 2012, http://mentalfloss.com/article/32042/corn -flakes-were-invented-part-anti-masturbation-crusade (accessed August 26, 2015).

32. J. H. Kellogg, "Plain Facts for Old and Young: Embracing the History and Natural Hygiene of Organic Life," in Woloson, *Refined Tastes*, p. 139.

33. Author phone interview with John Gibbs, August 4, 2015.

34. Author interview with Robert Tuck, June 2, 2015.

CHAPTER 16: THE PENNY CANDY EXPLOSION

1. "Lessons in Common Things," *Ohio Journal of Education* (May 1857), in *A Century of Panic and Pleasure*, Samira Kawash (London: Faber and Faber, 2013), p. 36.

2. Charles Dickens, *The Mystery of Edwin Drood*, chap. 3 (New York: Hurd and Houghton, 1871).

3. "It Looks Too Real," *Minneapolis Journal*, November 4, 1902, p. 8.

4. Sarah Tyson Rorer, "Why Sweets Are Not Good for Children," *Ladies Home Journal*, March 1906, p. 38.

5. "Tips on Candy: Never Pay Less than Forty Cents a Pound If You Want a Pure Article," *Daily Yellowstone Journal*, June 26, 1891, p. 2.

6. "Sweets for the Children," *Camden Chronicle*, August 5, 1904, p. 7.

7. *The Oxford Encyclopedia of Food and Drink in America*, ed. Andrew F. Smith, vol. 1 (New York: Oxford University Press, 2004), p. 177.

8. "Merchants Store 100 Tons of Tainted Candy," *Pittsburgh Post*, October 2, 1906, p. 1.

9. "Youth Is Victim of Strangely Poisoned Candy," *Salt Lake Tribune*, October 7, 1910, p. 4.

10. "State Chemist Says Candy Is Generally Pure," *Courier*, March 16, 1913, p. 4.

11. Frederic J. Haskin, "The Confectionery Trade," *El Paso Herald*, July 2, 1910, p. 44.

12. Author interview with Ethel Weiss, June 4, 2015.

13. Laura Mason, *Sugar-Plums and Sherbet: The Prehistory of Sweets* (Devon: Prospect Books, 2004), p. 122.

14. Ivan Day, "Sugar-Plums and Comfits," HistoricFood.com, http://www.historic food.com/Comfits.htm (accessed August 26, 2015).

15. Mason, *Sugar-Plums and Sherbet*, pp. 128–29.

16. Day, "Sugar-Plums and Comfits."

17. Samira Kawash, "Sugar Plums: They're Not What You Think They Are," *Atlantic*, December 22, 2010, http://www.theatlantic.com/health/archive/2010/12/sugar -plums-theyre-not-what-you-think-they-are/68385/ (accessed August 26, 2015).

18. Ibid.

19. "Ferrara Pan Candy Company," Encyclopedia.com, http://www.encyclopedia .com/doc/1G2-2690600049.html (accessed August 26, 2015).

20. "Jawbreaker," How Products Are Made, http://www.madehow.com/Volume-6/ Jawbreaker.html (accessed August 2, 2015).

21. "The Right Number," *Monroe City (MO) Democrat*, November 17, 1910, p. 5.

22. Ronnie Reese, "Nello V. Ferrara, 1918–2012: Ferrara Pan Exec Created Lemonhead and Atomic Fire Ball candies," *Chicago Tribune*, February 10, 2012, http://

articles.chicagotribune.com/2012-02-10/news/ct-met-ferrara-obit-20120210_1_candy
-capital-ferrara-pan-candy-lyric-opera (accessed November 3, 2015).

23. "Jawbreaker."

24. "The Oleaginous History of Wax Lips," American Oil and Gas Historical
Society, http://aoghs.org/products/an-oleaginous-history-of-wax-lips/ (accessed August
26, 2015).

25. "J. W. Glenn," *International Confectioner* 30, no. 1 (January 1921), p. 71.

26. "The Oleaginous History of Wax Lips."

27. James M. O'Neill, "A Jelly Bean Mystery Is Solved," *Philadelphia Inquirer*,
April 20, 2000, http://articles.philly.com/2000-04-20/living/25592558_1_jelly-bean
-food-science-easter-candy (accessed August 26, 2015).

28. Ad in *Brooklyn Daily Eagle*, October 2, 1898, p. 13.

29. Author phone interview with David Klein.

30. "Fun Facts about Jelly Belly," Jelly Belly, https://jellybelly.com/Info/funstuff/
fun_facts (accessed August 26, 2015).

31. Author phone interview with David Klein, June 28, 2015.

32. "Clarence A. Crane," Ohio History Connection, http://www.ohiohistorycentral
.org/w/Clarence_A._Crane (accessed August 26, 2015).

33. "Young Poet Is Drowned Sailing to New York, Delphos" *Daily Herald*, April
28, 1932, p. 1.

34. "Clarence A. Crane."

35. "A Brief History of Gouverneur, New York," Gouverneur, NY 13642, http://
www.gouverneurny.us/gouv_history.htm (accessed August 26, 2015).

36. "The Life Saver Candy Sweet Book Story," Greenwich Library Historically
Speaking, http://www.greenwichlibrary.org/blog/historically_speaking/2012/05/the-life
-saver-candy-story.html (accessed August 26, 2015).

37. Joan Monahan, "Life Savers: A Summer Candy Celebrates a Hole Lot
of History," *Ledger*, June 26, 2007, http://www.theledger.com/article/20070626/
COLUMNISTS/706260318 (accessed August 26, 2015).

38. "A Brief History of Gouverneur."

39. Carl White, "The Life Saver Candy Sweet Book Story," Historically Speaking,
May 9, 2012, http://www.greenwichlibrary.org/blog/historically_speaking/2012/05/the
-life-saver-candy-story.html (accessed August 29, 2015).

40. Author interview with Camilla Dhanak, June 15, 2013.

CHAPTER 17: THE HISTORY OF AN AMERICAN-MADE PASSION

1. Jennifer P. Mathews, *Chicle: The Chewing Gum of the Americas, from the Ancient Maya to William Wrigley* (Tucson, AZ: University of Arizona Press, 2009), p. 8.

2. "Antonio López de Santa Anna: A Man and His Times," PBS: US-Mexican War 1846–1848, http://www.pbs.org/kera/usmexicanwar/prelude/sa_antonio.html (accessed August 20, 2015).

3. "Thomas Adams Dead. Brooklyn Man Who Made Fortune in Chewing Gum Business," *New York Times*, February 8, 1905. http://query.nytimes.com/mem/archive -free/pdf?res=9A06E6D7163DE733A2575BC0A9649C946497D6CF (accessed August 27, 2015).

4. Mary Bellis, "The History of Chewing Gum and Bubble Gum, Part Two: Thomas Adams," About.com: Inventors, http://inventors.about.com/library/inventors/ bladams.htm (accessed August 20, 2015).

5. Ibid.

6. Mathews, *Chicle*, pp. 41–42.

7. Bellis, "History of Chewing Gum."

8. "Adams, Thomas, Jr.," *National Cyclopaedia of American Biography*, vol. 21 (New York: James T. White, 1931), p. 191.

9. "The Chewing Gum King," Brooklyn Public Library, http://brooklynology .brooklynpubliclibrary.org/post/2011/09/07/The-Chewing-Gum-King.aspx (accessed August 27, 2015).

10. "Charles Feltman Inventor of the Hot Dog," Coney Island Project, Hall of Fame, http://www.coneyislandhistory.org/index.php?g=hall_of_fame&s=feltman (accessed August 27, 2015).

11. "Chewing Gum King."

12. Mary Koegel, "Something to Chew On," National Digital Newpaper Program, Kentucky Edition, February 1, 2010, http://kyndnp.blogspot.com/2010/02/something -to-chew-on.html (accessed August 27, 2015).

13. Mathews, *Chicle*, p. 48.

14. "White, William John (1850 - 1923)," Biographical Directory of the United States Congress, http://bioguide.congress.gov/scripts/biodisplay.pl?index=W000398 (accessed August 27, 2015).

15. "American Chicle Company," Encyclopedia of Cleveland History, http://ech .cwru.edu/ech-cgi/article.pl?id=ACC1 (accessed August 27, 2015).

16. "Dr. E. E. Beeman Dead Chewing: Chewing Gum King Gave Up Medicine to Become a Manufacturer," *New York Times*, November 7, 1906, http://query.nytimes .com/mem/archive-free/pdf?_r=1&res=9E06EFD9173EE733A25754C0A9679D9467 97D6CF (accessed August 27, 2015).

17. "Beeman, Edwin E.," Encyclopedia of Cleveland History, July 10, 1997, http://ech.case.edu/cgi/article.pl?id=BEE (Accessed: August 21, 2015).

18. Ibid.

19. James Trager, The New York Chronology: *The Ultimate Compendium of Events, People, and Anecdotes from the Dutch to the Present* (Collins Reference, 2010), p. 262.

20. "Beech-Nut Nutrition Corporation," Company-Histories.com, http://www.company-histories.com/BeechNut-Nutrition-Corporation-Company-History.html (accessed August 27, 2015).

21. Mathews, *Chicle*, p. 48.

22. "PITCAIRN PCA-2 AUTOGIRO NC10780: Chewing Gum," Davis-Monthan Aviation Field Register, Revised, November 23, 2014, http://www.dmairfield.org/airplanes/NC10780/index.html#autogiro (accessed August 27, 2015).

23. "Beech-Nut Nutrition Corporation."

24. "26 Clark Bars: A Mighty Money-Maker in Candy Bars & Chewing Gum, Clark Co. Declares Another Dividend," *Bulletin Index*, December 1935, p. 26.

25. Shelley Wigglesworth, "The Teaberry Plant: A Native to New England," *Yankee*, November 2013, http://www.yankeemagazine.com/gardening-advice-ideas/teaberry-plant (accessed August 27, 201)

26. Roland Anderson with Rick Kuczur, "A Short Note," Rolan Anderson, http://www.rolandanderson.se/teaberry.php (accessed August 27, 2015).

27. "Thomas Adams," p. 191.

28. Mathews, *Chicle*, p. 43.

29. "American Chicle Company."

30. "Fleer Corporation," Company-History.com, http://www.company-histories.com/Fleer-Corporation-Company-History.html (accessed August 27, 2015).

31. Ibid.

32. Abby Goodnough, "W. E. Diemer, Bubble Gum Inventor Dies at 93," *New York Times*, January 12, 1998, http://www.nytimes.com/1998/01/12/us/we-diemer-bubble-gum-inventor-dies-at-93.html (accessed August 27, 2015).

33. "Fleer Corporation."

34. "Frank H. Fleer Dead," *Manning Times*, November 2, 1921, p. 2.

35. Goodnough, "W. E. Diemer."

36. "Wm. Wrigley Jr. Company," Company-History.com, http://www.company-histories.com/Wm-Wrigley-Jr-Company-Company-History.html (accessed August 27, 2015).

37. Paul Lukas, "Doubleminting Money Creative and Pervasive Marketing Built the Chicago Gum Giant," CNN-Money, March 1, 2014, http://money.cnn.com/magazines/fsb/fsb_archive/2004/03/01/363860/index.htm (accessed August 27, 2015).

38. "Wm. Wrigley Jr. Company."

39. "Wrigley's Rule for Results," *Richmond Daily Register*, March 7, 1921, p. 6.

40. Freeman Tilden, "Fortunes from Small Change," *Evening (Washington, DC) Star*, January 23, 1916, p. 6.

41. "Wrigley on Prosperity," *Richmond (KY) Daily Register*, April 20, 1922, p. 2.

42. "Wm. Wrigley Jr. Company."

43. "What Chicle Is. Where It Comes From," *Arizona Republican*, June 30, 1918, p. 7.

44. "Across the Boarder," *Arizona Oasis*, April 15, 1911, p. 3.

45. Mathews, *Chicle*, pp. 72–89.

46. "May Check Gum Chewing," *Wenatchee Daily World*, November 3, 1909, p. 3.

47. Laurent Thomet, *"Daredevil Chewing Gum Makers Stick to Maya Chicle,"* AFP *News,* https://sg.news.yahoo.com/daredevil-chewing-gum-makers-stick-maya -chicle-081332594.html (accessed August 27, 2015).

CHAPTER 18: STILL WRAPPED IN BAG AND BASKET

1. "Tootsie Roll Industries Inc.," Reference for Business, http://www.referencefor business.com/history2/85/Tootsie-Roll-Industries-Inc.html (accessed August 28, 2015).

2. "Tootsie," Dictionary.com, http://dictionary.reference.com/browse/tootsie (accessed August 28, 2015).

3. "Tootsie Roll Tragedy: The Real Leo Hirschfeld Story," Candy Professor, February 3, 2010, http://candyprofessor.com/2010/02/03/tootsie-roll-mystery/ #comments (accessed August 28, 2015).

4. Samira Kawash, "Tootsie Roll," in *The Oxford Companion to Sugar and Sweets*, ed. Darra Goldstein (New York: Oxford University Press, 2015), p. 738.

5. Laura Mason, *Sweets and Sweet Shops* (Oxford: Shire Publications, 1999), pp. 18–19.

6. "About Caramel," Food Timeline, http://foodtimeline.org/foodcandy.html #caramel (accessed August 28, 2015).

7. John F. Mariani, *Encyclopedia of American Food and Drink* (New York: Lebhar-Friedman, 1999), p. 255.

8. Artemas Ward, The Grocer's Encyclopedia: The Encyclopedia of Foods & Beverages (New York: Baker & Taylor, 1911), p. 106.

9. Evan Morris, From Altoids to Zima: The Surprising Stories Behind 125 Famous Brand Names (New York: Simon and Schuster, 2004), p. 59.

10. Jim Willard, "Sugar Daddy Has a Sweet History," *Reporter Herald*, February 21, 2003, http://www.reporterherald.com/ci_22623737/sugar-daddy-has-sweet-history (accessed August 28, 2015).

11. "About the Company," NECCO, http://www.necco.com/About.aspx (accessed August 28, 2015).

12. "History," Squirrel Brand, http://www.squirrelbrand.com/history/ (accessed August 28, 2015).

13. "Heath Candy," Robinson Chamber of Commerce Heath Museum and Confectionery, http://www.robinsonchamber.org/index.php/about-robinson/heath-candy/ (accessed August 28, 2015).

14. Ray Broekel, *The Great American Candy Bar Book* (Boston: Houghton Mifflin, 1982), pp. 31–33; "Fox Cross Company," Cambridge Historical Society, http://www.cambridge history.org/discover/candy/foxcross.html (accessed August 28, 2015).

15. "Museum/History," Bonomo Turkish Taffy, http://www.bonomoturkishtaffy.com/MuseumHistory_ep_40.html (accessed August 28, 2015).

16. Laurnie Wilson, "Pixy Stix Fix" Candy Favorites, http://www.candyfavorites.com/history-pixy-stix-candy (accessed August 28, 2015).

17. "Circus Peanuts," Urban Dictionary, http://www.urbandictionary.com/define.php?term=Circus+Peanuts (accessed August 28, 2015); John Sewer, "In Candy World, Circus Peanut Is a Riddle Wrapped in Marshmallow inside Orange Shell," *USA Today*, October 20, 2006, http://usatoday30.usatoday.com/money/industries/food/2006-07-27-circus-peanut_x.htm (accessed August 28, 2015).

18. Karen Pinchin, "The Story behind a Uniquely Canadian Holiday Treat," *Globe and Mail*, December 17, 2013, http://www.theglobeandmail.com/life/holiday-guide/holiday-survival-guide/the-story-behind-a-uniquely-canadian-holiday-treat/article16002345/ (accessed August 28, 2015); "The Original Chicken Bones," Ganong, https://ganong.com/product-category/product-type/chicken-bones/(accessed August 28, 2015).

19. Author phone interview with Wilma Green, August 5, 2015.

20. Nancy E. V. Bryk, "Lollipop," How Products Are Made, http://www.madehow.com/Volume-6/Lollipop.html#ixzz3iEBXABRd (accessed August 28, 2015).

21. Samira Kawash, "Lollipop," in *The Oxford Companion to Sugar and Sweets*, ed. Darra Goldstein (New York: Oxford University Press, 2015), pp. 413–14.

22. "New Haven Gives the Lollipop its Name—Today in History: October 13," Connecticut History, http://connecticuthistory.org/new-haven-gives-the-lollipop-its-name-today-in-history/#sthash.SipLiDc5.dpuf (accessed August 28, 2015).

23. Bryk, "Lollipop."

CHAPTER 19: CANDY BOWLS AND ICE CREAM TRUCKS

1. Author interview with her mother, June 4, 2015.

2. Girl Scouts of the United States of America, "Tramping and Trailing with the Girl Scouts," (New York: Girl Scouts, 1927), p. 71.

3. Author phone interview with Howard Nachamie, August 2, 2015.

4. "Brief History of Ice Cream Truck," Mental Floss, http://mentalfloss.com/article/52281/brief-history-ice-cream-truck (accessed August 28, 2015).

5. "Our Story," Good Humor, http://www.goodhumor.com/article (accessed August 28, 2015).

6. Jeri Quinzio, "The Good Humor Man," in *The Oxford Companion to Sugar and Sweets*, ed. Darra Goldstein (New York: Oxford University Press, 2015), p. 307.

7. Ibid., pp. 307–308.

8. "Our Story."

9. Quinzio, "Good Humor Man," pp. 307–308.

INDEX